THE GARDEN MAKERS

THE GARDEN MAKERS

*The Great Tradition of Garden Design
from 1600 to the Present Day*

GEORGE PLUMPTRE

RANDOM
HOUSE

The true gardener has abiding faith and must express it, if only
by planting an acorn where the *genius loci* calls for an oak
Fletcher Steele

For Hermione

Published in Great Britain by
Pavilion Books Limited

Library of Congress Cataloguing information is available

ISBN 0-679-43014-8

Manufactured in Italy

24689753

First U.S. Edition

Page 2: *Anglo-American unity in garden design*
achieved a notable peak in the work of the American designer
Beatrix Farrand at Dartington Hall.

CONTENTS

INTRODUCTION

THE CREATION OF GARDENS and the development of garden styles through successive periods have been dominated by personalities, both amateur and professional, whose work, either in one garden or in a great many, has been of seminal importance. Looked at another way, no garden can be truly understood or appreciated without some knowledge of the guiding hand behind its creation and the human, social legacy from one generation to another that has been responsible for evolving garden styles. The intention of *The Garden Makers* is to bring together the major figures through successive periods of garden making from 1600 to the present day, combining factual and biographical details for reference with a critical appreciation and description of each individual's work. By virtue of the introductory essays at the beginning of each period and the general chronological progression the book aims to demonstrate how often it was personal connections which were responsible for the changes from one period to another and how a number of gardens reveal the cumulative work of different generations. Castle Howard in Yorkshire, for instance, has gardens and a surrounding landscape containing work from the late-17th and early-18th centuries, the mid-19th century and the late-20th century.

The heroic landscape: John Vanbrugh's Temple of the Four Winds at Castle Howard, with the dome of Hawksmoor's mausoleum in the distance.

The choice of individuals and gardens included has been partly dictated by one or two basic factors. The book has a deliberate Anglo-American emphasis and does not attempt to cover in any detail garden making in continental Europe or other parts of the world. Therefore where people included did work elsewhere, for instance the 20th-century designer Russell Page, this is mentioned in general terms but without any quantity of specific information about individual gardens. Also, the gardens or landscapes included in the resumé at the beginning of each person's entry and subsequently discussed in the main section of text are limited to those where a recognizable amount of evidence survives. This limitation of the book's contents aims to give *The Garden Makers* tangible relevance today as opposed to a primarily historical interest.

The focus on England and America reveals how at many different times and through the work and influence of a number of individuals the development of garden making in the two countries has been closely interrelated throughout three hundred years. For nearly a century from the establishment of the first colonies in the New World American gardens grew out of the ideas brought over from England and which were applied to the particular requirements of the growing communities. In return, by the late-seventeenth century the first signs were appearing that the New World would prove to be the most valuable source of plants imported to be grown in English gardens, parks and woods and this has remained true, allowing for the popularity of plants originating from parts of China and South-East Asia from the mid-19th century for a period of roughly a century, ever since.

The changing selection of plants available to garden makers has without fail had an influence upon their work and the trade in plants accounts for the few individuals included in the book who, rather than creating one or more specific gardens, had a wider and often longer-lasting influence by personally introducing plants of special significance. In more general terms, it is most interesting to see how the leading people in the creation of American gardens, such as Thomas Jefferson in the 18th century, Andrew Jackson Downing in the 19th and Beatrix Farrand in the 20th, all greatly admired aspects of English garden making, had first-hand knowledge of the English garden and were acquainted with leading English gardeners, and yet without fail the influence has been tempered and adapted to social and landscape conditions in America. Finally, since the work of Thomas Church and his contemporaries between the wars and more especially after World War II, modern American gardens and landscapes have assumed international leadership and initiated the ideas and styles which have been subsequently followed elsewhere.

As well as intending to give a brief overview of each successive period the introductions allow for the inclusion of a number of people, such as craftsmen and architects who designed garden ornaments or garden buildings, who do not have an individual entry. The introductions also aim to pull together and discuss certain general trends and developments, be it the social and economic conditions in 18th-century England which combined with fashionable aesthetics to bring about the landscape movement, the growing importance of public parks during the 19th century and their first designs by garden makers such as John Claudius Loudon and Joseph Paxton, or later the emerging profession of landscape architecture which was initially born out of the application of garden design to large-scale public landscapes. From the late-19th century in America and more widely during the 20th century the interrelationship of garden design and landscape architecture has been of immense significance as is best shown in the work of individuals who have practised in both spheres, such as Frederick Law Olmsted, Thomas Mawson, Geoffrey Jellicoe, Brenda Colvin and the partnership of Wolfgang Oehme and James van Sweden.

The treatment of individual entries has not been decided by a set formula, so that as well as an element of variety garden makers have been discussed in a manner most relevant to their particular work. Therefore for instance, where it is the creation of one garden that is important, such as Lawrence Johnston's Hidcote, the garden is described in some detail. Lancelot 'Capability' Brown, on the other hand designed over eighty parks and gardens which still survive and therefore his career is discussed in more general terms with an emphasis on the techniques that he applied and an assessment of his overall impact on the 18th-century landscape movement.

Although there are biographies of some seventy individuals, and some three hundred and fifty gardens and landscapes are mentioned, a book of this nature can never hope to be comprehensive. In addition, where people are not perhaps immediately obvious candidates for inclusion an element of personal preference is applied and as a result there will be some appearances or absences which do not meet with universal approval. Nonetheless it is hoped that the book provides a new and thoroughly contemporary look at the garden history of nearly four centuries, showing who in the past was responsible for what we can still see and enjoy and coming right up to date to the present day.

GEORGE PLUMPTRE 1993

THE FIRST PROFESSIONALS
1600-1690

IT IS NOT UNTIL THE VERY BEGINNING of the 17th century that the personalities involved in gardens begin to assume importance and clearly recognized status. During the 16th century the garden had been steadily emerging from the mediaeval *hortus conclusus* – the protected enclosures where productivity and visual beauty combined in often unambitious and largely anonymous simplicity. Some splendid gardens were created during the reigns of both Henry VIII and Elizabeth I, but none survive today in any recognizable form. Exclusively created by the monarchy and leading members of the court, gardens such as Hampton Court and Nonsuch demonstrated with their brightly coloured flower gardens, their mounts and painted heraldic beasts the vibrancy which the Tudors so enjoyed and which offset the discomfort and drabness of much of their existence. By the standards of what was to follow, however, they were unsophisticated; the gardening world, still in a state of immaturity, was only starting to show the signs of a development that would gather pace during the following century.

In simple terms, the two decisive influences on British gardens were the renaissance and the lure of new varieties of plants found overseas. The renaissance not only elevated

The Pond Garden at Hampton Court, created on the
site of the palace's early-Tudor garden.

garden design and the individuals involved to a position of prestige within the arts, it expanded the significance of gardens and the whole spectrum of possibilities – architectural, ornamental and horticultural – beyond all previously conceived limits. Gardens, in particular those of the Stuart monarchs and the aristocrats of their courts, began to indicate both the power of their owners and fashionable taste and, as the inspiration for these gardens came from continental Europe, so there arose the demand for men with knowledge of French and Italian gardens. Many of the leading gardeners in England were Frenchmen; as designers of royal gardens the Huguenot brothers Salomon and Isaac de Caus (*q.v.* p. 16) were followed by André, Claude and Gabriel Mollet, while the first English royal gardener, Charles II's gardener John Rose, was trained in France.

Encouraged by their monarchs, wealthy and cultivated aristocrats at the apex of political and social life, became increasingly interested in gardens and their lead stimulated a surge of activity: in the creation of gardens, and their ability to reflect status; in the application of high quality architecture and craftsmanship to the design and ornamentation of gardens; in gardening literature; and in the advance of horticulture. In the vanguard were Sir Francis Bacon, who began the restoration of his father's garden at Gorhambury near St Albans in 1608, and in 1625 published his celebrated essay *On Gardens*; and the Earl of Pembroke whose garden at Wilton House, designed during the 1630s by Isaac de Caus and regularly visited by Charles I, was the most splendid and influential pre-Civil War garden in the country. The growing interest in individual plants was demonstrated by the Earl of Danby who masterminded and financed the foundation of the Oxford Botanic Garden in 1621. Their lead was taken up through the century by other men such as Sir Thomas Hanmer, Sir Christopher Hatton (*q.v.* p. 20) and Sir William Temple, but most notably by John Evelyn (*q.v.* p. 18).

Stylistically, gardens of the early decades of the 17th century were influenced by the renaissance principle that they should be both physically and decoratively harmonious with the house, to present a satisfying combined picture. Although only drawings and attributed gateways survive as testimony to Inigo Jones's influence upon English garden design it is clear that the Palladian architectural style that he brought to England advocated a garden that complemented the details of a house and included statues, buildings, fountains and other architectural elements. And yet, as Roy Strong pointed out in *The Renaissance Garden in England*, pre-Civil War gardens, even the grandest such as Wilton, covering impressive areas, were almost always still enclosed by walls, giving no contact with surrounding landscape other than that provided by the occasional view-point or belvedere. Renaissance principles were limited to the architecture, ornament and the arrangement of adjoining formal areas.

During the years of the Cromwellian interregnum in the middle of the 17th century, when the royalist cause had been lost in the battles of the Civil War, most English aristocrats, other than the relatively small number who actively supported the Parliamentarians, either escaped to the continent or sought out anonymity in their country seats. One influential figure who chose the latter course was Sir Thomas Hanmer, who retired to his family seat at Bettisfield in Wales, cultivated his garden and kept a *Garden Book*, the manuscript of which was discovered and published in 1933. Hanmer's gardening interests were primarily horticultural and his garden contained a wide variety of flowers and fruit. He was an early advocate of the cedar of Lebanon, introduced to England during the middle of the century.

By the time of the Restoration of Charles II in 1660 the influence of the French style of gardening was at its zenith. Vaux-le-Vicomte, the magnificent palace and garden created for the French finance minister Nicholas Fouquet by the architect Louis le Vau, the sculptor Charles le Brun and the garden designer André le Nôtre, was completed in 1661. After the almost immediate downfall of Fouquet the same trio began work on the apotheosis of French grandeur and formality at Versailles for Louis XIV. Charles II, wanting to compete, spent much of his reign trying to entice le Nôtre to England, and although he failed, the royal gardens at Hampton Court, St James's and Greenwich were all in the French style and set the standard to be copied by aristocratic members of the court. Yet, outside the royal gardens, the French style only percolated to a limited extent, producing specific features rather than the adoption of a whole concept of garden design. Neither English topography, society nor taste were suited to such regimented grandeur.

More significant, the post-restoration years witnessed the first stirring of the English landowning classes' real interest in the development of their country estates. Initially, in conjunction with the French influence, this led to the development of formal woodland gardens or *bosquets*, beyond the previous geometric confines of the garden, and avenues extending on axes from gardens immediately around a house – remnants of which can be seen at Boughton House in Northamptonshire. During these decades the relationship between garden and estate was to take on increasing importance, not least as advocated by John Evelyn (*q.v.* p. 18). He presented the decoration and management of the garden as being, with ornamental woodlands, the intrinsic link between a house and its surrounding estate, thereby laying the practical foundations of an ethos of landscape which was to dominate English garden thinking for over a century and to have dramatic and wide-reaching influence in other countries.

During the pre-Civil War era the burgeoning interest in plants and horticulture also influenced the development of English gardens. At a time when the individual qualities of different plants, especially rare and unusual ones, was becoming increasingly prized, the elder John Tradescant (*q.v.* p. 21) was a pioneering figure as gardener, plant collector – and founder of the first dynasty of English gardeners. Working for a succession of aristocratic employers – notably Robert Cecil, Earl of Salisbury – he spent much of his time collecting plants for their gardens from the continent; and once the earliest colonies had established a foothold in North America, the quest for plants soon extended across the Atlantic. Under Tradescant the botanical interest in plants was given practical horticultural application and was no longer limited to description and illustration as it had been in books such as John Gerard's *Herbal*, first published in 1597.

Tradescant the elder never visited North America himself, but his son, also John (*q.v.* p. 22), was the first important plant collector to visit the colonies, making three trips, the last in 1654. By the Restoration it was increasingly evident that there were enormous horticultural riches to be found in the vast tracts of the New World, and the most influential figure in the transatlantic plant trade was the aristocratic Henry Compton who was appointed Bishop of London in 1675. The garden of his Fulham Palace soon acquired the most extensive collection of North American trees and shrubs to be found in England, many of them collected by John Banister (*q.v.* p. 16) whom Compton sent to America with a dual brief as clergyman and plant collector. The trees and plants in Compton's garden provided much of the material for his friend John Ray's *Historia Plantarum Generalis*, one of the most important botanical books of the late 17th century.

For some years Bishop Compton's gardener at Fulham was George London, and their relationship and London's early career illustrate how the garden world during the years after the Restoration was establishing a network of patrons, gardeners, craftsmen and garden writers, between whom links and contact were regular and often personal. As a young man George London had been connected with the royal gardener, John Rose, on whose advice he had trained for a time in France. Shortly after his return in 1681 he began working for Henry Compton, and a few years later he established with three partners the Brompton Nursery, which was to become during its peak years around the turn of the 18th century one of the most famous and successful nurseries in gardening history. London's original partners were all leading gardeners: William Looker who had been

Queen Henrietta Maria's gardener; Moses Cook and John Field, who had respectively been responsible for two of the period's most renowned gardens, the Earl of Essex's Cassiobury and the Duke of Bedford's Woburn Abbey. The nursery's most influential supporter during its early years was none other than John Evelyn, whose aristocratic gardening friends and contacts soon provided the backbone of the nursery's trade.

Horticulturally, English gardening was far closer to the Dutch than to the French – in its international trade in plants; its nurserymen and collectors; its desire for improved species whether of forest or fruit trees; and in its natural enjoyment of flower gardening. Dutch influence grew after the Restoration and naturally came to the fore with the arrival in England in 1688 of a gardening-mad Dutch monarch, William III. Although similarly geometric in their formality to French gardens the more intimate scale of Dutch gardens was better suited to the average English garden; while as plantsmen – whether in the development of tulips or the propagation of new species brought back by their traders in the East and West Indies – the Dutch had established themselves as without rivals in Europe. Flower parterres, topiary and long rectangular canals, usually without the grandiose fountains of French gardens, were key elements of Dutch gardens which were soon adopted in England and carried on into the 18th century by George London in partnership with Henry Wise (*q.v.* p. 46).

By the end of the 17th century England had absorbed influences from Italy, France and Holland and yet retained a clear measure of independence from all of them – not least because a legacy of the Civil War was an acute awareness of the dichotomy between ornate French Roman Catholicism and the more reserved Dutch Protestantism. At the same time England had established gardening contact with America, initiating a trade in plants which was to expand rapidly and later produce a flow of ideas back across the Atlantic. Gardens had become fashionable, socially and philosophically important, a growing element of the national identity and way of life. Head gardeners were among the most senior figures in grand households and often developed relationships of extraordinary familiarity and mutual respect with their masters, while nurserymen became increasingly prosperous. Although elements of 17th-century gardening, and even gardens that had been created, were to be threatened and in many cases destroyed in the sweeping landscapes of the 18th century, what survived was an infrastructure built up through the century, of skills, knowledge and interest and of personal connections, which provided the platform for the rise to primacy of English gardens and their future extensive influence abroad.

THE REV JOHN BANISTER (*1654-92*)

As a missionary and plant collector John Banister was the first of a distinguished line of churchmen botanists whose plant introductions have played a significant part in the development of British gardens. At a time when the introduction of new plants from North America was gathering pace, Banister was sent to Virginia by that most influential gardening figure of the time, Henry Compton, Bishop of London, whose duties as bishop included responsibility for the Anglican church in the American colonies and whose interest in horticulture was to result in the garden at Fulham Palace containing an unrivalled collection of trees, shrubs and perennials introduced from North America.

It was Banister's dual qualifications as a clergyman and natural historian that made him an ideal candidate for Compton to dispatch across the Atlantic. He travelled first to the West Indies and on to Virginia around 1680, remaining there until his death in 1692. His most significant contribution to the horticultural knowledge of the time was the production of the first-ever catalogue of American plants. During the 1680s the botanist John Ray was compiling his *Historia Plantarum*, a major work of the 17th century which included descriptions of all known plants, and Banister's catalogue of American plants was incorporated into the second edition of Ray's work, published in 1688.

More specifically Banister introduced a number of plants – especially ornamental trees – which have enjoyed enduring success and which gave at the time a clear indication of the huge potential of American plants for Britain. Among these were *Magnolia virginiana*, the Sweet Bay, the first magnolia to be cultivated in Britain; *Liquidambar styraciflua*, the Sweet Gum and *Quercus coccinea*, the Scarlet Oak, both especially prized for autumn foliage; and *Acer negundo*, the Box Elder, one of the most successful maples. Banister died in 1692, as the result of an accident on a plant collecting trip; at the untimely age of forty-two he was, as Miles Hadfield recorded, 'probably the first plant collector to sacrifice his life in pursuit of his vocation.[1] Combining plant collecting with clerical duties and an all-round interest in natural history, Banister's contribution to the development of gardening by the introduction of plants does not compare with those of the collectors who followed during the 18th and 19th century. Nonetheless, the importance of his career, his collecting, his connection with one of the most important horticultural patrons of the period, and his writing, all demonstrate how the collection and introduction of new plants was becoming an integral and increasingly influential part of the evolving garden world.

ISAAC DE CAUS (*1590-1648*)

WILTON HOUSE, *Wiltshire*

Isaac de caus was born in France of Huguenot parents. He followed in the footsteps of his brother Salomon, becoming a central figure in the development of English gardens during the first half of the 17th century. Salomon's work for James I's wife, Anne of Denmark, and for their eldest son, Prince Henry, had marked the arrival of Italian and French renaissance influences in England that would remain prevalent throughout most of the rest of the century. After leaving France for England in 1613, Isaac continued to work in a similar style and to influence garden design through the reign of Charles I and the Civil War years. The de Caus were architects and engineers, not horticulturalists, and established these skills – so fundamental to the renaissance garden – as cornerstones of English garden design. Tudor traditions were not entirely discarded, surviving in garden detail throughout the 17th century, but the work of the de Caus brothers elevated the potential scale and architectural range of English gardens to a new plane, introducing ideas that were to make gardens, along with the other decorative arts, more closely influenced by continental Europe than at any subsequent period. It was a natural progression from their work to that of André Mollet and, more especially, to the influence of André le Nôtre during the reign of Charles II.

The de Caus's engineering skills and the styles that they developed brought to England many of the most intricate features of Italian and French renaissance gardens: automata, elaborate fountains and grottoes. Nothing of Salomon's work survives from his major gardens such as Somerset House and Greenwich for Queen Anne, or Hatfield House (see John Tradescant p. 21) for Robert Cecil. Surviving features of Isaac's most important garden, at Wilton, are tantalizingly few and none remains in its original place, but extensive documentation, in particular Isaac's own *Le Jardin de Wilton*, published *c.* 1645, gives us a vivid picture of what was undoubtedly the most splendid and influential pre-Civil War garden in the country.

Philip, 4th Earl of Pembroke, who commissioned de Caus to work at Wilton, was a brilliant figure of the Carolean court. Not only did his seat in Wiltshire become an intellectual focal-point of the age, but the king, Charles I, 'did love Wilton above all places, and came thither every summer.'[1] De Caus's garden was laid out between 1632 and 1633 and extended from the south front of the house (which de Caus designed with Inigo Jones 1634-5; it was burnt down ten years later): a walled rectangle of some $9^1/_2$ acres.

Surviving plans and descriptions of the layout show a broad central path leading through three successive pairs of rectangles; the first containing four *parterres de broderie*, at the time scarcely known in English gardens, the second containing closely planted groves or wilderness through which the River Nadder flowed, and the third formally planted with orchards.

Enclosed arcades ran along the outsides of the areas of wilderness and orchard. The position of the venerable cedars that still stand on the south lawn at Wilton, and are known to have been among the earliest grown in England, makes it probable that they were planted in the wilderness areas of de Caus's plan.

Integral to the design was a series of formally arranged statues. At the centre of each of the four areas of *parterre de broderie* were figures of Venus and Cupid, Diana, Susanna and Cleopatra, by Nicholas Stone, most of which survive at Wilton in different positions. Statues of Bacchus and Flora stood at the centre of the two areas of wilderness, while the most impressive, the gladiator by Herbert le Sueur, stood in the centre of the main path between the two areas of orchard.

(During the 18th century the statue was given to Sir Robert Walpole by the 8th Earl of Pembroke and it stands at the foot of the staircase of Houghton Hall, Walpole's great house in Norfolk.)

Furthest from the house, set in the centre of a raised, balustraded terrace, stood de Caus's *tour de force*, the grotto. Every visitor to Wilton was spellbound; a certain Lieutenant Hammond who went there in 1635 rudely described de Caus as 'the fat Dutch keeper' but agreed that he was 'an ingenious artist'[2], and the reputation of the grotto continued for well over half a century. The pedimented façade that survives today in the woodland garden at Wilton gives an indication of its decorative intricacy, as does the *jet d'eau* of wonderful craftsmanship with tritons and other mythological figures in white marble relief that was moved from the grotto's interior to the loggia of the 19th-century Italian garden.

Like many of his contemporary craftsmen and artists, de Caus is a shadowy figure, with few surviving biographical details, though we do know that at some time after the outbreak of the Civil War he returned to France where he died in 1648.

There is no question that he was highly accomplished as architect, engineer and artist in an all-round manner truly representative of the renaissance, but apart from Wilton, where he emerged fully into the limelight, definite attributions of his work are scarce. At Wilton, however, guided by the most cultivated of patrons, and probably advised at different times by Inigo Jones, he created a garden of primary importance in England's historical evolution.

JOHN EVELYN (1620-1705)

ALBURY PARK, *Surrey*; EUSTON HALL, *Suffolk*

JOHN EVELYN was a highly cultivated gentleman virtuoso whose interests and knowledge ranged through all aspects of the arts and science. In 1664 he published *Sylva, or a Discourse of Forest Trees* which, as Miles Hadfield wrote, 'remained the standard work on trees for over a century'.[1] Hadfield went on to comment that Evelyn 'takes his place in our history as the father of the great movement to plant ornamental trees and woodlands in and around our gardens rather than as a horticulturalist.'[2]

Evelyn's royalist sympathies as a young man forced him to leave the country in 1641 and he travelled on the continent for the next eleven years. During this long enforced absence from England he indulged his wideranging interest in art and science, recording the many famous people and places that he encountered – as well as descriptions of gardens and references to specific plants – in the diary which he wrote throughout most of his life. After his return to England in 1652 he created gardens at two homes, Sayes Court in Kent and subsequently the family home of Wotton in Surrey, although no traces of either survive today.

Evelyn was also a founder member of the Royal Society; indeed *Sylva* was originally written as a paper for the society in response to the problem of a shortage of timber for shipbuilding, which the society had been asked to give advice upon. Nearly two centuries later Disraeli wrote, 'Enquire of the Admiralty how the fleets of Nelson have been constructed and they can tell you that it was the oaks which the genius of Evelyn planted.'[3]

Evelyn's first-hand knowledge of French and Italian gardens and wide circle of wealthy friends and acquaintances meant that he was much in demand to give advice on the planning of gardens during the decades after the Restoration, and although most have disappeared, major features survive at one of the most impressive, Albury in Surrey, designed by Evelyn for Henry Howard, later Duke of Norfolk. His great terraces, half a mile long and originally held up by a brick retaining wall, still remain today.

At Euston Hall in Suffolk, where he worked for the restoration politician, the Earl of Arlington. Evelyn was responsible for the great axial avenues which originally swept away from both sides of the house to link the house with the park – at that time a mile away. Apparently looking forward to the 18th century, Evelyn wrote: 'I persuaded him to bring his park so neere as to comprehend his house within it, which he resolv'd upon.'[4] In the 18th century William Kent (*q.v.* p. 41) removed the first sections of both avenues to open up the parkland around the house and create an opportunity for architectural features on the rises on each side. Closer to the house, Evelyn also suggested the walks through the pleasure grounds which survive today, leading to the church and to the river.

Both during his lifetime and more particularly after his death, Evelyn's influence upon gardening taste and practice was primarily through his writing. His monumental encyclopaedia, *Elysium Britannicum*, first compiled during the 1650s and regularly added to thereafter, was never published, but it provided material for a number of subsequent publications such as his *Sylva*. Among his other most widely read horticultural works were *Kalendarium Hortense*, 'The Gardener's Almanack directing what he is to do monthly through the year, and what fruits and flowers are in their prime', and *The Compleat Gard'ner*, published in 1693, a translation of the French original by one of the leading French horticulturalists of the 17th century, Jean-Baptiste de la Quintinie, who created the *potager* in Louis XIV's garden at Versailles. The intensely practical nature of Evelyn's writing marked a fundamental departure from the more purely scientific and botanical work of contemporaries such as John Parkinson and John Ray. This practicality was also reflected in his all-round involvement in the gardening world of the late 17th century and Stephen Switzer (*q.v.* p. 50) reflected the general opinion of his contemporaries when he wrote of Evelyn in 1715: 'If he was not the greatest master in practice, 'tis to him due the theoretical part of gardening.'[5]

Euston Hall, where John Evelyn advised on the planting of park avenues and the siting of paths through pleasure grounds around the house.

CHRISTOPHER HATTON, IV,
Viscount Hatton of Gretton (1632-1706)

KIRBY HALL, *Northamptonshire*

CHRISTOPHER HATTON IV inherited Kirby Hall in Northamptonshire in 1670, but at the time was serving as Governor of Guernsey and unable to return to England for ten years. After he did so in 1680 he devoted himself to Kirby and hardly left it until his death in 1706; indeed in three different years he was summoned by the House of Lords to explain his failure to attend. His years at Kirby witnessed the halcyon era of what had been for four generations one of the great houses of Tudor and Stuart England, a political and social focal point comparable to Burghley and Hatfield. Yet after Hatton's death Kirby remained unoccupied and by the early 19th century it was uninhabitable.

As well as reversing the generally debt-ridden state of Kirby, Hatton's major contribution was in replanning and extending the gardens. As happened with other important gardens, the neglect that followed his death ensured the survival of the garden's layout until 1930, when Kirby was taken over by the Office of Works. The significance of this survival is explained by Miles Hadfield: 'Since Kirby never suffered from the eighteenth- and nineteenth-century "improvers", the officers of the Ministry of Works have, by skimming the accretions from the original stone edgings, recently unearthed the skeleton of this garden. Today it is, perhaps, the only place where, prompted by the official plan, we can visualize with little difficulty a Restoration garden.'[1] Since Hadfield wrote this the continuing archaeology and restoration work has revealed important features of the original Elizabethan garden which Hatton developed.

Christopher Hatton's garden at Kirby was of particular interest because, while its design was classically geometric in the manner that dominated the 17th century, he filled it with quantities of horticultural treasures, many of them new varieties imported from overseas. His enthusiasm for plants resulted in part from his close relationship with his brother, Charles Hatton, one of the most admired and knowledgeable gardening figures of the 17th century; in 1686 John Ray dedicated to Charles his *Historia Plantarum*, arguably the most significant horticultural book of the 17th century.

Charles Hatton acted as his brother's agent in London, selecting and passing on plants gathered through his wide circle of horticultural friends, including leading nurserymen and plant collectors. It is fortunate that most of his copious correspondence with his brother at Kirby survives, providing evidence of the plants that he was acquiring and sending on to Kirby: passion flowers, seeds of the soap tree from China, a rare kind of hyacinth, bay trees and quantities of fruit trees, both native and exotic. The instructions and personal comments that accompanied the various plants enliven the correspondence as well. In the case of the passion flowers (two, in pots), Charles instructed that careful layering by the gardener would ensure that 'this time twelve months you may have twenty';[2] and on another occasion he wrote with satisfaction, 'I am glad your Lordship likes the *Helleborus albus flore-atrorabeate*. You laughed at me when I was at Kirby for liking it.'[3]

Hatton probably inherited the design of the Great Garden but we know from his brother's correspondence that he made significant alterations, including realigning the garden's main east-west axis at right-angles to the house to north-south; laying gravel paths that divided the beds and stretched along the terraces on the north, west and south sides of the garden; and adding fountains, statues and urns. The south terrace wall was removed to allow the garden, while keeping the basic rectangular proportions, to extend southwards, initially as far as a small stream which was partly canalized, and subsequently beyond to the new orchard and wilderness.

It is not hard to imagine Hatton during the latter years of his life – a cultivated, patrician country gentleman, immersed in extending and improving his garden, planting unusual varieties of trees in his wilderness, such as oaks from Virginia recommended by Henry Compton, Bishop of London, when he visited Kirby in 1688. Three hundred years later all of Hatton's plants have disappeared and the orchard and wilderness have returned to farmland. But the combination of archaeological and architectural remains and documentary evidence provide a remarkably clear picture of this 17th century garden, which greatly assists the restoration currently being carried out by English Heritage. When this is completed, it will include the reintroduction of plants mentioned in Hatton's correspondence with his brother.

JOHN TRADESCANT the Elder (?1570-1638)

CRANBORNE MANOR, *Dorset;* HATFIELD HOUSE, *Hertfordshire*

JOHN TRADESCANT rose from origins so obscure that his definite date of birth is not known, to become the most important and influential gardener of his time, with the post of Keeper of His Majesty (Charles I)'s Gardens. Prior to achieving this position the major years of his career were spent working for a succession of aristocratic patrons: Robert and William Cecil, Earls of Salisbury; Lord Wotton; and George Villiers, Duke of Buckingham. Tradescant became one of the first of a distinguished line of men who were both knowledgeable horticulturalists and garden designers.

Englishmen were increasingly travelling abroad for commercial and political reasons at this time; Tradescant too travelled extensively, on horticultural business for his patrons, and became the first serious plant collector. After a number of trips to the continent, in particular to Holland, he became in 1618 the first English botanist to travel to Russia, collecting and compiling the first catalogue of the country's plants.

Even allowing for the many plants that Tradescant brought back from his journeys to the continent, and the importance of new species – such as the larch (*Larix decidua*), collected in Russia – the most significant of his plant introductions came from North America, where the new colonies were in their infancy. Tradescant himself never travelled to North America but in 1637, the year before his death, he had the satisfaction of sending his son, John Tradescant the younger (*q.v.* p. 22). However, in addition to bringing in valuable new introductions, Tradescant was also pioneering what became the richest horticultural trade route for England. In 1617 he joined the Virginia Company which financed and organized the collection and transportation of new trees and plants to England. Some, such as the spiderwort, *Tradescantia virginiana*, were named after him. In 1626 the Tradescants moved to a house in Lambeth and began the garden which became home for the many plant introductions made by both father and son. Here, too, the elder Tradescant housed his collection of curiosities, later added to by his son, and now in the Ashmolean Museum in Oxford.

Plants introduced by Tradescant are now found in gardens all over Britain, but evidence of his work only survives in the two gardens of his Cecil patrons, Hatfield House and Cranborne Manor. Jacobean Hatfield, built for Robert Cecil, 1st Earl of Salisbury, was one of the grandest houses in England and although Tradescant was not involved in the architectural features of the garden, or the spectacular water features, the general design and all of the planting were under his control. Today, despite major changes by successive generations, the total extent of the gardens – 18ha/45½ acres – remains exactly as it was when originally laid out during Tradescant's time. The present Marchioness of Salisbury has restored an essentially 17th-century character to the garden at Hatfield, with formal terraces on the east side, areas of small-scale geometric planting on the west side and a sunken knot garden in front of the surviving wing of the original Tudor palace. She sees Tradescant as the figure of primary importance in Hatfield's garden history and, in her own words, her aim has been 'to make the garden more closely connected to and harmonious with the house, as it would have been when the house was originally built and the garden made in the early 17th century.' Many of Tradescant's meticulous records, plant lists and diaries of his expeditions abroad survive in the Hatfield library, and these have enabled Lady Salisbury to restore the garden and reintroduce individual plants with the utmost accuracy.

Cranborne in Dorset had been a royal hunting lodge since King John's reign before it was given by James I to his Treasurer, Robert Cecil. Because the delightful house has always been the Cecils' second home, the garden has seen remarkably little alteration to its essential structure, planned by Tradescant for Robert Cecil. His plan survives, clearly showing long avenues of lime and beech trees stretching away to north and south – as they do today. The south avenue is still beech, although they are not the original trees, while the limes to the north were replaced with Cornish elms; killed by Dutch elm disease these were replaced by plane trees during the 1970s. The south front has the main walled courtyard with its Jacobean gatehouse opposite the house; on the north front a renaissance arched porch and balustraded terrace look down to a walled garden, part of which is still an orchard as it was in 1610 when Tradescant presented a bill for £2 2s 10d for supplying fruit trees.

The most intriguing features of Tradescant's garden to survive lie to the west of the house. A bowling green, with a narrow allée between yew hedges on one side, lies between the house and the Mount Garden raised up beside the garden's boundary yew hedge. Mounts to provide an elevated view over gardens – or as here out to surrounding countryside – were important features of Tudor and early Stuart gardens, but the one at Cranborne, enclosed by tall cylindrical yews, is a rare survivor.

As at Hatfield, the present Lady Salisbury has painstakingly replanted many parts of the Cranborne garden with plants listed by Tradescant, such as large double-flowered white roses which he recorded supplying for the garden, and the 'Crown Imperial' fritillaries and the primroses in the small knot garden that she has made. The plants at both Hatfield and Cranborne, the surviving evi-

dence of his garden designs, and his journeys as a plant collector all emphatically confirm the reputation that Tradescant enjoyed among his contemporaries and which he has retained ever since; decidedly one of the founding figures of British gardening.

JOHN TRANDESCANT the Younger (1608-62)

JOHN TRADESCANT THE YOUNGER quickly earned a reputation for plant collecting and for the important and successful introduction to Britain of trees and plants from North America. By the time he was of school age his father's career had prospered sufficiently for him to gain a place as a scholar at King's School, Canterbury. On leaving school in 1623 he immediately began working for his father, assisting in the collection of plants, and in 1626 the family moved to the house in Lambeth.

In 1637, the year before his father's death, Tradescant made the first of three plant-collecting trips to North America, working principally in Virginia. Subsequent visits were made in 1642 and 1654 and the quantity and importance of the plants collected or introduced for successful cultivation in England were confirmed in 1656 when he published *Musaeum Tradescantianum*, listing all the plants in the Lambeth garden. Among his most significant introductions from North America were two of the most distinguished of ornamental trees: the tulip tree (*Liriodendron tulipifera*) – for which John Evelyn (*q.v.* p. 18) gives him credit – and the swamp cypress (*Taxodium disticum*).

Tradescant inherited his father's house and garden in Lambeth, and both father and son – along with John the younger's son, also John – are buried in the churchyard of St Mary's, Lambeth, adjacent to the front gates of Lambeth Palace. In a fitting tribute the deconsecrated church became the property of the newly founded Tradescant Trust in 1976. The interior of the church became a Museum of Garden History and the Tradescant connection with the family's most significant patron was perpetuated

The mound garden at Cranborne Manor was originally created by John Tradescant the elder.

when the present Marchioness of Salisbury designed a small knot and flower garden in one part of the churchyard, using many plants with a Tradescant association.

EDMUND WALLER (*1606-1687*)

HALL BARN, *Buckinghamshire*

EDMUND WALLER and Hall Barn together represent a gem of English garden history; an intriguing and enigmatic personality and a garden of rare historical importance and quality, the earliest surviving example of a formal landscape in England, subtly adapting the French grandeur of Versailles.

Waller is best remembered as a poet but his talents were numerous and his whole career stamped with self-confident opportunism. He followed the well trodden path for upper-class scholars from Eton to King's College, Cambridge, thereafter entering parliament at a precociously early age – he himself recorded that he was sixteen at the time. In 1630 he caused something of a sensation by eloping with Anne Banks, the only daughter of a rich City of London merchant, whom he married the following year. She was always sickly and in 1634 died after giving birth to a son, which left Waller an enviably rich and youthful widower; according to Christopher Hussey, 'the richest poet known to English literature with the exception of Rogers'.[1] During the next few years much of Waller's poetry was designed to further his courtship of Lady Dorothy Sydney – 'Sacharissa', as he addressed her – but she eventually married an earl and Waller himself a more modest second wife, Mary Bressy. His parliamentary career was outspoken and equivocal, swinging from support of parliament to siding with King Charles. As the Civil War deepened, his position became increasingly tenuous and eventually, in 1644, he was imprisoned and fined £10,000 by parliament.

A year later Waller went into exile on the continent and it was during the next seven years – spent mainly in France – that his interest in gardening was aroused. 1646 found him in Italy in the company of John Evelyn (*q.v.* p. 18) who recorded that he travelled from Venice 'in the company of Mr Waller (the celebrated poet) now newly gotten out of England after the Parliament had extremely worried him.'[2] Eventually Waller set up in Paris where he remained living in considerable style until 1651 when, pardoned by parliament, he was able to return to England and his home at Beaconsfield.

Some time between his return and death in 1687 Waller built the original house at Hall Barn, which survives as the present main block, and laid out the garden. Waller called his garden the Grove, and its design marks a clear departure from the renaissance parterres of early Carolean gardens to a more expansive style inspired by France. One of the most radical features of the plan was the manner in which the link between house and garden was almost incidental; the house's south front faces at an angle across lawns sloping down to a formal canal known as the lake, beyond which lies the Grove, its delights completely hidden from the house. Here Waller laid out a series of long *allées* and walks, closely following the site's terrain and cutting through woodland to a series of focalpoints and junctions. From the lawn below the house a broad walk stretches the length of the canal, while beyond the far bank lies an open area of meadow, bounded on its two upper sides by the Grove.

Perhaps the most evocative surviving features of Waller's original garden are two massive yew hedges. One runs from the house down to the lake; the second stretches along the far side of the open grass meadow to the west of the lake and at one point is broken by a small castellated gothick temple. It was the great size of the hedges and their uneven, bulging walls that prompted Christopher Hussey to comment that as well as being, 'the most magnificent and authentically dated of their kind', they are 'symbolic of Waller's gardens at Hall Barn as a whole, which represent a first transitional phase from the old formal artifice of the enclosed Stuart garden towards the romantic naturalism of the eighteenth century.'[3]

Some forty years after Waller's death in 1687, a description of a visit to Hall Barn by Lord Percival in 1724 confirms the extent of Waller's work and helps to identify it from later 18th-century additions. 'Friday morning left Beaconsfield; we went half a mile out of our way to see Hall Barn, Mr Waller's house . . . we spent a full hour and half in viewing the gardens, which you will think are fine when I tell you that they put us in mind of those at Versailles. He has 80 acres in garden and wood, but the last is so managed as justly to be counted part of the former. From the parterre you have terraces and gravelled walks that lead up to and quite thro' the wood, in which several lesser ones cross the principal one, of different breadths, but all well gravelled and for the most part green sodded on all sides. The wood consists of tall beech trees and thick underwood, at least 30 feet high. The narrow winding walks and paths cut in it are innumerable; a woman in full health cannot walk them all, for which reason my wife was carry'd in a Windsor chair like those at Versailles, by which means she lost nothing worth seeing. The walks are terminated by Ha-hah's, over which you see a fine country and prospects every time you come to the extremity of the close winding walks that shut out the sun.'[4]

The Mr Waller referred to by Lord Percival was the poet's grandson, Harry Waller, who was also the stepson of John Aislabie (*q.v.* p. 32), thus making a connection between Hall Barn and Aislabie's later Studley Royal, one of the foremost early 18th-century landscapes. During Harry Waller's time at Hall Barn the classical statues that stand in prominent positions were added to the garden, as were two important buildings designed by Colen Campbell. Campbell's Great Room, positioned at the head of the lake, was burnt down during the 19th century and replaced with the more modest building that survives today, but he also designed the delightful Temple of Venus, an open rotunda which stands on high ground near the south-western edge of the Grove and provides the focal-point of the two main *allées*. The obelisk, too, was almost certainly designed by Colen Campbell and notable for its relief panels with cartouches of garden tools.

The storms of 1987 and 1990 devastated the garden at Hall Barn, cutting great swathes through the beech woodland of Edmund Waller's Grove. Clearance and replanting is already well under way, thanks to the determination of Lord Burnham, whose family have lived at Hall Barn since 1882. And yet, although the sense of enclosure that previously existed has temporarily disappeared, Waller's pattern of *allées* survives quite clearly and with it the raison-d'être of his garden. At the time of its creation Waller described his Grove as 'the creature of his own taste . . . the peculiar scene of his daily wanderings'[5]; more significantly, it was one of the earliest examples of a style of gardening that was to evolve into the English landscape of the 18th century.

THE EMERGENCE
OF AN ENGLISH STYLE
1690–1740

B Y THE LAST YEARS OF THE 17TH CENTURY formal gardening in England was coming under threat from various directions. While the woodland gardens of rides and *allées* cut through plantations or *bosquets* were still formal in their axial design – like Edmund Waller's garden at Hall Barn (*q.v.* p. 24), and Bramham Park in Yorkshire – the manner in which the concept of the garden had begun to be extended beyond regimented geometric enclosures marked the beginnings of the move from garden to landscape. At the same time a quite new inspiration was forthcoming from the continent, the heroic inspiration of landscapes of classical antiquity as presented in the paintings of Claude and Poussin. Gardening should abandon the constraining limitations of formal parterres and should take into account the 'painterly' view of nature, extolling her qualities, albeit in an idealized, romanticized way.

The practice of George London and Henry Wise (*q.v.* p. 46) and their Brompton Nurseries, which had grown increasingly powerful throughout the reigns of William and Mary and Queen Anne, provided a substantial target against which attacks on the formal style could be concentrated. As London and Wise's parterres became larger and more intricate –

Bramham Park was laid out slightly later than Hall Barn
and combines similar formal views with early
signs of the landscape style that followed.

27

and to many eyes more contrived – they became more vulnerable to attack, as was demonstrated by Joseph Addison in *The Spectator* in 1712. Having reiterated Sir William Temple's earlier observations on how Chinese gardens took their inspiration from nature, Addison continued: 'Our British gardeners, on the contrary, instead of humouring nature, love to deviate from it as much as possible. Our trees rise in cones, globes and pyramids. We see the marks of the scissors upon every plant and bush. I do not know whether I am singular in my opinion, but, for my own part, I would rather look upon a tree in all its luxuriancy, than when it is thus cut and trimmed into a mathematical figure . . . but as our great modellers of gardens have their magazines of plants to dispose of, it is very natural for them to contrive a plan that may most turn to their own profit, in taking off their evergreens and the like moveable plants, with which their shops are plentifully stocked.'[1]

Addison's insinuation that London and Wise's practice was organized to ensure the lining of their own pockets may have been unjustified, but he was certainly not 'singular in his opinion'. The importance which gardens and their development had assumed was amply confirmed by the degree to which the subject exercised the minds of other leading writers, statesmen, artists and intellectuals of the early 18th century. In 1710 the Earl of Shaftesbury had published *The Moralists*, in which he advocated a respect for nature as an essential factor of human life; but without doubt the most influential voice – and pen – to be raised was that of the poet Alexander Pope, who illustrated his precepts with his own garden at Twickenham. Amongst gardeners too there was a mood for change, notably in two of London and Wise's former apprentices, Stephen Switzer (*q.v.* p. 50) and Charles Bridgeman (*q.v.* p. 36), whose writing and designs were in marked contrast to the style of their former employers and partners.

In addition to the stylistic and philosophical impetus for change were weighty social and economic factors. The early Hanoverian reigns witnessed both the declining prestige of the Crown and the effective grasp of political power by a Whig oligarchy. Enclosure and improved farming methods, the forerunners of the Industrial Revolution, emphasised the importance of agriculture and hence of the estates owned by the landed aristocrats. With the growing fashion for Palladian architecture championed by the Earl of Burlington and practised by his brilliant protégé, William Kent (*q.v.* p. 41), an ideal was being presented to potential garden makers of a profitable landed estate where nature and classical architecture existed in perfect harmony.

In the longer term the reaction against 'unnatural' formality in gardens was to produce the extremes of 'Capability' Brown's (*q.v.* p. 62) apparently effortless park landscapes and a hankering after wild nature in the picturesque movement. In the first few decades of the 18th century, however, the result was a fusion of wonderful quality, as Tom Turner has pointed out when analysing the progressive change in gardens during these decades: 'Each of these evolutionary steps, all of which were taken between 1709 and 1748, marks a slight swing of the pendulum from rationalism to empiricism, from geometrical symmetry and regularity to asymmetry and the use of serpentine curves. Some of the finest 18th-century gardens were made when the pendulum reached the mid-point between the two poles. Duncombe (1713-50), Studley Royal (1715-30) and Rousham (1726-39) are brilliant examples of the way in which a disciplined and imaginative design concept can be developed from an intuitive response to a sense of place.'[2]

The heroic and classical landscapes that were being laid out had little room for horticulture. Silviculture, however, encouraged by the writing of John Evelyn (*q.v.* p. 18) and Stephen Switzer (*q.v.* p. 50) in particular and offering long-term economic benefits as well as fitting into the concept of large-scale landscape, was to assume increasing importance.

With these new concepts of landscape came a broad spectrum of craftsmanship, producing ornamental decorations and fixtures of unsurpassed quality in English gardening history. Many of the artists came to England from the continent. The Frenchman Jean Tijou, whose mastery of wrought ironwork brought the craft to a peak, arrived in England around 1690 at the beginning of William and Mary's reign and their patronage dominated his career. At Hampton Court he made the highly decorative gates and, most notably, the screen of twelve panels at the garden's riverside which brilliantly adapted the Dutch fashion for *clairvoyées* to a style of richer ornament. Tijou trained Robert Bakewell who emerged as probably the most skilful English ironworker and whose finest work was the superb rococo Birdcage Arbour at Melbourne Hall in Derbyshire. The arbour is only one of the ornamental highlights at Melbourne; it also has the finest single work by Jan (or John) van Nost, the lead Four Seasons urn. Van Nost came to England from Flanders and established a highly successful workshop in London, producing finely worked lead statues as well as occasionally more sumptuous and decorative pieces such as the Four Seasons urn. Melbourne also has statues by him of Perseus and Andromeda, and van Nost provided the various lead figures for William Kent's garden at Rousham. At Rousham, too, is Peter Scheemakers' outstanding piece of garden sculpture, the marble group of a Lion Attacking a Horse. Scheemakers, whose work was with that of Michael Rysbrack the most fashionable of the period, established a considerable reputation reproducing such famous antique statues as garden pieces. Like van Nost, both he and Rysbrack came from

Flanders – from Antwerp. Much of their work consisted of busts and tomb sculptures, where their only real rival was the Frenchman, Louis François Roubiliac. Considering the fierce rivalry between them for most of their careers, it is enjoyable that one of their few recorded joint commissions was to produce the sixteen busts for Kent's Temple of British Worthies at Stowe.

The close involvement of such craftsmen in gardens was partly prompted by the desire to recreate landscapes of classical antiquity. It also clearly demonstrates the degree to which gardens and their decoration had assumed a position of primary artistic importance during the early 18th century. The work of Vanbrugh at Castle Howard, the creation of the garden at Stowe and the career of William Kent are perhaps the three most emphatic factors in this development which by the 1740s had elevated the English landscape to a pinnacle of quality. Horticulture may to an extent have been squeezed out of the 18th-century garden, but it was by no means completely ignored by leading gardeners of the time, as is best illustrated by that influential figure, Alexander Pope. Because of his reputation and success as a writer and his enormous circle of the friends among the most fashionable and important aristocrats and artists of the day, Pope's influence on artistic taste was probably greater than that of any of his contemporaries. His contribution to gardening was summed up by Miles Hadfield: 'There can be no doubt that he had not only a brilliant visual imagination in which the English countryside was singularly in accord with the classical scene, but also a great keenness about the practical side of horticulture.'[3] This was borne out in Pope's own garden at Twickenham, where as well as the famous decorative features such as the grotto and shell temple he had a vineyard, a kitchen garden, a stove and an orangery. His correspondence too has many mentions of individual plants. To his friend Lord Digby he wrote in 1723, 'How thrive your garden plants? how look the trees? how spring the brocoli and finochio? hard names to spell'.[4]

Pope's writing and gardening confirmed the extent to which horticultural interest survived alongside the developing landscape movement, albeit in a subsidiary role. This was the period that saw Philip Miller (*q.v.* p. 49) elevate the Apothecaries' Garden in Chelsea to being among the foremost botanical gardens in Europe, and which saw the flow of new and exotic plants into Britain from overseas – from America in particular, largely through Peter Collinson, who by the 1730s had built up a thriving supply from collectors – increase rapidly.

The Temple of Piety overlooking the Moon ponds: the centrepiece
of John Aislabie's landscape at Studley Royal.

JOHN AISLABIE (1670-1742)

STUDLEY ROYAL, *Yorkshire*

IT IS ONE OF THE MOST ENJOYABLE IRONIES of garden history that the disgrace of a Chancellor of the Exchequer brought about one of the great achievements of landscape gardening. Influenced by the outgoing formality of the 17th century and looking forward to the high romanticism of the picturesque movement, Studley Royal bridges the gap between periods in a totally individual manner; nowhere else is a balance of formality, natural landscape and bravado so emphatically achieved.

John Aislabie, a Yorkshire gentleman whose father was killed in a duel, appeared to have crowned an ambitious political career when he was appointed Chancellor of the Exchequer in 1718. But within three years the appointment had led to his downfall. As Chancellor he championed official support for the South Sea Company's scheme to pay off the National Debt; when the infamous 'Bubble' burst in 1720, leaving a host of speculative investors bankrupt, Aislabie was widely held responsible. At his trial in 1721 he convinced the court that he had not made a significant personal fortune out of the South Sea scheme and was allowed to retain his property, but his political career was over. Chastened and not a little resentful – especially towards Sir Robert Walpole whom he suspected of master-minding his downfall – Aislabie retired to the estate he so nearly lost, Studley Royal in Yorkshire. During the next twenty years he proved himself a more lasting success as a gardener than as a politician, an amateur whose assistance from professionals was only advisory.

Amateur he may have been, but Aislabie moved in political and social circles where garden design was held in high regard. He knew Sir John Vanbrugh who had begun work on Castle Howard, also in Yorkshire, for Lord Carlisle in 1699, the year that Aislabie had inherited the Studley estate; he was a friend and neighbour of Robert Bingley, Lord Benson, who was transforming his own house and garden, Bramham Park. In 1712 Aislabie's name

appeared among the two hundred subscribers to *The Theory and Practice of Gardening*, a translation of the influential book of the same title by the Frenchman, Dezallier d'Argenville, made by John James (*q.v.* p. 40). Not least of the connections that could have motivated his work at Studley would have been his marriage to the widowed daughter-in-law of Edmund Waller (*q.v.* p. 24) which introduced him to the latter's garden at Hall Barn and where he undoubted strongly influenced or, most likely, had a direct hand in the development and embellishment of the original garden by his stepson, Harry Waller.

Aislabie's interest in his property at Studley was initially and dramatically aroused in 1716 when the existing Tudor house was destroyed by fire. He rebuilt the house in competent classical style and the lack of evidence of any architect suggests that the work was substantially his own. A more ambitious architectural achievement was the magnificent quadrangular stable block that he built to the south-west of the house, in which Christopher Hussey detected clear influence of Vanbrugh.[1] The stables pointed to Aislabie's love of the Turf which, with his garden, became twin passions after his enforced retirement from public life. When his house was destroyed by a second fire at the end of World War II the stable block was converted into a house.

Aislabie's landscape design at Studley Royal broke new ground. In taking a landscape of naturally romantic scenery and moulding it into a humanized but still primarily natural state, he made a dramatic departure from most accepted gardening practices of his time, as demonstrated in the work of London and Wise (*q.v.* p. 46) and Charles Bridgeman (*q.v.* p. 36). It is no coincidence that comparable work was being carried out at the same time nearby in Yorkshire — in Thomas Duncombe's terrace overlooking the Rye valley near Helmsley and in Vanbrugh's theatrical siting of the Temple of the Four Winds and the Mausoleum at Castle Howard.

The setting for Aislabie's landscape was the valley of the River Skell, where it flows between steeply wooded sides from Fountains Abbey past the park surrounding

Studley Royal – a distance of 1.75 km/1 mile. He immediately took the radical step of ignoring the house; it stood detached and out of sight at a distance of nearly 1 km/^{1}/$_2$ a mile. Aislabie's design was pure landscape, dependant upon its own qualities for its success.

On the edge of the park he created a large lake by damming the stream, the balustraded dam being broken in the centre by a cascade between a pair of Palladian fishing temples. Above, where the valley opens out, he formalized the stream into a long canal along one edge of the valley and filled the rest of the open area with moon pools – a circular pool flanked on either side by crescent-shaped ones. On the far side, standing amongst trees on the valley's edge a Temple of Piety overlooks them. Aislabie wanted part of the landscape to be viewed from above, so he built a pathway along the wooded west side of the valley, with cuttings through the trees giving views of the moon pools and the Temple of Piety. On the wooded banks he added architectural features, of which the Banqueting House in a clearing on the west side and a prospect tower on the east survive.

Above the pools, the canalized river turns and opens into a small lake before making a sharp right-angle turn to reveal today John Aislabie's dramatically conceived climax: an uninterrupted vista of over 1 km/^{1}/$_2$ a mile along the flat open valley to the abbey ruin.

In fact, despite repeated attempts, Aislabie failed to acquire the Fountains Abbey estate which included this stretch of the river during his lifetime. It was not until 1768 that his son William succeeded in buying it and was able to bring his father's work to the desired conclusion by landscaping the abbey vista, in the process turning down 'Capability' Brown's suggestion that he should be commissioned to complete the design, and carrying out the work himself with a skill that Christopher Hussey commended: 'Aislabie had the formal sense to grasp that the great east front of the abbey closing the straight vale would gain immensely in dignity by having an uninterrupted approach while the vertical mass of tower on the right needed a corresponding upright on the left, which was

provided by the straight canalized river. This rectangular design he framed with parallel woods upon the slopes on either side. The majesty of this vista of straight lines, emphasising the remoteness – the unattainable remoteness – and beauty of the Middle Ages is unforgettable.'[2]

William Aislabie's other major contribution to 18th-century garden design was the creation of the romantic landscape at Hackfall Park close to Studley Royal. Set in a dramatic natural gorge with a stream and wooded hills, and created during the middle of the century, Hackfall was an early example of the emerging fashion for picturesque, romantic scenes. Since 1987 the Hackfall Trust has been undertaking an extensive programme of restoration to the landscape's buildings.

In the context of its period Studley Royal with its envisaged finale was breathtakingly original. Even when the landscape movement blossomed into full flower towards the middle of the 18th century and subsequently acquired a taste for the kind of picturesque scene exemplified by Fountains Abbey, nothing really comparable to Aislabie's work was created. Preserved today with the loss only of some extraneous, and mostly later, architectural features, it still commands the verdict of Christopher Hussey, writing in the 1930s: 'Studley Royal, Fountains Abbey and Hall, and the grand layout of woodland and water in the valley connecting them, form together one of the most romantic places in England'.[3]

GUILLAUME BEAUMONT (c. 1650-1729)

LEVENS HALL, Cumbria

GUILLAUME BEAUMONT and the garden he created at Levens Hall in Cumbria provide an enjoyable curiosity in gardening history: an individual about whom relatively little is known and a garden and park which in some aspects were traditional and conservative by the standards of the late 17th century and in others surprisingly innovative.

Today Levens is renowned for the topiary parterre to one side of the house, its enormous specimens of yew and box clipped into fantastic shapes. But this was only one feature of the design that Beaumont made for his friend and patron, Colonel James Grahme, Keeper of the Privy Purse to James II, whose retirement to the north was no doubt precipitated by the sudden downfall and exile of the monarch in 1688.

It is known that Beaumont was born in France and spent his early life there, and it has been claimed, but never proven, that he was a pupil of le Nôtre. Since he was interested in gardening it is likely that he knew the French royal gardener's work, but his creation at Levens could hardly be described as derivative of the French style; it is altogether too individual. Grahme purchased Levens and its estate in 1688, when he was already well acquainted with Beaumont, and shortly afterwards commissioned him to begin work on the garden. Beaumont first came to Levens in 1692 and lived much of the rest of his life there. The modest house that he occupied still stands close to the stables. Beaumont is known to have advised on a number of other English gardens, some belonging to distinguished aristocrats, as well as on Hampton Court for James II, but all recognizeable evidence of his work at these places such as Edenhall and Greystoke Castle in Cumbria, and Nunnington in Yorkshire, has disappeared.

One key connection which bore fruit at Levens was Grahme's friendship with John Evelyn (q.v. p. 18). Evelyn was constantly advocating the use of yew, as in this passage from *Sylva*: 'Being three years old you may transplant them, and form them into standards, knobs, walks, hedges etc, in all of which works they succeed marvellous well, and are worth our patience for their perennial verdure and durableness.'

Nowhere could Evelyn's advice have been more faithfully followed or his descriptions more accurately realized, for Beaumont planted yew extensively, both in hedges and individually in the topiary parterre. His overall plan divided the garden into what he described as 'quarters', although there were five main areas in all: the topiary

parterre to one side of the house, and beyond a yew hedge on one side of the parterre, a large rectangle divided into four by a beech rondel with axial beech *allées* leading off at right-angles. These survive today, the clipped beech hedging now grown to a massive thickness of some fifteen feet.

One of the beech *allées* leads off towards the edge of the garden where Beaumont's design moves sharply away from the traditional. The boundary with parkland beyond is formed by a stone 'bastion', essentially a short ditch and retaining wall which was to become known during the early 18th century as the ha-ha. Beaumont's use of the device was a radical innovation, providing unbroken visual links between the garden and parkland, where traditional formality was preserved with a sycamore avenue stretching away from the bastion into the distance.

Beaumont's designs extended to the main park, now separated from the house and garden by the A6 – but mercifully saved in 1969 from the imminent threat of being cut in half by a new dual-carriageway road. Here Beaumont gave Levens its most ambitious feature, which also survives today: an oak avenue, extending for over a mile roughly parallel to the valley of the River Kent. While the avenue was quite in the spirit of the period, in one decisive aspect it heralded the vogue for the picturesque that was to emerge in the later 18th century. At its far end it terminated in a seat and viewing-point looking out over the River Kent where it made a right-angle turn into a steep and rugged gorge. Such a scene was guaranteed to excite any enthusiast of the Picturesque, such as William Sawrey Gilpin (q.v. p. 110) who visited Levens during the early 19th century and described the park as, 'A happy combination of everything that is lovely and great in landskip.'

Guillaume Beaumont retained his house at Levens until the end of his life, though during his last years he appears to have subsided into alcoholism which probably brought about his eventual death. He would, however, have had the opportunity to see the yew and box specimens in the parterre beginning to take on their

Guillaume Beaumont's topiary garden at Levens Hall
survives as a curiosity from the period when gardens
were moving towards landscape.

fascinating individual shapes. Today, closely grouped within the pattern of box-edged enclosures, they provide a memorable picture in front of the gaunt stone house. Subsequent planting, in particular since World War II, has done nothing to detract from Beaumont's original layout which survives, with its parterre, rondel, bastion and avenues, as a delightful peculiarity of the late 17th century.

CHARLES BRIDGEMAN (*d. 1738*)

CHISWICK HOUSE, *London*; CLAREMONT, *Surrey*; KENSINGTON GARDENS, *London*; ROUSHAM HOUSE, *Oxfordshire*; STOWE, *Buckinghamshire*

A LACK OF BIOGRAPHICAL DETAILS, an apparent personal reticence and the fact that most of his work was altered or destroyed by his successors later in the 18th century have all conspired against Bridgeman's reputation being as substantial as it clearly deserves to be. Although he left no written descriptions of his life or work, he was an expert draughtsman and some of his plans do fortunately survive. We also know that two contemporary arbiters of taste, Alexander Pope and Horace Walpole, both held his gardening talents in high esteem.

Pope conceded that Bridgeman was, 'another man of the virtuoso class as well as I (and in my motions, of the higher kind of class, since gardening is more antique and nearer God's own work than poetry)'; while Walpole wrote in his essay *On Modern Gardening*, published in 1780: 'After London and Wise Bridgeman was the next most fashionable designer of gardens', adding that he had 'Many detached thoughts, that strongly indicate the dawn of modern taste'.[1]

Bridgeman's origins – even his date of birth – are unknown and he first appears sometime during the early 1700s, working under George London and Henry Wise (*q.v.* p. 46), the leading gardening partnership during the reigns of William and Mary and Queen Anne. Bridgeman's work during the next two decades until his death in 1738 demonstrated a style of gardening that was integral to the evolution of the landscape movement. While it retained characteristics and details of formality – avenues, regular-shaped pools and straight paths, it was also asymmetrical, acknowledged the visual link between garden and surrounding countryside that Walpole delighted in, and was on a scale that extended beyond the conventionally accepted boundaries of garden.

Miles Hadfield suggests that Bridgeman's connection with London and Wise may have been brought about by his reputation for simplifying the elaborate designs of early 18th-century gardens, in order to make them more economic to maintain. Certainly, in 1727 Bridgeman and Wise were commissioned to carry out a survey of the running costs of the royal gardens, concluding that they were excessively expensive to run. Nevertheless, the next year Bridgeman succeeded Wise in the prestigious post as royal gardener, at which he remained until his death ten years later. The garden Bridgeman created for George II at Richmond was completely destroyed by 'Capability' Brown during the 1760s, but the Round Pond in Kensington Gardens, made for George II's wife Caroline, remains.

However, the innovative aspects of Bridgeman's work were demonstrated more clearly in the designs he made for a series of aristocratic clients. He was a member of the St Luke's club, as were several of the leading artists of the day, many of whom were also involved in garden work – such as William Kent (*q.v.* p. 41), Michael Rysbrack the sculptor, Grinling Gibbons and James Gibbs – and this facilitated his introduction to successive patrons. But without question the most significant of his associations was his friendship with Pope and Vanbrugh (*q.v.* p. 52). Pope was, until his death in 1744, the central figure in the field of gardening and landscape, at the hub of patrons, architects and designers. Bridgeman had two main assets: his practical gardening knowledge, and his professional training as a surveyor which enabled him to cope with large-scale designs. Bridgeman was employed as designer at both Stowe and Claremont, with Vanbrugh as architect, and it is clear that he was much influenced by Vanbrugh's panache and vision.

Bridgeman continued to work at Stowe for the 1st Viscount Cobham from 1715 until shortly before his death in 1738. Although – as at Rousham – virtually all of the detail of his design such as planting, paths and vistas was subsequently altered, what survives quite clearly is the scale of the basic plan and the association of different areas. The two main pieces of water which he created – the Octagon Lake in the main central southward axis and the Eleven-Lake immediately to the west – had Bridgeman's formal edges naturalized but remained integral features of the later landscape. Equally important, the ha-ha with which he enclosed the west and south boundaries of his layout, running between theatrical bastions to suit his patron's military enthusiasm, remains the boundary between garden and farmland beyond. At Levens Beaumont had used a narrow ha-ha to allow for an unbroken vista from garden to park avenue, but his extensive use of a ha-ha as a garden boundary, allowing unbroken views and connection with the countryside beyond, was one of the earliest single pointers to the evolution of garden into landscape.

Claremont in Surrey was the home of Sir John Vanbrugh until 1711 when he sold it to Sir Thomas Pelham-Holles, later Earl of Clare and 1st Duke of Newcastle, who employed Vanbrugh and Bridgeman to develop the garden. Here again, under the patronage of a leading political and social figure, Bridgeman worked in partnership with Vanbrugh to create a scene which, like his work at Stowe, clearly belongs to the transitional period from formal enclosed garden to informal, outward-looking landscape. Central to the design was his grass-terraced amphitheatre, a unique feature covering some 1.75ha/4 acres, whose outstanding restoration by the National Trust during the late 1970s rescued it from steady destruction by encroaching laurels. In Bridgeman's original plan the amphitheatre overlooked a circular lake that was subsequently enlarged and naturalized by William Kent.

At Chiswick House Bridgeman was employed by Lord Burlington during the early 1720s, prior to Kent's involvement, and may have been responsible for the garden's original main axis from the house to the north-west which formed the central line of a *patte d'oie* whose three arms led to the focal points of a temple, a column and a bridge.

The garden of Rousham House has become acknowledged as Kent's outstanding work, escaping subsequent alteration and surviving as he designed it between 1738 and 1741. But, as at both Stowe and Claremont, and to some extent at Chiswick, Kent was able to work around an earlier design by Bridgeman, who was employed by Rousham's owner, Sir Robert Dormer, during the same period that he was working at Claremont. A more extensive description of Rousham appears in Kent's entry (*q.v.* p. 41), but a plan of *c.* 1715-20 by Bridgeman reveals how closely Kent's new design fitted into the existing area and shape of the garden. Some of Bridgeman's features were retained and survive, notably the 'natural theatre' (a modest version of the Claremont amphitheatre), the bowling green lawn immediately to the north of the house, which leads towards the main area of garden above the River Cherwell, and the central formal vista through the woodland part of the garden.

At a time when attitudes to gardening and garden design were in a state of flux, when most of the impetus for change was literary, artistic or allegorical, rather than horticultural, Bridgeman was a rare professional who could convert ideas onto paper and into reality. No single figure was so intimately involved in bridging the gap between the geometric formality of London and Wise's gardens and the classically inspired landscapes of William Kent.

MARK CATESBY (*1683-1749*)

Mark catesby's career as a plant collector in America is of particular interest in that it illustrates the progress from the pioneering days of the Tradescants (*q.v.* p. 21) to those of the early 18th century. Born and brought up in Suffolk, not far from the home of the botanical author John Ray with whom he became acquainted at an early age, Catesby first travelled to Virginia in 1712. His most important patron in England to whom he sent seeds was once again Henry Compton, Bishop of London. Catesby remained in America until 1719 but three years later, in 1722, he was sent again under very different auspices. During the 18th century major plant-collecting or exploratory expeditions came increasingly under the patronage and control of the leading scientific institutions, and this time Catesby was dispatched and financed by members of the Royal Society including Sir Hans Sloane.

Catesby's work greatly strengthened the horticultural link between the two countries. Two of his introductions from America were among the most impressive ornamental trees ever to come into England – *Magnolia grandiflora* and *Catalpa bignonioides*. Equally significant were two major publications. The first, the first important illustrated natural history of the United States, was *The Natural History of Carolina, Florida, and the Bahama Islands* (1730-47), for which he not only drew the series of plates depicting birds and plants together, but etched and engraved them as well. More specifically horticultural and relevant to the Anglo-American trade in plants was the posthumously published *Hortus Europae Americanus* – 'A Collection of 85 Curious Shrubs and Trees, the Produce of North America and adapted to the Climates and Soils of Great Britain, Ireland and most Parts of Europe, etc.'

THOMAS BROWNE DUNCOMBE (*c. 1650-1720*) and
THOMAS DUNCOMBE, (*c. 1720-99*)

DUNCOMBE PARK, *Yorkshire;* RIEVAULX TERRACE, *Yorkshire*

FOR CHRISTOPHER HUSSEY the two terraces at Duncombe and Rievaulx, both overlooking the valley of the River Rye and separated by a distance of some three miles, are 'perhaps the most spectacularly beautiful among English landscape conceptions of the eighteenth century.'[1] Indeed, if the English landscape movement achieved an aesthetic pinnacle, a simplicity and yet grandeur in conception producing a perfect and elevating marriage of architecture and landscape then it is here. The terraces are the work of two generations of the same family, father and grandson. While the first – Duncombe – undoubtedly inspired the second and there are obvious similarities, the two are subtly different in a manner that illustrates changing attitudes during the forty years between their creation.

The site of Duncombe Park and its garden was inherited in 1711 by Ursula, the sister of Sir Charles Duncombe, MP for Helmsley and Lord Mayor of London, who had purchased Helmsley Castle and its estate of some 40,000 acres for £90,000. Ursula married Thomas Browne, a city of London partner of her brother's, who, given the fortune that his wife had inherited, not surprisingly assumed the surname of Duncombe. The first hint of future developments at Duncombe came with the new Palladian mansion, whose east front looked straight out to magnificent views across the wooded escarpment dropping to the River Rye beyond.

The architect was William Wakefield, a Yorkshire gentleman, but it has been suggested – and it seems very likely – that Vanbrugh (*q.v.* p. 52), who at the time was working at Castle Howard some ten miles away to the east, may have influenced the siting of the house. With or without Vanbrugh, Duncombe showed clearly that he knew what he wanted in the garden. It has been suggested by Christopher Hussey that Charles Bridgeman was involved in its design, but there is no documentary evidence and it seems more likely that Duncombe himself was largely responsible for the layout.

To the east of the house a flat, open square lawn was cut between flanking woods and a sundial incorporating a life-size lead statue of Father Time (attributed to John van Nost) set on the far side. From here Duncombe created his terrace, which sweeps away to left and right, curving along

The terrace at Rievaulx leads to temples at
both ends, here the Ionic temple, to which the
Duncombe family journeyed for picnics.

the line of the escarpment for a total distance of 1 km/half-a-mile. The perspective of the terrace is naturally enhanced by the curtains of trees that extend along both sides of the satisfyingly broad expanse of grass, and through cuttings in the trees on the escarpment side, spectacular views to the river meandering far below are suddenly and unexpectedly revealed. The shortest arm of the terrace extends north where the focal point is a domed open rotunda with Ionic columns, attributed to Vanbrugh and most likely to have been to his design as it closely resembles the one at Stowe. Similarly, the bastioned, curving ha-ha wall below the temple is a very similar arrangement to that at Stowe. At the far, southern, end of the terrace is a circular, closed Tuscan temple. This was most probably designed later, *c.* 1730, by Sir Thomas Robinson, and bears strong similarities with the Mausoleum at Castle Howard, designed by Hawksmoor, but whose completion in 1729 was overseen by Robinson for his father-in-law, the 3rd Earl of Carlisle, as a result of Hawksmoor's old age.

Given that it was begun at a time when London and Wise were still laying out enclosed and highly stylized parterres, and when John James (*q.v.* p. 40) was celebrating the formal principles of André le Nôtre in his translation of *The Theory and Practice of Gardening*, Duncombe's terrace and its landscape implications were dramatic. Yorkshire was the cradle of the English landscape movement, yet it predated John Aislabie's work at Studley Royal (*q.v.* p. 32) by over a decade, and even Vanbrugh's grandiose work at Castle Howard came some years afterwards.

Fortunately Duncombe's terrace remains unaltered and its quality is complemented rather than rivalled by the terrace created by his grandson at Rievaulx. Thomas married the granddaughter of the builder of Castle Howard, Lord Carlisle, and the appreciation of landscape which they jointly inherited was triumphantly demonstrated in the Rievaulx terrace. Begun in 1754, it is superficially similar to the one at Duncombe: a wide, curving grass sweep extending for 1 km/half-a-mile along a similar escarpment

overlooking the Rye valley, with a domed Tuscan temple at one end and a Palladian banqueting house with an Ionic portico at the other, both with richly decorated interiors and probably designed by Thomas's cousin, Sir Thomas Robinson.

But in inspiration and composition Rievaulx marks a decisive departure from its neighbour. First, it has no connection with a house and was created as a feature of pure landscape in its own right. Second, it was sited and designed specifically to afford a series of thirteen wonderfully picturesque vistas through cuttings in the trees to the ruins of the medieval Cistercian Rievaulx Abbey below. Third, whereas at Duncombe the terrace is a regular curve with the flanking woods making a neat curtain boundary, here at Rievaulx the width of the terrace is irregular as the tree-line advances and recedes, and the curve is less pronounced. This constantly changing perspective, emphasised by the succession of vistas to the abbey ruins below, was described by Arthur Young as 'moving variation' when he visited Rievaulx in 1770.

That the Duncombe terrace and the Rievaulx terrace were laid out by the same family on the same estate serves to increase their unique interest, and although the viaduct once planned by Thomas Duncombe and his Howard wife to link the two terraces was never built, their impact is perhaps the more dramatic as separate and yet intrinsically linked landscapes.

JOHN JAMES (*1672-1746*)

WARBROOK HOUSE, *Hampshire*

TRADITION HAS ALWAYS HAD IT that large-scale formal gardening was introduced to Britain during the late 17th century through English admiration for the work of André le Nôtre in France. Many Englishmen had visited le Nôtre's gardens while in enforced exile in France during the Civil War and Protectorate; others, in the years after the Restoration. But it was not until 1712, when John James published his translation of Dezallier d'Argenville's *The Theory and Practice of Gardening*, which set out in detail the principles advocated by le Nôtre, that his ideas were made available to a far wider audience. First published anonymously in France in 1709, the book incorporated plans, engravings and descriptions by Jean-Baptiste Alexandre Le Blond, one of le Nôtre most accomplished pupils who later worked on the Peterhof Gardens in Russia for Peter the Great.

James's translation remained one of the most widely read and influential books throughout the 18th century, with subsequent editions appearing in 1722, 1723 and 1743. Among the distinguished and aristocratic list of 236 subscribers to the original edition were the names of James Johnston of Orleans House in Twickenham, to whom the book was dedicated, John Aislabie of Studley Royal, James Brydges of Canons (who became Duke of Chandos) of Canons, the Earl of Carlisle of Castle Howard, Thomas Coke of Melbourne and the Earl of Pembroke of Wilton. In Christopher Hussey's opinion, James, 'far more than le Nôtre, should be recognised as responsible for encouraging the "grand manner" of gardening in England.'[1]

James was born in Hampshire, the son of a clergyman and well enough educated to be able to claim in later life that, 'no person pretending to Architecture among us, Sir Christopher Wren accepted, has had the advantage of a better education in the Latin, Italian and French tongues.'[2] And yet, although a competent and conscientious architect – he received a number of commissions as a result of his trustworthiness as much as his building skills – he was throughout his career eclipsed by his more brilliant contemporaries: Wren, Hawksmoor, Vanbrugh and Gibbs. As Clerk of the Works at Greenwich Palace he never achieved the senior position of surveyor, and was subordinate to Wren, Hawksmoor, Vanbrugh, Colen Campbell and Thomas Ripley. Nor has James's reputation as an architect been helped by the fact that all of his most important houses, in particular Orleans House, Twickenham, have been destroyed.

His own house, Warbrook House, Eversley, in Hampshire, however, fortunately does survive, together with its garden, which James built and laid out for himself in 1724. The house was considerably extended during the 1930s by Lord Gerald Wellesley and Trenwith Wills, who added identical pedimented east and west façades but left James's original building unaltered. It was in front of the west façade that James created a garden, putting into practice a number of the principles outlined in *The Theory and Practice of Gardening*.

On a level site – which James maintained was ideal for a garden unless the ground could be terraced – he created a long central vista cut through groves of oak and scots pine, with a formal canal into which the River Warbrook was neatly diverted. Two narrower vistas extended at angles from the house on either side of the canal, completing a *patte d'oie* at Hampton Court. The whole scheme was unmistakeably French in inspiration and survives today, remarkably little altered, as a rare example of early 18th-century formality.

James's family life presented regular disappointments, culminating during the 1730s in the collapse of a printing venture initiated by his brother, in which he had been persuaded to invest heavily. As a result, both Warbrook and his house in Greenwich had to be sold on his death, in order to provide for his wife and for his widowed daughter-in-law.

William Kent (1685-1748)

Badminton House, *Avon*; Chiswick House, *London*; Claremont, *Surrey*; Euston Hall, *Suffolk*; Holkham Hall, *Norfolk*; Rousham House, *Oxfordshire*; Shotover House, *Oxfordshire*; Stowe, *Buckinghamshire*

Even from a distance of nearly three hundred years William Kent stands out as an appealing character, an artistic all-rounder of extraordinary accomplishment whose career, whether as landscape gardener, painter, interior decorator or architect was buoyed up and furthered by a rich mixture of self-confidence, charm and talent. Brimming with enthusiasm and energy, he threw himself into almost every department of the arts and, with few exceptions, strode from success to success. Nine years in Italy from the age of twenty-five gave him an appreciation and understanding of Italian, especially Roman, architecture, painting and gardens that were to provide an unending source of inspiration in his later career.

His other skills notwithstanding, it was as a landscape gardener that Kent was most innovative. He had an intensely visual approach to the subject. There is no evidence that he drew up plans for any of his projects, or wrote down his ideas, other than in letters; but far from proving a limitation, this allowed him the freedom to create the landscapes of painters, in particular the painters of heroic imaginary landscapes: Claude Lorrain, Gaspard Poussin and Salvator Rosa. It was exactly this freshness of approach compared, for instance, with the more restrained professionalism of Charles Bridgeman (q.v. p. 36) that enabled the landscape movement to accelerate from its tentative beginnings.

Born into a humble family in Bridlington, North Yorkshire, Kent worked as an apprentice to a coach painter in Hull. It appears that he did not complete his apprenticeship. Instead, travelled to London in search of patrons to further his career as a painter. Helped by his talent and charm, in 1710 he was sent to Italy by an unknown benefactor to study and to buy antiquities and paintings, but shortly after arriving in Rome he gained the support of three patrons who were to finance his early years in Italy: Sir William Wentworth, Burrell Massingberd and Sir John Chester.

During his time in Italy Kent gained an introduction that was to dominate the rest of his life, to Richard Boyle, 3rd Earl of Burlington. Burlington, a wealthy young aristocrat, soon to become the arbiter of architectural taste in England, was the most influential protagonist of Palladianism. When he returned from Italy in 1719 Kent accompanied him as his protegé and companion, and the rest of Kent's life revolved around Burlington, his family and circle of friends. They affectionately named Kent 'Signor', Burlington House in London became his home, and when he died he was buried in their family vault at Chiswick House.

Burlington introduced Kent to a social circle that included the most influential and progressive aristocratic patrons of the arts, as well as architects and artists, and among these the most significant for Kent's career as a landscape designer was Alexander Pope. The poet had begun his garden at Twickenham soon after acquiring his villa there in 1719. Kent had just returned from Italy and was quickly establishing himself as a decorator, designer of interiors and furniture and – later – as an architect. Through their friendship Kent became intimately acquainted with the planning and execution of Pope's garden, and, more importantly, with Pope's ideas about gardening and landscape: 'all gardening is landscape painting . . . the lights and shades in gardening are managed by disposing the thick grove work, the thin and the openings, in a proper manner, of which the eye is generally the properest judge . . . you may distance things by darkening them, and by narrowing the plantation more and more towards the end, in the same manner as they do in painting . . .'[1].

Kent's first essay as a gardener was, not surprisingly, for Lord Burlington at Chiswick House. Here he followed in the steps of Charles Bridgeman, as he was to do at Claremont, Rousham and Stowe, and at Chiswick he gave more than a hint of the innovative effect he would have on the evolution of the English landscape. Christopher Thacker describes Kent's naturalized canal or lake at Chiswick as being 'the earliest example of a lake designed to appear "natural" in Western Europe', and the cascade at the south-east end of the lake as 'the earliest example of a design for a deliberately ruined garden feature in Western Europe'.[2] Kent's *exedra*, too, was a bold indication of the classically inspired but original approach he was to take towards garden architecture.

It was while he was working for Frederick, Prince of Wales at Carlton House (a direct result of Burlington's

The octagonal pool with the rill leading off, at Rousham House, William Kent's gardening masterpiece.

influence and of Kent's successful interior decoration at Kensington Palace) that contemporaries began to note the signs of a new departure in gardening. The gentleman architect Sir Thomas Robinson wrote in a letter to his father-in-law, Lord Carlisle: 'There is a new taste in gardening just arisen, which has been practised with so great success at the Prince's garden in town, that a general alteration of some of the most considerable gardens in the kingdom is begun, after Mr Kent's notion of gardening, viz. to lay them out, and work without either level or line. By this means I really think the 12 acres the Prince's garden consists of, is more diversified and of greater variety than anything of that compass I ever saw; and this method of gardening is the more agreeable, as when finished it has the appearance of beautiful nature, and without being told one would imagine art had no part in the finishing, and is, according to what one hears of the Chinese, entirely after their model for works of this nature, where they never plant straight lines or make regular design.'[3]

The Carlton House gardens have long disappeared but Kent was soon to enhance his reputation by adding to and altering the designs of Charles Bridgeman at Claremont, Stowe and Rousham. It could be argued that Bridgeman was as important in the evolution of gardens by virtue of his designs which provided Kent with a basis on which to work as he was in his own right, for in all three cases Bridgeman's work, which went some way towards transporting garden into landscape and yet remained firmly encased in formality, enabled Kent to see clearly how this could and should be carried to a conclusion. Unencumbered by the need to work to a detailed plan, as in all three cases he was presented with an existing one by Bridgeman from which to develop his ideas, Kent merely produced delightful, atmospheric sketches of suggested scenes or architectural details, and the detailed planning was left to whichever humble craftsman was employed to implement his designs.

At Claremont, Kent's alterations were limited to naturalizing Bridgeman's formal pond into a lake with an island and pavilion and softening the formal lines of some of the paths and planting. At Stowe, his was only one of a host of contributions to this most richly varied canvas of the 18th century landscape; albeit among the most important, with his creation of the valley known as the Elysian Fields, where classical allegory and the politics of Stowe's owner Lord Cobham merged in his Temple of Ancient Virtue looking down across the winding River Styx to his Temple of British Worthies. Kent also built a Temple of Modern Virtue as a ruin, demonstrating Cobham's antipathy to Walpole and his government, but this has disappeared.

Rousham was – and remains – Kent's universally acknowledged masterpiece. For Horace Walpole it was 'the most engaging of all Kent's works . . . pure Kentissimo'[4]. He was again working on an existing Bridgeman 'transitional' design, and possibly because of the more intimate scale of the place compared to most of his commissions, possibly because of the topography and setting or the fact that he was given a broad brief to re-model both house and garden, whatever the reason, Kent synthesized a variety of influences and his own genius in a supremely harmonious manner.

The garden was planned to be enjoyed via a set route from the house, designed to reveal scenes which transported the inspiration of classical Italy into the setting of an English rural landscape. To the north and out of sight of the house the ground drops to the River Cherwell in a gentle slope to a crook in the river formed by two pronounced bends. In front of the house a broad bowling green terminates in a superb sculpture of A Lion Attacking a Horse by Peter Scheemakers; beyond it the ground drops sharply to the river while the view extends into the countryside, to the 'eye-catcher' on a distant hill. From the far corner of the bowling green Kent's path leads downhill and across a terrace adorned with a Dying Gladiator, again by Scheemakers. From here, too, there are extensive views out across the river.

Beyond the terrace is the Venus Vale, perhaps the heart of Kent's creation: a small valley enclosed by trees, with cascades decorated with classical lead figures from

John van Nost's workshop and an octagon pond. From the bottom of the valley the water flows through grove-like woodland in a deliberately serpentine rill to the cold bath and on to a small doric temple named after its builder, William Townesend. The temple stands on the edge of an open clearing and looks out to the Heyford Bridge crossing the river in the far distance. Kent emphasized further these outward vistas of the garden by transforming an old mill cottage into a gothick Temple of the Mill and adding a sham arched ruin, the 'eye-catcher', on a hilltop beyond, both of which are visible from a number of positions in the garden.

On another edge of the clearing a statue of Apollo stands at the end of the long walk which leads back through woodland towards the unseen house and the Praeneste, a unique piece of garden architecture and totally characteristic of Kent in its inspiration, position and design. The severely Palladian seven-arched arcade, looking out across the river to the countryside beyond, stands beneath the terrace with the Dying Gladiator and yet is completely invisible from above; the surprise of its appearance on the return journey is entirely as Kent intended. It is also an ingenious architectural device to cross the narrow neck of slope above the river's main bend.

It has often been claimed that Kent's horticultural knowledge was virtually non existent but at Rousham he displayed a clear sensitivity to the varying character and effect of different trees, most notably – and innovatively – in his blending of coniferous evergreens with native species such as beech and oak. As with his other work, Kent was not present to supervise the actual planting or the application of his design, as Michael Wilson describes: 'The making of the garden at Rousham was not a simple matter. It involved, amongst other things, moving tons of earth, planting numerous (5 m) 15ft conifers, re-aligning a road, widening the river and establishing a ha-ha . . .. In November 1738 we find White (the steward) expressing the hope, in a letter, that Kent can soon be cajoled into paying a visit: "The time Mr Kent will be most wanted . . . will be about the beginning of next February, could he then be prevailed upon to take a trip down".'[5]

Only at Rousham did Kent have the opportunity to create a complete landscape; by and large his commissions were architectural or for alterations to specific areas of landscape or planting schemes. His buildings demonstrated an individuality and vigour ideally suited to garden architecture, and nowhere more so than at Euston Hall in Suffolk where he was employed by the 2nd Duke of Grafton in the 1740s. The duke's predecessor, the Earl of Arlington, had been advised by John Evelyn (q.v. p. 18) in the extensive planting of his park, and Evelyn had been responsible for the two magnificent avenues which stretched up the slopes on both sides of the house and on over ridges into the distance. Kent did away with the avenues from house to ridge, flanking the vista more informally with clumps of trees in a way that clearly heralds the style of 'Capability' Brown (q.v. p. 62). To the west he built a pedimented gateway on the ridge, with the remaining lime avenue known as the Duke's Ride stretching beyond. To the east the effect is even more spectacular: from the forecourt gates and railings an open slope of parkland leads up to the crest where an avenue of beech begins.

A stretch by Kent, which shows that at some stage he suggested the duke should build a new Palladian house half way up the slope to the east, has as its focal point on the ridge a building which evolved into the Temple, one of Kent's most impressive pieces of garden architecture. Built as a banqueting house, not actually where shown on the drawing but further along the ridge, it is a domed octagon, with lesser rooms on either side of a central dining room whose interior Kent also decorated. The Temple has clear similarities with Kent's Worcester Lodge at Badminton, built around the same time for the Duke of Beaufort, whose aunt had been the wife of the Duke of Grafton. Both the Temple and Worcester Lodge are Kent in assured maturity, a few years before his death, and it would not have escaped the notice of his contemporaries that two of his last commissions were for dukes, and for two of the grandest parks in England.

Kent died in 1748 aged sixty-three after a splendidly varied and productive career during which he had been acclaimed by aristocratic and intellectual society and had achieved the prestigious position of deputy surveyor in the office of works, a post he took on in 1735 and retained for the rest of his life. Although his output as a landscape designer was in some ways limited, we are fortunate that so much of what he did survives today, and it was enough for Horace Walpole to call him, 'The father of modern gardening. He leapt the fence and saw that all nature was a garden.'[6] Throughout the rest of the 18th century and beyond, the influence of Kent's garden designs was enormous – on amateurs such as Henry Hoare at Stourhead (*q.v.* p. 73) or Charles Hamilton at Painshill (*q.v.* p. 72); on 'Capability' Brown himself (*q.v.* p. 62); and on the disciples of the picturesque movement. Looking at Rousham, it is easy to understand why.

GEORGE LONDON (*d. 1713*) and HENRY WISE (*1653-1738*)

BLENHEIM PALACE, *Oxfordshire*; HAMPTON COURT, *London*; MELBOURNE HALL, *Derbyshire*

THE PARTNERSHIP of London and Wise owned and ran the Brompton Nurseries from 1689 and it was here that their reputation was established. Subsequently their joint names have become synonymous with the period of formal gardening during the reigns of William and Mary and Queen Anne which not only reached a peak of detailed grandeur at places such as Blenheim, Chatsworth and Longleat, but provided the prime example against which the landscape movement was to react. The success of George London's early career rested on his admiration for the gardens of André le Nôtre, but by the end of the century his plan for the formal treatment of Ray Wood at Castle Howard was being rejected by his client, the Earl of

Carlisle, in favour of a more natural scheme; and in 1727, the year before his retirement, Henry Wise was working on a survey of the running costs of the royal gardens in conjunction with Charles Bridgeman (*q.v.* p. 36) who, with another London and Wise trainee, Stephen Switzer (*q.v.* p. 50), was instrumental in the move away from the formality of the classic London and Wise layout to the more natural landscape.

Prior to the establishment of his partnership with Wise, George London emerges as the senior figure, despite origins of such obscurity that the place and date of his birth are not known. It is known that at some stage he visited France, gaining first-hand knowledge of André le Nôtre's gardens and becoming acquainted with John Rose, who studied under le Nôtre and became Charles II's gardener at St James's Palace from 1666 until his death in 1677. On returning to England, London became gardener to Henry Compton, Bishop of London, at Fulham Palace, and in 1688 he played his part in the Glorious Revolution when he assisted Compton (the only bishop to have signed the invitation to William of Orange) in organizing the escape of the then Princess Anne from London and accompanying her to safety in Nottingham. In 1681, while still working for the bishop, he joined three other partners – Roger Looker, Moses Cook and John Field, all leading gardeners of the day – in establishing the Brompton Nurseries on a site of some one hundred acres where the museums of South Kensington stand today. After the death or retirement of his three partners, London took on Wise in 1687 and the firm became a partnership under their joint names in 1689.

Their reputation was based partly on royal connections. London had been made superintendant of the royal gardens under William and Mary, and in 1702 Wise was appointed official gardener to Queen Anne. During both reigns Hampton Court was the most prestigous of the royal residences, and here most of the work that was carried out for William III, such as London's Great Fountain Garden, the semi-circular parterre with fountains between Wren's new east façade, and the *patte d'oie* of lime avenues

The main vista at Melbourne Hall, laid out by
the leading English exponents of formal gardens,
George London and Henry Wise.

and central canal beyond, was subsequently altered for Queen Anne by Wise. The great chestnut avenue across Bushy Park that Wise planted in 1699, forming the northern approach to the palace, was retained and survives today. The area known as the Wilderness that the firm planted immediately to the north of the palace, incorporating the famous maze, also survives in its basic layout and style of planting.

Like many successful partnerships, it was to some extent a union of opposites, with London probably the more likeable and Wise the more practical and ambitious; certainly London was first and foremost a designer and gardener, while Wise was an astute businessman as well as a horticulturalist. Within a period of a few years the increased workload led to a clear division of duties, with London tending to travel the country, apparently thinking nothing of riding 100 km/60 miles within a day to visit and advise their impressive array of aristocratic clients, and Wise concentrating upon the royal gardening duties and the management of the nursery.

Their most ambitious projects were enormous parterres for their grandest clients, such as Lord Weymouth at Longleat, the Duke of Devonshire at Chatsworth (these two predominantly London's work), and the Duchess of Marlborough at Blenheim (where Wise was almost exclusively involved). Virtually all traces of these have disappeared; at Blenheim only the walls and pools in the kitchen garden survive. Indeed it was against the stylized formality, the neat rows of tightly clipped trees and hedges, the intricate patterns of box and gravel around statues and fountains, that the early protagonists of a more natural style of gardening, such as Joseph Addison, first reacted.

It is one of the partnership's most delightful creations and one on a relatively small scale that presents the best surviving example of their work: Melbourne Hall in Derbyshire, where they worked for Thomas Coke, vice-chamberlain to Queen Anne, from 1696. London died in 1714 but Wise continued to advise Coke until the latter's death in 1725. Although the parterres that once covered the terraces descending in front of the house have disappeared, the rest of the garden has remained remarkably little altered due to neglect and irregular occupation by Coke's successors.

Melbourne has often been described as a copy of the work of André le Nôtre, but while he was probably the main inspiration – Coke had travelled extensively in France and Holland and had recorded his admiration for le Nôtre – the garden has greater originality than this suggests. Its charm lies in the combination of the layout and the display of work of two of the outstanding craftsmen of the period, Robert Bakewell and John van Nost. From the house the main sweep of garden descends in grass terraces to a large circular pool, the Great Basin, on the far side of which stands the domed and partly gilded Birdcage Arbour, the most ornate and impressive piece of wrought-iron work in any English garden, created by Robert Bakewell whose smithy was in the village of Melbourne. Extending down one side of the terraces is a tunnel of yew some 185m/200 yds long, originally planted before London and Wise's time but most probably extended by them to form a complete boundary on this side of the garden. At the far end of the tunnel a line of three smaller circular pools provide the link with the second area of garden in gently rising woodland. From each pool straight formal *allées* are cut through the beech and lime wood, neatly lined with beech and hornbeam hedges. Here are the *bosquets* that certainly link Melbourne to French formality, a regular pattern within a woodland setting. Although there has inevitably been extensive replanting – especially of the hedges – the layout and the plants used are as originally planned by London and Wise, assisted by references in their papers at Melbourne: '600 large limes at a shilling each, 2,000 hornbeams . . .'.

The main central *allée*, known as Crow Walk, leads gently uphill to the focal point of Melbourne's second ornamental masterpiece, the enormous Four Seasons lead urn made by van Nost in his London workshops. Van Nost also supplied many lead figures to adorn different parts of the garden: cherubs for fountains in the pools, pairs of winged *amorini*, and life-size figures of Mercury, Perseus and Andromeda, and a kneeling slave.

George London died in 1714, the year after his long-standing patron and employer, Henry Compton. The style of gardening of which he had been a leading exponent was dying too; formality, whether in intricate parterres or woodland *bosquets*, was being increasingly challenged by the gardening cognoscenti.

Wise, faced with a shrinking demand for the thousands of plants the nursery produced, and without his seemingly inexhaustible partner, was soon to get rid of the Brompton nursery. In 1715, a year after George I's accession, his prestige, too, received a blow when Vanbrugh was given the new position of 'surveyor of the gardens and waters belonging to the several palaces within that part of Great Britain known as England! The unquestioned primacy that Wise had enjoyed over the royal gardens for more than a decade had ended. He remained active as royal gardener, responsible for maintenance rather than for improvements and in an atmosphere clouded by wrangling over the management of the royal gardens and debts owed by the Duchess of Marlborough and his former partner Joseph Carpenter.

He had purchased Warwick Priory with its estate in 1709, and David Green describes how: 'From the midst of this turmoil Wise must have longed to retire, to cut his losses, nurse his ailments and plan his own garden at Warwick. But the Priory was not yet empty; and some money matters still needed to be set in order, including debts due from Blenheim.' Eventually, in 1727, the year of George I's death, Wise gained vacant possession of the Priory and was able to give up: 'In his day no one had been more active. Now in his evening he would be content to potter and, if he chose to experiment, it should be within the walls of his own grounds at Warwick.'[1]

Today, almost all of London and Wise's work has disappeared, but it is worth remembering, in addition to their garden designs, the importance of the Brompton Nurseries as marking a decisive step forward for the commercial aspects of gardening. London and Wise had offered their many patrons and clients a well-organized and complete service and their unquestioned skill was delightfully recorded in a short poem, attributed to 'a labourer employed in Mr Wise's garden at Brompton':

> *If he who the first garden made*
> *Had put in Wise to keep it,*
> *Made Adam but a labourer there*
> *And Eve to weed and sweep it;*
> *Then men and plants had never died,*
> *Nor the first fruits been rotten;*
> *Brompton had never then been known*
> *Nor Eden e'er forgotten.*

PHILIP MILLER (1691-1771)

APOTHECARIES GARDEN, *Chelsea, London*

IN THE VIEW OF Miles Hadfield, Philip Miller was, 'the greatest British gardener of the period.'[1] The claim is based upon Miller's encyclopaedic knowledge of plants, the success and influence of his book, The *Gardener's Dictionary*, published in 1731, and upon his work as curator of the Apothecaries Garden in Chelsea (now the Chelsea Physic Garden) which he elevated from a botanical garden of no significance to one that claimed the foremost reputation in Europe. Only after Miller's retirement in 1770 and death the following year, was Chelsea's supremacy challenged and surpassed by the rise of the Royal Botanic Garden at Kew.

Miller came from a Scottish family but was brought up in or around London and at an early age began to work for his father, a market-gardener. Branching out on his own as a florist in what is today Pimlico, he was brought to the notice of Sir Hans Sloane who engineered his appointment in 1722 as curator at Chelsea, when he (Sloane) passed over ownership of the land to the Apothecaries Company – and was thus in a strong position to exert his influence. By a combination of ceaseless activity, contact with botanists and gardeners all over the continent, and skill as a plantsman, in a relatively short time Miller transformed the garden's fortunes. In 1736 he was even visited by Carl Linnaeus who was already working towards the publication in 1753 of his *Species Plantarum*, acknowledged ever since as the definitive starting-point for all botanical nomenclature. Miller, who was both opinionated and stubborn, at first disagreed with Linnaeus on a number of nomenclature details, but in the later editions of his *Gardener's Dictionary* he acknowledged Linnaeus's binomial system of consistently two-word names for species by making the necessary alterations.

Miller's *Gardener's Dictionary* does not rival Linnaeus's book as a work of botanical scholarship, but was without question among the most widely read and influential gardening books in 18th-century England. It combined descriptions of plants and trees with suggested principles of garden design taken from Dezallier d'Argenville's *La Théorie et la Pratique du Jardinage*. Dezallier d'Argenville's book, translated into English and published by John James (*q.v.* p. 40) in 1712, celebrated the formal principles of André le Nôtre and, as Miles Hadfield wrote about Miller's *Dictionary*: 'The wide circulation of these precepts makes one realize their importance and one can only conclude that they were largely followed by the unfashionable long after the sinuous lines of "nature" had become the mode in smart quarters.'[2]

Miller's *Dictionary* influenced gardens all over the country, and also advised on gardens. But it was within the confines of the Apothecaries Garden that he carried out his most important horticultural work, notably with the advances that he made in raising unusual plants, germinating seeds from tropical countries, cross-fertilizing, and specializing in plants with medical use. Most prestigious among new plants introduced from abroad and first grown in Britain by Miller at Chelsea was *Ailanthus altissima*, the 'Tree of Heaven' from China. In a number of instances the fruits of his work were exported abroad, for instance when he developed new seed for cotton plantations in Georgia – still at the time a British colony. His influence and methods are today the principles that guide the Chelsea Physic Garden, which remains what he made it – a rare repository of unusual and exotic plants and a centre of scientific horticultural research.

STEPHEN SWITZER (1682-1745)

CIRENCESTER PARK, *Gloucestershire;* EBBERSTON HALL, *Yorkshire;* NOSTELL PRIORY, *Yorkshire*

DESPITE HIS CONTINENTAL-SOUNDING SURNAME, Switzer was an Englishman, born in the Hampshire village of East Stratton. His involvement in gardening began at an early age, during the 1690s, when he was apprenticed to London and Wise (*q.v.* p. 46) at their Brompton Nurseries. It is interesting that both Switzer and Charles Bridgeman (*q.v.* p. 36), who were later to take early – if tentative – steps away from French formality and clearly delineated gardens, began their careers working for London and Wise. As the most successful and prestigious gardening partnership of the day, London and Wise were able to introduce their protégés to a circle of potential patrons and connections that were to prove of great importance in future years. And yet, it was the very formality of London and Wise's style stressing the integral relationship of the garden to its house but not to the landscape beyond, which provided a focus for reaction from Switzer, Bridgeman and the other early advocates of the landscape style at the turn of the century.

In Switzer's case this was clearly demonstrated at Castle Howard. Early on in his planning, Lord Carlisle had asked George London to devise a plan for Ray Wood, an area of some 24 ha/60 acres. London's response, a series of formal walks in the pattern of a star, was rejected by Lord Carlisle – probably under the influence of Vanbrugh who first appeared at Castle Howard in 1699 – in favour of a decisively less regular, more natural scheme. Switzer's verdict was unequivocably in support of the peer rather than his employer: 'Mr London designed a star, which would have spoiled the wood, but that his Lordship's superlative genius prevented it, and to the great advancement of the design, has given it that labyrinth-diverting model we now see it.'[1]

Nevertheless, and despite any reservations he may have had about their style of gardening, Switzer remained with London and Wise for a number of years, and in 1715 considerably enhanced his career and future reputation with the publication of *The Nobleman, Gentleman, and Gardener's Recreation*. The book was subtitled 'An Introduction to Gardening, Planting, Agriculture and the other Business and Pleasures of a Country Life', which in itself suggests a desire to make the garden outward-looking and related to the surrounding countryside. Three years later it reappeared as the first of his three volumes of *Ichnographia Rustica*, one of the most important garden books of the 18th century, which gave detailed advice on all aspects of gardening and design; practical instruction mixed with Switzer's own, often trenchant opinions, and illustrated with a series of plans that bear witness to his high standard of draughtsmanship. Certainly the author had no illusions about the quality of his work, prefacing a new edition in 1742 with the words: 'with above fifty Copper Plates, done by the best Hands, which, though first published above twenty years ago, has given rise to every thing of the kind, which has been done since.'[2]

The most significant sections of *Ichnographia Rustica* are where Switzer advocates a natural style that goes beyond the previously accepted confines of the garden: 'All the adjacent country should be laid open to view and that the eye should not be bounded with high walls, woods misplaced, and several obstructions as they are seen in too many places, by which the eye is as it were imprisoned and the feet fettered in the midst of the extensive charms of nature and the voluminous tracts of a pleasant country.'[3]

In simple terms, what Switzer was proposing was a staging-post between strictly geometric formality and the 'natural' landscape of William Kent (*q.v.* p. 41) – a style in which major axial lines combined with lesser 'serpentine' walks, and in which the treatment of water was still essentially formal. He was, however, sympathetic to contemporary moves to link gardening with agriculture and tree planting, producing as an end result a designed or planned landscape that might involve large areas of an estate. Just the immediate surroundings of a house.

At Nostell Priory in Yorkshire, Switzer's limited amount of work was the subject of considerable later alteration by 'Capability' Brown (*q.v.* p. 62). The garden which best illustrates his ideas, as set out in *Ichnographia Rustica*, is Cirencester Park, where Switzer almost certainly advised its energetic owner, the 1st Earl Bathurst, and where great avenues stride through blocks of woodland, linked by rides and highlighted by a series of architectural features. Lord Bathurst was also assisted in his impressive planting schemes and in the adornment of his woodland rides by his close friend and frequent visitor to Cirencester, the poet Alexander Pope.

The most intriguing garden with which Switzer's name is linked is that of Ebberston Hall in Yorkshire, where today only the bones survive of what was perhaps the most delightful English version of an Italian villa and water garden, reminiscent of the Palazzo Farnese's *casino* at Caprarola. Christopher Hussey in particular was convinced that Ebberston was Switzer's work, and since we know that Switzer enjoyed a thriving northern practice and was particularly interested in the treatment of water (in 1734 he published *An Universal System of Water and Waterworks, Philosophical and Practical*), it seems likely that he had a major hand in the design. The villa itself, built in 1718 by Colen Campbell for William Thompson, MP for Scarborough, survives, as does one of the original flanking pavilions. On the house's north front a first-floor loggia originally looked onto a water garden where a stream fed by a spring high above in the limestone ran into a series of pools and then around an island into a formal canal some 380 metres/1,200 feet long. Close to the house the water flowed over a cascade between stone urns and disappeared beneath the ground. Today, the water has long ceased to flow but one pool survives, as do the body of the canal and the urns on either side of the cascade's dam.

Switzer remained an all-round professional gardener throughout his life; as well as designing and writing, he established himself as a nurseryman and supplier of seeds at Millbank in 1724. Competitive and dogmatic, he was too closely dependent upon his trade to risk radical departures in garden design, and he lived out of the mainstream of fashionable society whence most innovative ideas emanated. None the less, the combination of his writing and surviving work confirm a considerable influence, probably enhanced by his regularly extolling the virtues of his trade: 'Gardening is easy, quiet, and such as puts the Body nor Mind in those violent Agitations or precipitate and imminent Dangers that many other Exercises (in themselves very warrantable) do.'[3]

SIR JOHN VANBRUGH (1664-1726)

BLENHEIM PALACE, *Oxfordshire*; CASTLE HOWARD, *Yorkshire*; CLAREMONT, *Surrey*; STOWE, *Buckinghamshire*.

JOHN VANBRUGH was born the son of a merchant; in his career he was a vigorous and at times inspired amateur in a variety of fields. He first served as a soldier, when his adventuring ended with imprisonment in the Bastille; then earned his living as a playwright, when his plays – in particular *The Provok'd Wife* – were popular but condemned by some as outrageously immoral; and eventually, at the end of the century, turned his hand to architecture. During the next twenty-five years he designed a series of houses on an heroic scale; the best known of these are Castle Howard and Blenheim Palace. Apparently

untrained, he developed a style of baroque architecture that was unique in England, carrying it to heights of bravado.

As a result of his work at Castle Howard for Lord Carlisle, first lord of the treasury, he was appointed comptroller of the office of works in 1702, a position he retained until his death, apart from a period of some two years from 1713. Knighted in 1714, in recognition of work at Blenheim which he had begun for the Duchess of Marlborough in 1704, in 1715 he was also given the newly created position of surveyor of the royal gardens and water, and in 1716 he succeeded Wren as surveyor of Greenwich Hospital. He lived for most of the rest of his life at the castellated house he built for himself up the hill from Greenwich Park and appears, despite speculation, to have led a surprisingly contented domestic married life. His patrons, such as Lord Carlisle and Lord Cobham, for whom he worked at Stowe, were often also his friends, and he was a leading light of the Kit-Cat Club, where so many of the ideas that were to produce the landscape movement of the 18th century were first discussed.

Vanbrugh was concerned not only with the architectural appearance and construction of a house, but also with its setting; and it is here that his contribution to gardening – or, more correctly, to the development of the English landscape – lies. In his definitive work on *The Picturesque*, Christopher Hussey asserts: 'In the creative arts that were decisively affected by the picturesque, Vanbrugh stands out as the original innovator . . . .. At Castle Howard, at Eastbury, at Claremont, to take but the largest of Vanbrugh's schemes, enough of his work survives to prove that it was he who first conceived the approximation of gardens to painted landscape, with lakes, vistas, temples and woods worked into a composed whole.'[1]

Nowhere is this more emphatically demonstrated than at Castle Howard. To the east of the house the village of Henderskelfe was destroyed to clear the way for the major features of Vanbrugh's landscape. Following the line of the village street, curving upwards along the natural line of the hill, a broad grass walk lined with statues leads to the

Temple of the Four Winds – designed by Vanbrugh but not completed until two years after his death. To stand beside Vanbrugh's temple and look out to Hawksmoor's mausoleum with its vast dome and columns rising from a wooded eminence in the far distance is to witness the most monumental landscape scene created in England, one which has inspired a host of admiring descriptions. Horace Walpole's verdict is the most memorable, especially as he was not always an admirer of Vanbrugh's work: 'Nobody had told me that I should at one view see a palace, a town, a fortified city, temples on high places, woods worthy of being each a metropolis of the Druids, the noblest lawn on earth fenced by half the horizon, and a mausoleum that would tempt one to be buried alive.'[3]

Such grandeur of scale was continued at Blenheim with the bridge which Vanbrugh built across the River Glyme, although grandeur was the main bone of contention between the architect and Sarah, Duchess of Marlborough, who considered the bridge an extravagant folly. When Vanbrugh departed in 1716 after their final row it was still not finished and he never saw it completed; he returned to Blenheim once but was barred from the grounds. Partly because of these differences the colossal construction was never in harmony with its surroundings until fifty years later when 'Capability' Brown (q.v. p. 62) was inspired to dam the ineffective River Glyme and create a lake which happily submerged the lower part of the bridge and provided suitably noble surroundings. Another battle which Vanbrugh lost with the duchess was his attempt – in support of the picturesque – to preserve the remains of old Woodstock Manor; the duchess demolished them in 1723.

At both Claremont and Stowe Vanbrugh worked with Charles Bridgeman, and one suspects that the flamboyant architect had a strong influence upon the professional gardener. Vanbrugh himself lived at Claremont until 1711, when he sold it to Sir Thomas Pelham-Holles who became the Earl of Clare and eventually Duke of Newcastle. In 1715 the newly created duke commissioned Vanbrugh to build a new house (subsequently demolished) and lay out the garden in partnership with Bridgeman. Although not quite on the scale of Blenheim or Castle Howard, the castellated belvedere Vanbrugh built at Claremont on top of a small hill, looking down a straight grass vista to a bowling-green, was a picturesque folly which became a prototype for numerous similar buildings positioned in parks and gardens all over the country during the ensuing hundred years.

The majority of Vanbrugh's garden buildings at Stowe have been demolished, so it is fortunate that perhaps the most important, the rotunda, survives in its original position, albeit given a dome in the middle of the 18th century by Giovanni Battista Borra. It was positioned as the major focal point for the canal and avenues of Bridgeman's original design, standing on a slight rise which allowed for extensive views out to the surrounding countryside. A few years later its design was closely reproduced at one end of the Duncombe terrace in Yorkshire. At Stowe, also, given the bastioned walls that he had already built at both Castle Howard and Blenheim, it seems likely that Vanbrugh had an influence on the bastions built at the angles of Bridgeman's encircling ha-ha which marked the boundary of the garden and surrounding countryside.

Vanbrugh never trained as a garden designer, or indeed as an architect, but his inspiration was none the less hugely influential on English landscape and architecture. Perhaps only a man free from the limitations imposed by the petty details of professionalism could have envisaged such a scale of landscape as one finds at Castle Howard. His own aims were revealed when he wrote that he hoped the surroundings for his houses would always include, 'some plain but magnificent and durable monument'. It is hard to think of an architect whose work has proved more magnificently durable.

THE FLOWERING OF
THE LANDSCAPE MOVEMENT
1740-1820

WHEN CONSIDERED FROM THE PERSPECTIVE of the 20th century, the second half of the 18th century is clearly dominated by the career of 'Capability' Brown. His early training as a gardener was at Stowe, whose development, more than any other garden, marked the unfolding stages of the 18th-century landscape movement. From there, Brown launched into three decades of unparalleled productivity until his death in 1783. The quantity and scale of his commissions have left their mark. With the boundaries between garden and surrounding countryside already dismantled by Bridgeman, Kent and the other leading designers earlier in the century, Brown carried this to an extreme, landscaping huge parks, often of hundreds of acres, and in some cases whole estates. In his designs detail was subjected to overall form; simple if enormous compositions where the guiding influence was the serpentine 'line of beauty' as identified and illustrated by William Hogarth in his *Analysis of Beauty* published in 1753 and Edmund Burke's *A Philosophical Enquiry into the Origin of our Ideas of the Sublime and Beautiful*, published in 1757. But while they undoubtedly expressed this aesthetic quality, Brown's landscapes were neither allegorical nor consciously romantic. Intensely practical, his

Stowe, where successive work by Bridgeman, Vanbrugh,
Kent and Brown make it the most significant
eighteenth-century landscape.

work answered the economic, agricultural requirements of his landowning patrons as much as their social aspirations, and provided both status and revenue.

At the very beginning of the 18th century Sir John Vanbrugh had established the integral role of architecture in landscape gardens and his lead was followed right through the first three quarters of the century. Most garden architecture remained classical in style, but as the century progressed it often provided an outlet for gothic or Jacobean designs which would have been unacceptable for a major house. Architecture was not integral to Brown's landscape designs, but some of his most successful schemes nevertheless incorporated buildings designed by him, such as the Jacobean bath house at Burghley and the bridge at Scampston Hall. On occasions Brown's parks were given buildings by other architects, and many of the leading architects of the period made contributions to 18th-century gardens – such as James Gibbs at Stowe, Henry Flitcroft at Stourhead, and James Paine whose elegant, arched bridges became something of a trademark. In many instances, for example at Kedleston Hall, where Robert Adam also designed the three-arched bridge spanning the new lake, the architect's commission included both house and buildings in the surrounding landscape.

Magnificent architecture and Brown's expansive landscapes illustrate the seemingly unassailable social confidence of the 18th-century landowners who commissioned them, and yet they were not to everyone's taste. When Thomas Jefferson came to England in 1786 and visited several of the best-known gardens of the day, the comments in his *Garden Book* were often intensely critical; he found the expanses of park impressive but empty and left convinced that such a style would never be suitable for the recently formed United States of America. It was largely as a result of Jefferson's influence – and the example of his garden at Monticello – that the gardening style of the newly independent nation began to evolve at this time, combining a European admiration for classicism with a primary enjoyment of flower and vegetable gardens that stemmed from the traditions of old colonial gardens. Admiration for natural landscape also became an important constituent of American garden design, but not in the possessive manner of English landowners who liked to feel that they ruled everything they could see from the windows of their Palladian mansions.

One of the few places that Jefferson singled out for praise was the Leasowens near Birmingham, the former home of the poet and gardener, William Shenstone. Shenstone's property was a modest farm but between 1745 and his death in 1763 he had skilfully capitalized on the varying terrain of well wooded valleys with streams to create what became

one of the most visited and admired landscapes of the period. The importance of the Leasowens was that its circuit path was carefully planned to reveal a series of views to impressive natural scenery and to take in groves of trees, cascades and other features whose
appearance was also natural. In his landscape, classical allusion was not a dominant factor
but limited to various urns judiciously positioned along the path, each marked with a
suitable inscription.

Unfortunately, Shenstone's finances were never sufficient to support his projects at the
Leasowens, as Jefferson himself recorded: 'Shenstone had but three hundred pounds a
year, and ruined himself by what he did to this farm. It is said that he died of the heart-
aches which his debts occasioned him.'[1] However, his influence continued after his death
with the posthumous publication of *The Works in Verse and Prose of William Shenstone*,
which included the essay, *Some Unconnected Thoughts on Gardening*, in which Shenstone
divided gardeners into three distinct types: kitchen gardeners, parterre gardeners and
'landskip or picturesque' gardeners, and in identifying the third category, indicated clearly
the direction that the English landscape would take in the second half of the 18th century.

Shenstone was one of the most significant of the many talented amateurs who made a
major contribution to gardens during the 18th century. Another – also plagued by financial problems – was Charles Hamilton, whose garden at Painshill had a clearly landscaped
appearance and included architectural ornaments, but was, at the same time, firmly horticultural and on a restrained scale. Hamilton grew some of the first rhododendron varieties
to be seen in England – all from North America – as well as a number of outstanding
ornamental trees and shrubs, such as American oaks and swamp cypresses, acquired from
his friend Peter Collinson. By the middle of the 18th century Collinson's main supplier
from North America was John Bartram, who had the unique distinction of being the only
American to be made the king's botanist. He held this post from 1765 until his death in
1777, though the Declaration of Independence in 1776 had by that time made his
appointment somewhat obsolete.

Bartram was the most prolific supplier of plants from the United States, but at this
time there was a constant flow of plants and gardening ideas between individuals on both
sides of the Atlantic. One was the journalist, gardener, agriculturalist and social reformer
William Cobbett, who visited the United States for most of the 1790s and again in 1817
and published *The American Gardener* in 1821, followed by *The English Gardener* in 1829,
and his best known, most popular book, *Rural Rides* in 1830. Cobbett became an ardent
enthusiast for American plants which he sold from a nursery in Kensington and described

in his *Catalogue of American Trees, Shrubs and Seeds for Sale by Mr Cobbett*. He was responsible for popularizing the false acacia or locust tree which became one of the most widely-grown American trees in English gardens.

Socially far removed Cobbett was George Lyttelton, an aristocratic amateur who created an important garden at his family seat, Hagley Hall, and whose brother was governor of Carolina and a regular source of new plants. Lyttelton's landscape at Hagley was better known, however, for its affinity with the picturesque, in particular for the ruined castle that Sanderson Miller built in the grounds. Ruins of the kind erected by Miller constituted an important element in the picturesque movement, but Hagley was unashamedly eclectic in its architectural taste, also boasting an important neo-Grecian temple designed by James 'Athenian' Stuart.

Another leading protagonist of the picturesque during the middle of the century was the clergyman William Gilpin. Gilpin published his *Essay on Prints* in 1768 and, subsequently, *Remarks on Forest Trees (Relating Chiefly to Picturesque Beauty)* and a series of *Observations* on different parts of the country, whose locations – the valley of the River Wye, the Lake District and the Scottish Highlands – all indicated his preference for landscapes of naturally spectacular scenery in contrast to what some considered to be the stylized and artificial landscapes of 'Capability' Brown. However, the most vociferous and extreme championing of the picturesque came later in the century in the persons of Sir Uvedale Price and Richard Payne Knight. Both were fierce in their criticisms of 'Capability' Brown landscapes, which they considered bland, contrived and unexciting, and both published polemics criticising Brown and extolling the quality of rugged natural landscapes of mountains, of rushing streams and untamed woodland. They put their ideas into practice at their own homes, both in Herefordshire, Price's at Foxley and Knight's at nearby Downton Castle. But, initially having focused their criticism upon Brown and, to a lesser extent, upon Humphry Repton, Prince and Knight came to disagree between themselves over their interpretation of the picturesque. None the less this did nothing to diminish the importance of the movement in steering the English landscape away from dependence upon classical inspiration and from the seeming monopoly of the 'Brownian' style, to a closer affinity with natural scenery. By the last quarter of the century the fashion for the picturesque and for spectacular – often awesome – natural scenery had spread from the practitioners of landscape to literature, as can be seen in the poems of Thomas Gray and William Wordsworth and the novels of Jane Austen. Such enjoyment of natural rather than man-made large-scale landscape could be argued to have indirectly led to

Chatsworth, where the realisation of Brown's
expansive park setting caused the destruction of
London and Wise's most lavish formal garden.

gardens once again being considered as the immediate surroundings of a house rather than primarily its more expansive setting, and thus in part prepared the way for the return to ornamental gardening that came in the 19th century.

It is ironic that the man who began his career with the primary aim of taking up 'Capability' Brown's mantle, Humphry Repton, was later responsible both for the subtle reduction in the scale of landscape design and for reuniting it with pure gardening – a step that ushered in the new horticultural directions of the 19th century. Like others before and since, Repton's influence was not only widespread at the time, but was destined to last, as a result of his publications as well as his designs. Like Brown before him, Repton responded to social demands, and the garden-commissioning world of the early 1800s was subtly different to that of the mid 18th century. Patrician landowners had been joined by the Tory squirearchy and by new wealth from the Industrial Revolution; in addition, for much of the time that Repton was working, England was at war with France.

Repton's response to his clients' demands was what is described as 'the Transition Style', which allowed for a clearly subdivided composition of foreground, middleground and background. Ornamental flower gardening returned to the foreground around the house, usually within the architectural framework of a terrace, and provided an ideal launching-off point for parkland beyond, which eventually merged into the surrounding countryside. In Repton's earlier work, as he followed in the footsteps of his mentor, Brown, the parkland invariably dominated the design; yet even at this early stage a shift in scale was evident, not least because Repton was working predominantly at country seats rather than power houses at the apex of great landed estates. By the end of his career the change is in some cases dramatic. At Ashridge he designed a series of fifteen interconnecting flower gardens to one side of the house, including a circular rosarium, a magnolia and American garden, and a rockery. His own description illustrated the assured break away from the 18th century landscape: 'The novelty of this attempt to collect a number of gardens, differing from each other, may perhaps excite the critic's censure; but I hope there is no more absurdity in collecting gardens of different styles, dates, characters, and dimensions, in the same enclosure, than in placing the works of a Raphael and a Teniers in the same cabinet, or books sacred and profane in the same library'.[2] And it was from this standpoint that gardens were to develop through the 19th century.

WILLIAM AITON (1731-1793)

ROYAL BOTANIC GARDEN, *Kew*

NOT LONG BEFORE HIS DEATH in 1745, Stephen Switzer (*q.v.* p. 50) was complaining about the extent to which young Scottish gardeners were invading England and taking all the jobs. Had he lived a little longer William Aiton would have been a prime target for his complaint.

Having trained as a gardener in his native Lanarkshire, in 1754 Aiton travelled to London and began work at the Apothecaries Garden in Chelsea, then at the height of its fame under another Scotsman, Philip Miller (*q.v.* p. 49). In 1759, when Princess Augusta, the widow of George II's eldest son, Frederick, who lived at Kew House, established a small botanic garden under the control of Lord Bute, Aiton was appointed the first superintendent of the garden which some eight years later took on the official title of the Royal Botanic Garden, Kew.

During Princess Augusta's lifetime the botanic garden remained comparatively small, extending only to some 3.75ha/9 acres, but two years before Aiton's arrival William Chambers (*q.v.* p. 68), had begun landscaping the more extensive grounds and had added the various architectural features – notably the pagoda – for which Kew remains known to this day. After her death in 1771 George III joined the adjacent ground of Richmond Gardens, which had been used by his grandparents, George II and Queen Caroline, to the gardens of Kew House, thereby considerably extending the size. Bute was replaced as botanical adviser by the energetic naturalist, Sir Joseph Banks, but Aiton was retained as superintendent and a house was built for him in the garden. During the next twenty years Aiton and the legendary patrician entrepreneur Banks together launched Kew into its first golden period, seeing it overtake Chelsea in reputation and prestige and, of major significance to the garden's future, inaugurating in 1772 the first of many plant-collecting expeditions overseas. Perhaps not surprisingly, the first collector was another Scotsman, Francis Masson.

Apart from his efficient management of garden and plant collections, a major contribution was the publication in 1789 of Aiton's *Hortus Kewensis* which catalogued and described over 5,500 plants in cultivation at Kew. That the collection of plants had become so extensive in such a comparatively short period of time was largely thanks to Aiton, and the standards that he set as superintendent provided a lasting example for his successors, the first of whom was his son, William Townsend Aiton.

JOHN BARTRAM (1699-1770)

JOHN BARTRAM was a pioneering figure in the development of American gardens, the first great American plant collector and naturalist. He also had a considerable impact upon English gardens by virtue of the new species of plants that he dispatched across the Atlantic. Bartram's family were Quakers from Derbyshire who had settled in Pennsylvania, and Bartram, a shy, retiring countryman, remained in Pennsylvania all his life, farming but increasingly preoccupied with botanical work and with recording the results of his plant-collecting expeditions. Within America, his introductions from the wild had an enormous impact upon what became standard and popular garden plants, while in England he did more to satisfy the ever increasing demand for American plants – in particular trees – than any of his contemporaries. Bartram was among the most respected figures in early American scientific circles and was a friend of Benjamin Franklin, after whom he named perhaps the finest of his discoveries, *Franklinia alatamaha*, a tender late-summer flowering shrub that was never again seen in the wild, and remains a choice rarity among cultivated plants.

The most significant contact of Bartram's career was made at some point during the 1730s when he was recommended to Peter Collinson, a London cloth merchant and enthusiastic gardener, and the leading introducer of

American plants to England during the 18th century. Miles Hadfield estimates that of some three hundred new species of plants introduced to England from North America between 1735 and Collinson's death in 1768, two thirds came from his partnership with Bartram. Collinson organized a group of aristocratic patrons and subscribers whose support enabled Bartram to make annual plant-collecting trips all over North America. Each subscriber paid five guineas for every box containing a hundred selected seeds sent by Bartram. Eventually, such was Bartram's reputation in England that Collinson and his group succeeded in arranging for him to be appointed king's botanist in America, with a salary of £50 per annum and specific instructions to seek out new plants.

Collinson himself was in close contact with the Swedish botanist Linnaeus and forwarded to him any new plants that arrived from Bartram in need of identification. By the late 1740s Linnaeus considered Bartram to be the outstanding field botanist of the time, and his respect for Bartram's work was such that he instructed his student, Peter Kalm, to visit him during a trip to North America.

In 1728 Bartram bought a house close to Philadelphia with 2 ha/5 acres of garden sloping down to the River Schuylkill. Here he created the first botanic garden in the United States, filling it with the plants that he collected from most corners of the country. He was assisted in his plant collecting by his son William, who was also a talented artist and painted many of the discoveries. After his father's death William continued to look after the Philadelphia garden and plant collection, and within a few years of John Bartram's death had developed it into a nursery. He was soon supplying quantities of plants to George Washington (*q.v.* p. 89) for his garden at Mount Vernon. Both the garden and nursery survive today.

LANCELOT 'CAPABILITY' BROWN (1716-23)

ALNWICK CASTLE, *Northumberland*; ASHBURNHAM, *Sussex*; ASHRIDGE, *Hertfordshire*; AUDLEY END, *Essex*; AYNHOE PARK, *Northamptonshire*; BEECHWOOD, *Bedfordshire*; BELHUS, *Essex*; BENHAM, *Berkshire*; BERRINGTON HALL, *Herefordshire*; BLENHEIM PALACE, *Oxfordshire*; BOWOOD, *Wiltshire*; BROADLANDS, *Hampshire*; BROCKLESBY PARK, *Lincolnshire*; BURGHLEY HOUSE, *Lincolnshire*; BURTON CONSTABLE, *Yorkshire*; BURTON PYNSENT, *Somerset*; CADLAND, *Hampshire*; CASTLE ASHBY, *Northamptonshire*; CHARLECOTE PARK, *Warwickshire*; CHARLTON, *Wiltshire*; CHATSWORTH, *Derbyshire*; CHILHAM CASTLE, *Kent*; CHILLINGTON HALL, *West Midlands*; CLANDON PARK, *Surrey*; CLAREMONT, *Surrey*; COMPTON VERNEY, *Warwickshire*; COOMBE ABBEY, *West Midlands*; CORSHAM COURT, *Wiltshire*; COWDRAY PARK, *Sussex*; CROOME COURT, *Worcestershire*; DODDINGTON HALL, *Cheshire*; DODINGTON PARK, *Avon*; DYNEVOR (NEWTON) CASTLE, *Dyfed*; EATON HALL, *Cheshire*; EDGBASTON, *West Midlands*; ELVEDON, *Suffolk*; EUSTON HALL, *Suffolk*; FAWLEY COURT, *Oxfordshire*; GARRICK'S SHAKESPEARE TEMPLE, *London*; GRIMSTHORPE CASTLE, *Lincolnshire*; HAREWOOD HOUSE, *Yorkshire*; HEVENINGHAM HALL, *Suffolk*; HIGHCLERE CASTLE, *Berkshire*; HIMLEY HALL, *West Midlands*; HOLKHAM HALL, *Norfolk*; INGESTRE, *Staffordshire*; KEW GARDENS AND RICHMOND, *London*; KIDDINGTON HALL, *Oxfordshire*; KIMBERLEY HALL, *Norfolk*; KING'S WESTON, *Avon*; KIRTLINGTON PARK, *Oxfordshire*; KNOWSLEY HALL, *Lancashire*; LONGFORD CASTLE, *Wiltshire*; LONGLEAT, *Wiltshire*; LUTON HOO, *Bedfordshire*; MELTON CONSTABLE, *Norfolk*; MILTON ABBEY, *Dorset*; MOCCAS COURT, *Herefordshire*; MOOR PARK, *Hertfordshire*; NUNEHAM COURTENAY PARK, *Oxfordshire*; PACKINGTON HALL, *West Midlands*; PATSHULL, *West Midlands*; PETWORTH HOUSE, *Sussex*; PRIOR PARK, *Avon*; ROTHLEY, *Northumberland*; SANDBECK PARK, *Yorkshire*; SCAMPSTON HALL, *Yorkshire*; SHERBORNE CASTLE, *Dorset*; SLEDMERE HOUSE, *Yorkshire*; SOUTHILL PARK, *Bedfordshire*; STOWE, *Buckinghamshire*; SYON HOUSE, *Middlesex*; TEMPLE NEWSAM, *Yorkshire*; THORNDON HALL, *Essex*; TONG CASTLE, *West Midlands*; TRENTHAM PARK, *Staffordshire*; UGBROOKE, *Devon*; WAKEFIELD LODGE, *Northamptonshire*; WARWICK CASTLE, *Warwickshire*; WESTON

At Bowood Brown's park stretches away on all sides from the formal nineteenth-century terraces around the house.

PARK, *Staffordshire;* WIMBLEDON PARK, *London;* WIMPOLE HALL, *Cambridgeshire;* WOTTON HOUSE, *Buckinghamshire;* WREST PARK, *Bedfordshire.*

THE LIST OF PROPERTIES for which Lancelot 'Capability' Brown designed landscapes, and where his work still survives in a recognizable state or where features of particular interest remain, reads like a catalogue of the great houses of England. Even more remarkable is the fact that it represents something like half the total number of places where his designs were implemented. Purely on such statistical evidence Brown bestrides the history of English landscape like a colossus. During a career of some forty years he refined the concept of landscape to a degree whereby it became dependant upon three simple ingredients: trees, water and terrain – with only occasional architectural embellishment. Brown's method was so efficient that he has been accused – both by contemporaries and by subsequent observers – of working to an unimaginative formula. The other major criticism laid at his door concerns his destruction of existing formal gardens. The first charge can be repudiated by visiting even a small selection of his parks, which reveals that however often recognizable features were repeated, their application always varied according to the site. The second accusation is undoubtedly valid, but we must remember that Brown was, with the consent of his clients, sweeping away gardens that were widely considered to be old-fashioned and out-of-date and where owners specifically requested that he retain a particular feature – such as an avenue – he almost invariably complied with their wishes.

Brown's work is best appreciated when the priorities and principles that guided him are considered. His clients were almost exclusively Whig aristocrats, men who controlled English society and politics throughout most of the 18th century. By the middle of the century their country houses and surrounding estates were reflecting a harmonious balance of established self-assurance and good taste. Good taste involved an understated appreciation of nature, the enjoyment of a landscape that did not rely upon allegorical or heroic inspiration from the past, but which was carefully moulded to enhance the natural qualities of a particular site. The overall impression should be of serene naturalness and permanence.

Brown's response was all his clients could have wished. Emphasizing the importance of a house's setting and approach, he studied the topography of the surroundings, planning how best the full 'capabilities' could be realized. Certain techniques were applied regularly, such as perimeter belts of trees around a park or along a distant skyline, the judicious positioning of clumps of trees, damming a small stream to produce a lake and tucking the end of the water out of sight around a corner. But such similarities of approach were never allowed to obscure the individuality of the site. At Longleat you look up from the house; at Harewood you look down from the house; while at Petworth and Grimsthorpe it is the controlled presentation of expansive open space that is most impressive.

Lancelot Brown was born in 1716 in Kirkharle, Northumberland, into a yeoman farming family. He was educated at the local school in Cambo until he was sixteen when he left to work as a gardener for the local squire, Sir William Loraine. Seven years later he travelled south to Buckinghamshire, armed with a recommendation from Sir William. The move stood him in good stead, for after a few months assisting Sir Charles Browne to redesign Kiddington Hall, the head gardener's position at Stowe became vacant and Brown was taken on. It was a decisive step forward. Stowe was already the most talked about and fashionable garden of the day; the job brought Brown directly into contact with the work of William Kent (*q.v.* p. 41) (and quite possibly involved working with him); and it gave him an opening into the extensive circle of important Whigs who made up Lord Cobham's family, friends and acquaintances.

Brown's nine years at Stowe witnessed the two last major phases of the garden's development by Lord Cobham: the creation of the Queen's Valley east of Kent's Elysian Fields, and of the Grecian Valley north-east of the house. Kent himself was certainly still involved with the

Queen's Valley, where the central feature is the Gothic Temple designed by James Gibbs – another important contact. By the time the Grecian Valley was being planned it is likely that Brown himself had a hand in the design, as David Watkin suggests: 'In terms of so-called "natural landscape", this dog-legged or right-angled valley represents a decisive advance on the slightly earlier Queen's Valley, and perhaps contains the seeds of 'Capability' Brown's mature style.'[1]

Lord Cobham died in 1749 and two years later Brown moved to London. At Stowe he had not only been immersed in the foremost garden of the day, but his job had involved organizing the physical excavation and planting of the site, hiring men and costing the work. It was an invaluable training, as is shown throughout the rest of his career, when he demonstrated unfailing business acumen – working through sub-contractors, ordering trees from different suppliers instead of running his own nursery, and combining an ability to control costs with a scrupulous honesty – money paid on deposit was always returned if the eventual costs proved less than the original estimate. All of which, not surprisingly, endeared him to his clients.

By the time that he left Stowe Brown had already carried out a number of commissions elsewhere and within a short time of establishing himself in Hammersmith had become the leading landscape designer of the day, a position that he retained unchallenged until his death. During three decades of extraordinary productivity and hard work he travelled all over England, assessing sites, drawing up plans, organizing the delivery of trees and building materials and returning to check on progress or carry out subsequent work. It appears that he never worked in Cornwall or Nottinghamshire, although he may have been consulted at Thoresby Park; otherwise, every county in England and many in Wales received his attention to a greater or lesser degree.

Given the quantity of work, and the scale often involved Brown's technical achievements were at times astonishing. In order to achieve his ideal landscapes with their gentle contours, water, and a minimum of man-made interruptions, huge quantities of earth were often removed and resited, and tiny streams were dammed into lakes, their level assisted by extensive drainage systems which were also used to transform useless ground into picturesque grazing land. The lakes themselves, always serpentine in shape, had banks which were planned with just the right amount of drop, and curved easily away to a distant point where planting shrouded the far extremity of the water. Trees were planted by the thousand, native deciduous varieties predominating, in particular beech and oak, but with evergreens such as yew or holm oak used to provide contrast and winter foliage. If necessary whole villages were demolished and resited.

As if his landscape work did not keep him busy enough, Brown also designed a number of substantial new houses for clients, or made extensive alterations to existing ones. Croome Court, Broadlands and Claremont are three of his most impressive houses that survive; at Claremont Brown worked for the first time in partnership with his architect son-in-law Henry Holland. Croome in Worcestershire was one of Brown's earliest commissions after moving to Hammersmith and, while not as impressive in scale as Blenheim or Burghley, his success there provides, if anything, a more incisive reflection upon his character and talents. Brown's biographer, Dorothy Stroud, wrote of Croome: 'It would be hard to imagine a more uncompromising situation than that which faced Brown at Croome. The estate lies in the low plain which is bounded by the Avon and the Severn, and at that time the place was virtually a marsh . . . Sanderson Miller (*q.v.* p. 80) had suggested the possibility of draining the park itself and making it into a suitable site for a new mansion. This was the first problem which Brown was called upon to tackle, and he set about it by laying vast underground culverts from the foundations of the house to an artificial river which he contrived some distance away. The next step was to rebuild the house on a larger and grander scale, and for this he produced a dignified classical design in which it is easy to trace the influence of Kent and the Palladian principles which he had imbibed while at Stowe.'[2]

In addition to the house and park, Brown rebuilt the church at Croome. His client, Lord Coventry, was delighted and remained a firm friend and champion. As well as erecting a memorial to Brown beside the lake with the inscription, 'To the Memory of Lancelot Brown who by the powers of his inimitable and creative genius formed this garden scene out of a morass,' he later wrote to Humphry Repton (*q.v.* p. 81), 'I write from a house which he built for me which . . . is, perhaps, a model for every internal and domestic convenience. I may be partial to my place at Croome, which was entirely his creation and, I believe, originally as hopeless a spot as any in the island.'[3]

The work at Claremont may have been the first of many happy joint ventures with his son-in-law Henry Holland (whose father, a stonemason living in Fulham, had become one of Brown's first friends when he moved to Hammersmith), but it also provided the occasion for the most outspoken attack on Brown by a contemporary, William Chambers (*q.v.* p. 68). Chambers had himself tendered designs for a new house at Claremont for Lord Clive and no doubt the fact that Brown got the commission aroused his anger. Chambers used his published *A Dissertation on Oriental Gardening* (1772) as a vehicle for a swingeing criticism of Brown's work; it had some influence abroad but at home found little support.

In 1764 Brown was appointed surveyor to His Majesty's gardens and waters at Hampton Court, the position which Vanbrugh (*q.v.* p. 52) had first held. Brown's supporters had been lobbying for him to be appointed royal gardener since 1758, and it is clear that he considered himself to be an ideal candidate. As well as a salary of £2,000 per annum the position gave him an official residence, Wilderness House at Hampton Court, which remained his home – together with a small country house, Fenstanton in Huntingdonshire – for the rest of his life. It says much for Brown's easy relations with his clients that he bought Fenstanton in 1761 from Lord Northampton, for whom he worked at Castle Ashby. Indeed, the picture of Brown that is most readily conjured up by

contemporary descriptions and portraits is of an unfailingly agreeable character, kind, thoughtful and mentally alert, who achieved a fine balance between deference and friendship with his aristocratic patrons. Calm self-assurance rooted in certain knowledge of what they required and confidence in his ability to provide it demonstrates itself in the great majority of his projects. If the resulting figure emerges as something of a paragem this may in part explain the criticism that was levelled at him by some of his contemporaries and even more after his death by the leading disciples of the picturesque, such as Sir Uvedale Price and Richard Payne Knight. In 1794, eleven years after Brown's death, Price published his *Essay on the Picturesque* and Knight his poem *The Landscape*, both of which contains regular scarcely disguised attacks on Brown.

> '*Hence, hence! though haggard fiend, however call'd,*
> *Thin, meagre genius of the bare and bald;*
> *Thy spade and mattock here at length lay down,*
> *and follow to the tomb thy fav'rite Brown:*
> *Thy fav'rite Brown, whose innovating hand*
> *First dealt thy curses o'er this fertile land.*'[4]

Well before the end of his life Brown had achieved a prestige and reputation far beyond the expectations of his background and childhood. He referred to himself as Lancelot Brown *Esquire*, and his eldest son was sent to Eton where he quickly became known as 'Capey'. Despite his success he continued to lead a rigorously busy working life right up until his sudden death in 1783, which Horace Walpole recorded in his diary: 'February 6, 1783, about nine o'clock, died Lancelot Brown Esq., of Hampton-court aged 67. His death was probably occasioned by a violent blow he received falling in a fit in the street as he was returning from a visit at Lord Coventry's house in Piccadilly to the house of his son-in-law (Henry Holland) in Hertford Street. For thirty years he had laboured under a very troublesome asthma, (and) though he bore it with an uncommon degree of fortitude and good spirits . . . .

'His great and fine genius stood unrivalled and it was

The enormous lake at Chillington which Brown
created by building a dam, with James Paine's
bridge the perfect focal point of the view.

the peculiar felicity of it that it was allowed by all ranks and degrees of society in this country, and by many noble and great personages in other countries. Those who knew him best, or practised near him, were not able to determine whether the quickness of his eye, or its correctness, were most to be admired. It was comprehensive and elegant, and perhaps it may be said never to have failed him. Such, however, was the effect of his genius that when he was the happiest man, he will be least remembered; so closely did he copy nature that his works will be mistaken. His truth, his integrity, and his good humour were very effectual, and will hold a place in the memory of his friends, more likely to continue, though not less to be esteemed.'[5]

Two centuries after his death the evidence of Brown's work is still remarkably extensive, and despite later alterations and destruction his stamp upon the English countryside remains unmistakeable. Horace Walpole's comment that Brown's work was so close to nature as to be virtually indistinguishable became increasingly true as his landscapes grew steadily towards maturity. This slow maturing processes emphasizes the foresight with which Brown's landscapes were conceived, but also reflects the self-confidence and long-term assurance of both Brown and his patrons.

SIR WILLIAM CHAMBERS (1723-96)

BLENHEIM PALACE, *Oxfordshire*; ROYAL BOTANIC GARDENS, *Kew, Surrey*; WILTON HOUSE, *Wiltshire*

WILLIAM CHAMBERS'S career was one of contrasts, in which he produced both precise classical architecture and far more original and imaginative gardening ideas and designs – notably in his work at Kew for which he has always been best known. He achieved the highest official position as an architect and produced what became the standard book of reference on classical architecture, his *Treatise on Civil Architecture*. His views on garden style became an important influence on the European fashion for *chinoiserie* and the development of the picturesque movement, through his two publications *Designs of Chinese Buildings* and *A Dissertation on Oriental Gardening*. The latter was also used by Chambers as a vehicle for an attack on the work of 'Capability' Brown, among whose contemporary critics Chambers was the most outspoken and this element of personal combativeness, combined with his association with the widely disliked royal family, largely account for the lack of enthusiasm with which he and his work were received by many of his contemporaries.

Chambers's background was unconventional. He was born in Gothenburg in Sweden, the son of a Scottish merchant. His father sent him to stay with relatives at Ripon in Yorkshire where he went to school, but at the age of sixteen he returned to Sweden and joined the Swedish East India Company. In 1740 he made his first voyage overseas with the company and on two subsequent ones, in 1743-5 and 1748-9, visited the Far East. Between voyages he travelled in Britain, Holland and France. It would appear that the primary purpose of his employment with the trading company was financial – perhaps also under parental pressure – and Chambers himself wrote that the voyages allowed plenty of time for him to study 'modern languages, mathematics and the free arts, but chiefly civil architecture, for which latter I have from my earliest years felt the strongest inclination.'[1]

After the last trip, during which he visited Canton in China, Chambers left the company and moved to Paris where he spent a year studying architecture under J. F. Blondel. In 1750 he travelled to Italy where he was to spend five years, mainly in Rome but including visits to the most important cultural and architectural cities, with the overall aim to 'collect in all these places all that could serve and increase my knowledge of the science I had chosen for my study.'[2] While in Italy he became acquainted with a number of visiting British artists and architects and it may easily have been a connection thus established which resulted in Chambers being recommended by Carr of York to the Marquess of Bute as a suitable candidate to be architectural and drawing tutor to the future King George III, son of Augusta, Princess of Wales.

This connection was the foundation of Chambers's success, for he continued to enjoy royal patronage until the end of his career, most significantly in his appointment a series of increasingly prestigious official architectural positions whose patronage came under Crown control; first as one of two architects of the works in 1761 (with Robert Adam), subsequently as comptroller of the works in 1769 and as the first surveyor-general and comptroller of the office of works in 1782. In his official capacity he designed Somerset House and the royal state coach that is still used at coronations. In 1770, in recognition of his services, George III allowed him to use the title of knight when he was awarded the order of the Polar Star by Sweden – an appointment that came in for ridicule from many contemporaries.

After the death of her husband, Frederick, Prince of Wales, in 1751, Princess Augusta continued to develop the garden he had begun at Kew. In 1775, Chambers published his *Designs of Chinese Buildings*, based upon the sketches he had made while in Canton, and that year the princess commissioned him to landscape the Kew garden and to embellish it with a variety of buildings and temples. Christopher Hussey, not one of Chambers's admirers, gave his opinion of the situation in which Chambers found himself: 'Thus he was suddenly thrown into the most fashionable coterie where, as in all fashionable coteries, novelty is beyond all else required of an artist. He might do anything at Kew except copy Brown, the gardener to the rival royal faction at Richmond. Accordingly he elaborated a system of gardening which, he assured society, was the genuine Chinese style. Had he not been there? Had not he himself made drawings of pagodas on the spot? There was nobody to contradict him, save a missionary or two who had never heard of Kew.'[3]

Chambers worked on the various buildings at Kew between 1757 and 1763 and by the time he had finished had produced more than twenty. The majority were classical temples, but there was also an aviary, a menagerie and a Chinese temple. Today, three survivors clearly demonstrate the quality and variety of Chambers's architectural achievement for his royal patron. The best known is the Pagoda, built in 1761, 55m/163ft tall and constructed of ten octagonal storeys. Even without the coloured dragons that originally adorned the eighty corners of the ascending eaves, and less brilliantly coloured than when newly painted, it remains superbly theatrical, its position within the garden enhanced by the 19th-century landscaping by William Nesfield (*q.v.* p. 116).

At about the same time Chambers designed the Orangery, an outstanding example of the neo-classical revival. Earlier, he had made his main picturesque contribution to Kew with the Ruined Arch which he designed to 'imitate a Roman Antiquity, built of brick, with incrustations of stone'.[4] Yet, however apparent the quality of all three buildings may seem today, at the time they received scant praise, largely because of the unpopularity of Princess Augusta and her adviser Lord Bute. The *Universal Museum* dismissed the Pagoda, which had cost £12,000, in one sentence: 'In comparison with the stupendous originals which existed in the East, we must look upon that at Kew almost in the same light as the little models of the latter which we see in the toyshop.'

In addition to his royal duties, Chambers built up a clientele of aristocratic patrons. His first important commission was for the Earl of Pembroke at Wilton, where he built a triumphal arch and a *casino* as an eye-catcher across the River Nadder – the former being recorded as, 'the first work of Stone I executed in England'.[5] Thereafter Chambers worked for the Duke of Richmond at Goodwood and, during the 1760s, more extensively for the Duke of Marlborough at Blenheim where, as well as doing work in the house, he decorated Vanbrugh's East Gate and added in the park the three-arched New Bridge and small temples, including the Temple of Diana where Winston Churchill was later to propose marriage to his future wife, Clementine Hozier.

Chambers emerges as an abrasive and self-opinionated character, sensitive about his connection with the unpopular monarchy and even more unpopular Lord Bute, so it is perhaps no surprise that architectural rivalry goaded him into a publication for which he is almost as well known as for his buildings. In 1769 Robert Lord Clive (of India), for whom Chambers was rebuilding Walcot House in Shropshire, accepted plans by 'Capability' Brown for a new house at Claremont in Surrey in preference to those submitted by Chambers. Three years later Chambers's professional jealousy was made clear when he published a *Dissertation on Oriental Gardening*. In it he compared Brown and his style of landscape design unfavourably with the supposed quality of the Chinese gardens he described. Although parts of the book have some relevance to oriental gardening, it was in fact no more than the basis for a thinly disguised attack on Brown, and the main purpose of publishing the book was, as Miles Hadfield concludes, 'so that Chambers could give publicity to his personal views of gardening, by foisting them on to the innocent Chinese, and thereby indulge his venom towards "Capability" Brown.'[6]

Most of Chambers's contemporaries in England perceived the intention behind his dissertation and as a result its pronouncements were not taken very seriously. Nonetheless, it did have a strong influence on the continent, and its criticisms of Brown assumed significance for the later protagonists of the picturesque movement. For Chambers himself, already treated with circumspection because of his connection with a generally unpopular monarchy, the publication ensured that he remained an outsider to fashionable artistic circles and the architectural establishment.

Chambers's work at Kew demonstrates the combination of a high degree of technical skill with an adventurous feel for different architectural styles, but his theories on gardens and landscape have always remained questionable. When one of Brown's most ardent supporters, William Mason, published in 1774 his *Heroic Epistle to Sir William Chambers*, its opening lines gave opportunity for widespread mirth:

'Knight of the Polar Star! by Fortune plac'd
To shine the Cynosure of British taste; . . .
O, let the Muse attend they march sublime,
And with thy prose, caparision her rhyme;
Teach her, like thee, to gild her splendid song
With scenes of Yven-Ming and sayings of Li-Tsong;
Like thee to scorn Dame Nature's simple fence,
Leap each Ha Ha of truth and common sense.'

SIR FRANCIS DASHWOOD (1709-81)

WEST WYCOMBE PARK, *Buckinghamshire*

SIR FRANCIS DASHWOOD was among the most flamboyant of 18th-century Englishmen, a vigorous blend of hedonist and aesthete who was both the leading light of the infamous Hell-Fire Club and a founding member of the distinctly more intellectual Society of Dilettanti, as well as a Fellow of the Royal Society and Society of Antiquaries. Inheriting his baronetcy and a considerable fortune from his father at the age of sixteen, he subsequently acceded to the title of his mother's family as Baron le Despencer. After an extensive Grand Tour he returned to England where he became an active politician, holding the offices of postmaster-general and chancellor of the exchequer, but his most important work lay in the transformation of his home at West Wycombe, a house and landscape which became one of the most renowned and admired in England. Over a period of some forty years Dashwood employed professionals to assist him: first Maurice-Louis Jolivet and subsequently Richard Cook supplied plans for the park, while the architects John Donowell and Nicholas Revett, a member of the Society of Dilettanti, made significant additions to the house and designed the temples in the grounds. But in all the works the guiding hand was that of Dashwood himself, who desired that West Wycombe should be both a statement of his good taste and a suitably idyllic setting for the regular entertainments that he held.

*At Sir Francis Dashwood's West Wycombe the pillared facades
of the house were planned as part of the landscape.*

The house itself, positioned on one side of the valley, was redesigned in stages over nearly two decades, in such a manner as to act primarily as a decorative feature of the landscape, presenting a different face when viewed from various angles.

The north front was designed by Servandoni, who probably also built the east façade in 1754 or 1755. In 1760 John Donowell added the unique south front with its two-storeyed colonnade, and finally in 1770 or 1771 Revett added the west portico, modelled on the Temple of Bacchus at Telos, its primary function to serve as a temple façade rather than a part of the house.

The creation of the park, lying mainly in the valley and sweeping up to West Wycombe hill surmounted by a church, was similarly carried out in stages. Between 1735 and 1739 the small stream was dammed to make the lake with its island cascade and rock arch. The first three temples to be built – the temples of Venus, the Winds and Apollo – were probably all designed by Donowell, in 1748, 1759 and 1761. In 1770 Revett took over supervision of the work from Jolivet, and in 1775 added the Round Temple to the south-west of the house. In 1778-80 he built one of the most attractive of all 18th-century garden buildings, the Music Temple with its curving doric façade, standing on the island in the lake and perfectly positioned above the cascade which was simplified and had its supporting figures added.

West Wycombe was a leading example of the kind of idealized landscapes created by many gentleman-amateurs during the mid 18th century – landscapes such as Henry Hoare's Stourhead in Wiltshire, and Lord Fortesque's Castle Hill in Devon, developed after his death in 1851 by his half-brother whose sister married George Lyttelton of Hagley Hall. These allegorical layouts, decorated with temples and inspired by the ancient world and classical Italy, were designed for show and for social occasions in a manner quite different from the more subdued and 'natural' landscapes that 'Capability' Brown was creating at the time. But they depended above all on the personal taste of their owners.

THE HON CHARLES HAMILTON (*1704-86*)

BOWOOD, *Wiltshire;* PAINSHILL, *Surrey*

CHARLES HAMILTON, fourteenth child and youngest of nine sons of the 6th Earl of Abercorn, was one of the most brilliant stars in the firmament of 18th-century gardening, his work combining innovative planting and horticultural knowledge with the adventurous creation of an idealized, classically-inspired landscape. Unfortunately his financial resources as the youngest son in such a large family were always limited and only thirty-five years after acquiring the lease of Painshill in Surrey he was forced to sell and retire to Bath, where he built a house in the Royal Crescent and created a second noted garden during the last decade of his life.

After Oxford, Hamilton spent many years in Italy studying painting and acquiring antiquities. He returned to England early in the 1730s and joined the circle of Frederick, Prince of Wales, for whom he worked in various positions and through whom, in 1738, he acquired the lease of the Painshill property near Cobham in Surrey. Here, with the assistance of a number of distinguished architects, but all to his own plans and designs, he created one of the most eclectically brilliant and earliest naturalistic landscapes of the 18th century. Hamilton wished the visual impact of the garden to reproduce the qualities of the great landscape painters he had admired in Italy which he achieved by a combination of architectural and horticultural quality, engineering skill, and elements of ingenuity and surprise.

One of the few advantages that the Painshill site possessed was undulating terrain, but by taking water from the small River Mole by a waterwheel arrangement that he himself devised, Hamilton was able to fill the 6 ha/15 acre lake that he dug, and greatly increase the fertility of the poor soil. Through his landscape he created a series of scenes, each quite different in mood and visual impact. A five-arched bridge, ingeniously built of wood, spanned the water and at one end of the lake stood a gothick pavilion.

Robert Adam designed the ceiling and pedestal for a Temple of Bacchus; Henry Keene designed a Turkish Tent and a number of other buildings or part-buildings, including a Roman mausoleum, a hermitage – occupied – and a ruin, and most spectacular of all, the grotto disguised beneath a second smaller bridge.

Hamilton was not alone in planning the various architectural features at Painshill for specific effect; others were doing similar things in their own gardens and landscapes at this time. What singled out his work was the decisive importance of his planting, both in the planning of woodland walks and in the species he used. Along the walks seats were judiciously positioned to encourage visitors to enjoy a specific view or feature and some years after Hamilton had been forced to move, Sir Uvedale Price, the champion of the picturesque, wrote: 'At Pains Hill we have enjoyed the dear delight of getting to some spot where there were no traces of art, and no other walk or communication than a sheep track.'[1]

Hamilton's most innovative planting was of newly introduced and rare species, many of them from North America and acquired from his friend Peter Collinson, the London-based nurseryman who was constantly importing new varieties sent by collectors such as Mark Catesby (q.v. p. 37) and John Bartram (q.v. p. 61). As well as conifers, Hamilton may have been among the first English gardeners to plant in any quantity the rhododendrons and azaleas being imported from North America – plants that were later to revolutionize the appearance of gardens all over the country. In 1838 J. C. Loudon (q.v. p. 112) visited Painshill and recorded: 'Among the trees remaining are some remarkable fine silver cedars, pinasters and other pines, American oaks, cork trees and ilexes, a tupelo tree, tulip trees, deciduous cypresses, Lombardy and other poplars, etc. Here some of the first rhododendrons and azaleas introduced into England by Mr Thorburn, who was gardener to Mr Hamilton.'[2]

Such planting of new species in conjunction with classical-inspired architectural features to produce a picturesque landscape was an original step forward, and Hamilton took advantage of the rich harvest of plants becoming available from America and used them to best effect. He also desired his landscape to have practical features as well as ornamental ones, something which appealed to and possibly influenced Thomas Jefferson when he visited Painshill in 1786, and his vineyard apparently produced sparkling white wine. In this sense Painshill showed characteristics of the ornamental farms, *fermes ornées*, which had become fashionable by the mid 18th century and of which the best known examples were the Leasowens, created at Halesowen by William Shenstone, and Wooburn Farm, close to Chertsey in Surrey, created by Philip Southcote. Today Wooburn Farm has disappeared and only remnants of the Leasowens survive as part of a golf course. After neglect since World War II Painshill itself appeared doomed to decay until the foundation of the Painshill Park Trust which raised funds for an admirably extensive restoration, begun in 1981 and continued for a period of some ten years.

In addition to Painshill itself, Hamilton's wider influence was considerable, as he was frequently consulted by friends and acquaintances for advice about their gardens. At Bowood he designed the cascade at one end of 'Capability' Brown's lake in 1765, and may also have designed the Hermit's Cave; and it has also been suggested that he advised Henry Hoare (q.v. p. 73) on the exact siting of the Temple of Apollo at Stourhead, and later similarly advised William Beckford on planting around Fonthill Abbey in Wiltshire.

HENRY HOARE (1705-85)

STOURHEAD, *Wiltshire*

HENRY HOARE, grandson of the founder of the famous London bank, made at Stourhead in Wiltshire what is popularly considered the ideal landscape. Although Stourhead is very different from Studley Royal, both Henry

Overleaf: One of Hoare's planned views at Stourhead, across the lake to the Temple of Flora, the five-arched bridge and Stourton church.

Hoare and John Aislabie (*q.v.* p. 32) had similar reasons for wanting to create such a scene of arcadian beauty. Both men turned to landscape gardening as a release from disappointment; Aislabie's was financial and political, Hoare's was personal – his first wife died after less than one year of marriage and his second wife, Susan, also died prematurely in 1743, after some fifteen years of obviously happy marriage; their favourite daughter Anne also died young in 1759.

Henry Hoare inherited Stourhead, the estate bought by his family in 1714, on the death of his mother in 1741. His father had employed Colen Campbell to build the Palladian house in 1722, and after the death of his second wife Hoare began the creation of his landscape in a series of adjoining small valleys to the west of the house which is set up on a plateau and out of sight. Hoare had travelled extensively in Italy as a young man and was a devoted admirer of classical art and literature. He was also well acquainted with the major developments in gardens in England and on the continent. For a long time Hoare's landscape was believed to have been based on Virgil's *Aeneid* and the route around the lake planned as a journey, both visual and allegorical. It now seems more likely, as Christopher Thacker argues, that 'the recommended itinerary round the lake was simply given Virgilian overtones related to the sequence of features along the route'.[1] However it was planned, there is little question that the arrangement of features gave the place an unusual degree of unity, though the heart of this unity lies in the informally shaped 8 ha/20-acre lake which the whole landscape is planned. Hoare created the lake in the winding valleys, damming and linking together a series of small ponds fed by the source of the river Stour. On the surrounding hillsides he planted beeches, oaks and conifers, to grow up into hanging woodlands. The quality of Hoare's overall design at Stourhead is matched by the craftsmanship of the commissioned architecture and smaller ornaments. Most of the buildings were designed by Henry Flitcroft, the Palladian architect who had as a young man been assistant to Lord Burlington and was a close associate of

Kent (*q.v.* p. 41); statues were supplied by Michael Rysbrack and John Cheere. Together they were employed at Stourhead over a period of nearly thirty years as Hoare's landscape gradually developed and unfolded.

The original approach from the house gives no intimation of the landscape that lies ahead. Eventually a view of the lake appears and the path descends through woodland to the water's edge. Today the visitor embarks on the meandering journey around the lake from a lower level, passing on the way the various architectural features, of which the grotto is the most ingenious. Inside is a chamber, its roof encrusted with spars, whither Hoare diverted a series of springs from the neighbouring hillsides to emerge in a channel as the source of the river. Most of the flow rushes out beneath the prostrate sleeping figure of the Nymph of the Grot, a white-painted lead statue, while more water gushes symbolically from the River God's urn. The model for the grotto is clearly suggested by a quotation from Alexander Pope carved in marble in front of the nymph. Both figures were made by John Cheere and are lit from a hole in the ceiling, while in front of the nymph an encrusted opening looks out at water level across the lake. Emerging from the grotto the path continues along the lakeside, past the Watch Cottage that was given its picturesque appearance by Hoare's grandson, towards the destination of the outward journey and focal point of the whole landscape, the Pantheon, built by Flitcroft in 1754, the year that the lake was completed.

Positioned on the lakeside, the Pantheon, with its Corinthian portico and shallow dome, is obviously modelled on the famous original at Rome – which Hoare no doubt saw for himself – but more specific inspiration probably came from paintings, as David Watkin suggests: 'this building seems to have been inspired by the Pantheon temple in Claude's View of Delphi with a Procession, of which Hoare owned a version by Locatelli. Even closer to Stourhead is Claude's Coast View of Delos with Aeneas, which was one of six paintings illustrating the story of Aeneas. Claude shows a doric portico (corresponding to the Temple of Flora at Stourhead), a Pantheon and a bridge which are close not only in form but in their relationship to each other, to the corresponding buildings at Stourhead.[2] Inside the Pantheon was a collection of statues, notably Rysbrack's *Hercules*.

From the Pantheon the Temple of Flora is seen on the other side of the lake and, to one side, the five-arched bridge with the hamlet and church of Stourton beyond, which Hoare himself described in a letter to a friend: 'the bridge, village and church altogether will be a charming Gaspard (Poussin) picture at the end of the water.'[3] In 1765 this area was given another picturesque feature when Hoare erected the Bristol Cross that he had purchased and transported from the town. On the wooded hillside to the south of the lake Flitcroft built the Temple of Apollo in 1765, supposedly modelled on the circular Temple of Venus at Baalbek, and it is from this elevated position that the visitor originally gained the most complete picture of Hoare's landscape, although today the surrounding trees present too thick a screen.

In 1783, two years before his death, Hoare gave Stourhead to his grandson (and great-nephew, since the boy's parents were Hoare's daughter and nephew), Richard Colt Hoare. The same year Richard Colt Hoare married Hester Lyttelton whose uncle had created the landscape at Hagley Hall in Worcestershire, but his marriage also ended early, with the death of his wife two years later, and his only son predeceased him by two years. After many years abroad, Richard Colt Hoare returned to Stourhead where he planted a great variety of ornamental trees and shrubs, including many new introductions from the United States. There were rhododendrons among them, but the majority of those at Stourhead today were planted after 1894, by Sir Henry Hoare, the last member of the family to own the property, who was also responsible for extensive restoration to the buildings. Family sadness continued into the 20th century, for it was as a result of Sir Henry's only son being killed in 1917 that in 1946 Stourhead passed to the National Trust.

Some claim that the later planting of great banks of rhododendrons and azaleas are insensitive and unsuitable additions at Stourhead, detracting from the purity of Henry Hoare's original creation. They are certainly very much in evidence during spring and early summer, but at other times of the year the visitor is able to enjoy to a remarkable degree the landscape as Hoare originally planned it some two hundred and fifty years ago. At the time, Stourhead was one of the most complete statements of the landscape movement, for unlike Stowe, to which its classical allegory most closely relates, it was not the result of successive stages of development, but the complete realization of one man's vision of landscape.

THOMAS JEFFERSON (*1746-1826*)

MONTICELLO, *Virginia, USA; University of Virginia, USA*

IT IS NO COINCIDENCE that the two most influential figures in the development of American gardens during the 18th and early 19th centuries were the two foremost statesmen of the time – Thomas Jefferson, author of the Declaration of Independence and later President, and George Washington (*q.v.* p. 89), first President of the United States. Their homes and their surrounding gardens – Monticello and Mount Vernon – have acquired the status of shrines, and their views on garden design and planting were widely disseminated at a time when America was making the first tentative steps towards establishing a gardening tradition of its own.

Jefferson, whose agrarian, intensely democratic political philosophy was inextricably bound up with his ideas on landscape and horticulture, has been described by Geoffrey Jellicoe as, 'one of the last humanists in the Renaissance tradition'.[1] Deeply interested in philosophy, science and architecture throughout his life – which became increasingly dominated by politics until his retirement from the Presidency in 1809 – it was at Monticello, the home that he designed and built for himself close to his birthplace in Virginia, that his ideas on landscape and love of plants were applied. His *Garden Book* is one of the most valuable and revealing sources of information about gardening during the 18th century. It includes meticulous details of the plants that he acquired and where they came from, and where he sent plants in return; his comments upon current horticultural and agricultural practices; detailed horticultural and botanical correspondence; and the annual records of the performances of the vegetables and fruit in the Monticello garden.

In 1785 Jefferson succeeded Benjamin Franklin as minister in Paris, where he remained until 1790. These five years were of crucial influence upon his gardening and architectural ideas, for they allowed him time to travel in France and England and to familiarize himself with the style of the great houses, parks and gardens. Though impressed by French grandeur, he preferred the more rural enjoyment of landscape apparent in England, which he visited in 1786 in the company of John Adams, their itinerary including a number of the most renowned country houses and landscapes. The more broad-minded Jefferson was far more receptive to what he saw than the fiercely nationalistic Adams who encountered little that he felt to be praiseworthy: 'It will be long, I hope, before Ridings, Parks, Pleasure Grounds and ornamented farms grow so much in fashion in America. But Nature has done greater things and furnished nobler materials there. The oceans, islands, rivers, mountains, valleys are all laid out upon a larger scale.'[2] Jefferson, whose critical approach was tempered by his natural desire to absorb new knowledge, was impressed by English gardening techniques but found some of the great open sweeps of parkland impersonal.

In a short period of some six weeks in March and April the two men managed to visit a large proportion of the best-known gardens in England and none escaped Jefferson's keen analysis: Chiswick House; Hampton Court, which was 'old-fashioned'; Twickenham; Esher Place; Claremont, where there was 'nothing remarkable'; Painshill, where he did admire 'a Doric temple, beautiful';

Woburn; Caversham; Wootton; Stowe, where he recorded 'fifteen men and eighteen boys keeping the pleasure grounds . . ... The Corinthian arch has a very useless appearance, inasmuch as it has no pretention to any destination. Instead of being an object from the house, it is an obstacle to a very pleasing distant prospect'; the Leasowens where 'the walk through the wood is umbrageous and pleasing'; Hagley; Blenheim, where he did admit that 'the water here is very beautiful and very grand'[3]; Enfield Chase, Moor Park; and Kew.

Having experienced at first hand the fruits of the vigorous and long-established European gardening tradition, Jefferson returned home to transplant ideas into the very different soil of America. One decisive difference from the more insular, self-protective earlier gardens of the colonies, was a sense at Monticello of looking outward and of unity with the landscape beyond. The house, sited on a hill with views in three directions, was purely classical, with its garden stretching out in front on terraces which Jefferson cut into the descending hillside. Central to the garden's layout was the main oval lawn encircled by a winding path, along which Jefferson planned a series of contrasting flower-beds, with larger areas given over to carefully selected shrubberies. Along the terraces were his fruit and vegetable gardens and the progress of each area and individual plant was meticulously recorded in his garden diary. On one terrace he built an enchanting square brick pavilion with tall arched windows on all four sides, looking out over the wooded Virginia countryside.

As letters in the *Garden Book* indicate, Jefferson's friends often shared the produce of his garden. To John W. Eppes he writes in 1817: 'Mrs Eppes will receive herewith a box containing some calycanthuses, prickly locusts (*Robinia hispida*) a Snowberry bush and the sweet-scented curran . . . the Snowberry is beautiful in autumn and winter by its bunches of white snowberries. I send in a paper some sprout kale to be sowed and transplanted as cabbage. It has to remain in its place during winter and will give 2 or 3 successive crops of sprouts from the beginning of December to April, and is a fine, tender, sweet winter

Thomas Jefferson's garden at Monticello combined the appreciation of landscape that he had seen in Europe with traditional American flower-gardening.

vegetable . . . . PS. A Halesia sent, also purple and white figs.'[4]

However, while some of the confident, outward-looking aspects of European landscape were incorporated into the emerging American gardening tradition, they were blended with the domestic, productive gardening of the early colonials and their instinctive enjoyment of warm colours and flower gardening. At Monticello Jefferson grew almost exclusively indigenous American plants, and while he derived unending enjoyment from experimenting with species previously little known in cultivation, his example had considerable impact in demonstrating the riches of plant material that was available in the country. These riches were hugely increased when, in 1803, the Louisiana Purchase doubled the size of the country, extending it as far as the Rocky Mountains.

Between his retirement in 1809 and death in 1826 Jefferson lived most of the time at Monticello, and during the last years of his life realized a long-standing ambition when he founded the University of Virginia at the foot of the hill below Monticello. From the end of his main lawn he was able to look down upon the buildings and landscape of the university site that he himself had designed. Jefferson's work here provided the foundation for a tradition of good landscape design and architecture which has been such a noticeable feature of American universities ever since. Finally, a few months before his death he wrote in melancholy tones to Edward Livingston, 'worn down by time in bodily strength, unable to walk even into my garden without too much fatigue . . .'[5]

SANDERSON MILLER (1717-80)

FARNBOROUGH HALL, *Warwickshire*; HAGLEY HALL, *Worcestershire*; HONINGTON HALL, *Warwickshire*; PRIOR PARK, *Avon*; WIMPOLE HALL, *Cambridgeshire*; WROXTON ABBEY, *Oxfordshire*

AT THE AGE OF TWENTY, Sanderson Miller was left a considerable fortune by his father, a prosperous wool merchant from Banbury. Thus secure, the young man was able to set himself up as a country gentleman and, more importantly, as an amateur architect who was to play a central role in the gothic revival and the development of the picturesque landscape. After leaving Oxford before taking his degree, Sanderson Miller dabbled in architecture for pleasure rather than as necessary employment. He worked primarily for friends, usually providing sketches which were then adapted into formal plans by a resident mason or builder. He was happier designing a limited addition to a house or a theatrical eye-catcher for a park, than getting involved in the more demanding and detailed work of a complete house.

Radway Grange, the home Sanderson Miller inherited, overlooked the site of the Battle of Edgehill. This together with an enthusiasm for mediaeval history, stirred his interest in gothic architecture – which he first applied to Radway itself. Around 1745, and more dramatically, he constructed a gothic cottage and castellated tower at Edgehill, which soon acquired a widespread reputation. One of his first commissions after this was from his friend, the politician Sir George Lyttelton, later 1st Lord Lyttelton whose uncle was Lord Cobham of Stowe.

Lyttelton's home, Hagley Hall near Stourbridge, was close to William Shenstone's the Leasowens at Halesowen, and it may have been Shenstone who initially aroused Lyttelton's interest in improving the park at Hagley. The naturally picturesque site with its wooded hills and narrow valleys was the ideal setting for the 'sham' ruined castle that Miller built there in 1748, and the authenticity of the castle's mediaeval imagery was enhanced by the fact that it was built with stones from the ruined Halesowen Abbey nearby. The castle caused something of a sensation and a year later Lord Dacre – who was later to commission Miller to gothicize his Tudor house, Belhus in Essex – wrote to Miller: 'You have got everlasting fame by this castle at Hagley, so that I hear talk of nothing else.'[1] When Horace Walpole – whose own gothic essay, Strawberry Hill, is recognized as the main impetus for the gothic revival in Britain – visited Hagley in 1755, he sent a description of enormous enthusiasm to a friend: 'You might draw, but I can't describe the enchanting scenes of the park; it is a hill of three miles, but broke into all manner of beauty . . .. There is a ruined castle, built by Miller, that would get his freedom even of Strawberry: it has the true rust of the Baron's Wars . . .. I wore my eyes out with gazing, my feet with climbing, and my tongue and my vocabulary with commending.'[2]

The Hagley castle secured Miller's reputation as the leading exponent of gothic or ruined architecture as a landscape feature, and similar buildings became widely sought after among his circle of landowning friends and acquaintances. Through Lord Lyttelton he was commissioned by the Earl of Hardwicke, the lord chancellor, to design a ruined castle for the park at Wimpole Hall in Cambridgeshire. Drawings that Miller supplied around 1750 survive, but in the event the ruin was not erected for some twenty years, eventually being built by 'Capability' Brown (q.v. p. 62) for Lord Hardwicke's son as part of his extensive work at Wimpole. Miller's other important sham castle was built for Ralph Allen at Prior Park on Claverton Down above Bath around 1755. Allen later employed 'Capability' Brown to landscape the park and build a dramatically sited Palladian bridge at the bottom of the hill in front of the house.

Sanderson Miller's landscape work was not confined purely to gothic architecture. At a number of places close to his home at Radway, he carried out a variety of more extensive gardening commissions. At Wroxton Abbey near Banbury he was employed by Francis North, 1st Earl of Guilford, to add decorative architectural features to the natural landscape with which Lord Guilford had replaced the earlier formal garden made for his father by Tilleman Bobart. Miller's buildings included a gothic dovecot erected as an eye-catcher, the semi-ruined Drayton Arch and a temple on a mount; he also built a cascade. Much of his work at Wroxton has recently been restored.

Even closer to Miller's home was Farnborough Hall where he advised his friend William Holbeck on the creation of the great terrace which compares with those at Duncombe and Rievaulx in Yorkshire. The terrace extends away in a curving, uphill 'S' shape from the house for a distance of some 740 m/800 yards, with extensive views across the two lakes created by Holbeck to Edge Hill in the distance. Miller designed for the terrace an ionic temple, another wonderfully unusual elliptical temple with a domed upper room supported by doric columns, and an obelisk on the summit at the far end from the house. Later Miller built a cascade and grotto for another neighbour, Joseph Townshend, at Honington Hall near Shipston-on-Stour.

By the time of Miller's death in 1780 his reputation was secure as a leading innovator in the development of the English landscape. This had largely come about as a result of his financial circumstances which enabled him to indulge his personal architectural fancy at a time when picturesque features were becoming increasingly fashionable. It is fortunate that much of his work survives today; the castle at Hagley Hall is, for instance, as impressive a sight today as it must have been when completed in the middle of the 18th century.

HUMPHRY REPTON (1752-1818)

ABBOTS LEIGH, *Avon;* ANTONY HOUSE, *Cornwall;* ASHRIDGE PARK, *Hertfordshire;* ASHTON COURT, *Somerset;* ATTINGHAM PARK, *Shropshire;* BABWORTH, *Nottinghamshire;* BARNINGHAM HALL, *Norfolk;* BURLEY-ON-THE-HILL, *Leicestershire;* CASSIOBURY PARK, *Hertfordshire;* COBHAM HALL, *Kent;* CORSHAM COURT, *Wiltshire;* COURTEENHALL, *Northamptonshire;* CREWE HALL, *Cheshire;* CULFORD, *Suffolk;* DULLINGHAM, *Cambridgeshire;* DYRHAM PARK, *Avon;* ENDSLEIGH, *Devon;* GARNONS, *Herefordshire;* GAYHURST, *Buckinghamshire;* HAREWOOD HOUSE, *Yorkshire;* HASELLS HALL, *Bedfordshire;* HATCHLANDS, *Surrey;* HEATHFIELD PARK, *Sussex;* HOLKHAM HALL, *Norfolk;* LAMER, *Hertfordshire;* LATHOM HOUSE, *Lancashire;* LIVERMERE PARK,

Overleaf: Sanderson Miller's unusual elliptical temple at Farnborough Hall.

Suffolk; LONGLEAT, *Wiltshire;* LONGNOR HALL, *Shropshire;* LUSCOMBE CASTLE, *Devon;* MILTON, *Cambridgeshire;* MOCCAS COURT, *Herefordshire;* MULGRAVE CASTLE, *Yorkshire;* PANSHANGER, *Hertfordshire;* PLAS NEWYDD, *Anglesey;* PORT ELIOT, *Cornwall;* PRESTWOOD, *Staffordshire;* PURLEY HALL, *Berkshire;* RENDLESHAM HALL, *Suffolk;* RHUG HALL, *Clwyd;* RODE HALL, *Cheshire;* RUDDING PARK, *Yorkshire;* SARSDEN HOUSE, *Oxfordshire;* SEZINCOTE, *Gloucestershire;* SHARDELOES, *Buckinghamshire;* SHERINGHAM HALL, *Norfolk;* STANAGE PARK, *Powys;* SUFTON COURT, *Herefordshire;* TATTON PARK, *Cheshire;* TREGOTHNAN, *Cornwall;* TYRINGHAM, *Buckinghamshire;* UPPARK, *Sussex;* WELBECK ABBEY, *Nottinghamshire;* WENTWORTH WOODHOUSE, *Yorkshire;* WIMPOLE HALL, *Cambridgeshire;* WOBURN ABBEY, *Bedfordshire.*

IT WOULD APPEAR ALMOST TOO CONVENIENT to be able to say that Humphry Repton took up the development of landscape gardening where 'Capability' Brown left off, and subtly adapted it from the demands of Brown's grandly confident Whig aristocrats to those of the Regency squirarchy and the emerging prosperous middle classes. In broad terms, however, it was true. Beginning to practise in 1788, five years after Brown's death, and acutely conscious of the great man's mantle, Repton was, during the next thirty years, as tirelessly energetic as his predecessor travelling thousands of miles all over the country; from his home in East Anglia he worked as far afield as North Wales, Cornwall and Yorkshire, at least until a carriage accident in 1811 severely disabled him and confined him to a wheelchair for much of the time. Like Brown, he handled clients well and professionally, factors which played a large part in the quantity of his commissions. Although, as with Brown, much of Repton's work has either disappeared or been so altered and disfigured as to be unrecognizable, some of his most important landscapes still survive in a remarkably good state of repair, with their layout and planting clearly as originally planned.

Landscape gardening seemed at first an unlikely profession for Repton. He was born the son of a prosperous tax officer in Bury St Edmunds, and even while at school in Bury and subsequently in Norwich, his father was planning for his future as a merchant. As a result, when Humphry was aged twelve he was taken to Holland to learn Dutch and to absorb the ways of the most successful trading nation in Europe. He disliked the school at which he was deposited and left to live with the family of a Scottish banking friend of his father's, Zachary Hope, who had been asked to look after the boy. In the home of this sociable, cultivated family he was taught by a tutor, and given an education that concentrated on music and literature and on improving the boy's painting – enjoyable but not practical subjects for the career ahead of him. At the age of sixteen he returned to Norwich to work in the textile trade, employment for which he clearly had little enthusiasm but which lasted for five years. He married in 1773, aged twenty-one, and shortly afterwards his father set him up in business as a general merchant. Throughout his life Humphry retained an unfailingly generous and cheerful outlook on life; now, happily married and with a growing family, he worked at his trade out of sensibility to his parents' ambitions, but with little relish.

Release came in 1778 when both parents died and Repton decided to combine the proceeds of his business and his inheritance and settle down as a country gentleman near Aylsham. Unfortunately his finances were unable to sustain him and within a few years the need to find gainful employment became acute.

In retrospect, one can see that the foundations of Repton's career as a landscape gardener were laid during these years. He enjoyed a circle of cultivated friends and acquaintances at this time, in particular William Windham of Felbrigg Hall, who liked Repton's company, allowed him unlimited access to his library, and introduced him to many visitors. Through Windham, Repton met, among others, Richard Payne Knight the champion of the picturesque landscape, who was to figure largely in his future career, and Sir Joseph Banks the patrician explorer and botanist. It was also clear that for someone like Repton, who combined obvious artistic talent and appreciation of the arts with little material ambition, successful employment would only be found in an activity which he found enjoyable.

Towards the end of 1783 Repton's financial problems forced him to sell Old Hall, his home near Aylsham and move to a cottage in the Essex village of Hare Street, where he was to remain for the rest of his life. During the next few years he dabbled in a number of different occupations until, as Edward Hyams describes, his vocation apparently manifested itself during a sleepless night: 'his straits became such as to keep him awake at night despite his naturally buoyant temper. But that was the nadir, for during one such sleepless night it suddenly occurred to him that he would try his hand at landscape gardening. He had made something of Old Hall; he could draw and paint; he had an eye for "taste"; he had many friends among the landed gentry. "Capability" Brown had been dead for five years, and no artist of anything like equal merit had risen from the ranks of his imitators to take his place. He had read much of botany and architecture; Marsham and his own reading had taught him to understand the management of trees; he had listened to Joseph Banks's talks about plants. It must have seemed to him, as he thought of his chances, that it was extraordinary he had not thought of this solution before. He rose in the morning with his mind made up.'[1]

It is easy to attempt to force comparisons between Brown and Repton, and they embarked upon their careers in very different manners: Brown, a trained gardener who was by his early twenties working in the most important garden of the period for one of the most influential patrons in England; Repton, who, aged nearly forty and with no formal training, turned to garden design out of financial necessity and began by tapping his local circle of friends and acquaintances. But, as we shall see, once Repton started the ball rolling, his progress was very comparable to Brown's, commissions coming from personal recommendations from satisfied clients and leading to marked regional activity – one successful project often leading to others within a close vicinity.

In a remarkably short time Repton had propelled himself into an increasingly busy and successful career; but his confidence and grasp of landscape design and all its implications suggest that a very real talent had been lying dormant. As Miles Hadfield points out, Repton had the benefit of a broader general education and was far better read than the majority of his professional predecessors, and he used this knowledge and an acquisitive brain to the full. Within five years he had prepared the first of four major publications on garden design, which together give a more comprehensive and more beautifully illustrated record of his ideas and principles than is available for any other garden designer of comparable importance. The first was *Sketches and Hints on Landscape Gardening* which, by the time it was published in 1795, incorporated a subtle and amusing riposte to the bombastic publications the year before of Richard Payne Knight's *The Landscape* and Sir Uvedale Price's *Essay on the Picturesque* which contained attacks on 'Capability' Brown and, to a lesser extent, on Repton himself. In 1803 Repton published his most weighty work, *Observations on the Theory and Practice of Landscape Gardening*, followed in 1806 by the shorter essay, *An Inquiry into the Changes of Taste in Landscape Gardening*, and finally, in 1816, *Fragments on the Theory and Practice of Landscape Gardening*.

These publications spell out Repton's ideas about the kind of landscape and gardens that he was aspiring to create, and show too how even the smallest of details hardly ever escaped his notice. In *An Inquiry into Changes of Taste in Landscape Gardening* he gives a broad picture of his aims: 'The perfection of landscape gardening consists in the four following requisites: *First*, it must display the natural beauties, and hide the natural defects of every situation. *Secondly*, it should give the appearance of extent and freedom, by carefully disguising or hiding the boundary. *Thirdly*, it must studiously conceal every interference or art, however expensive, by which the natural scenery is improved; making the whole appear the production of nature only; and *fourthly*, all objects of mere convenience or comfort, if incapable of being made ornamental, or of becoming proper parts of the general scenery, must be removed or concealed.'[2]

More specific are his views on the problem of the 'browsing-line' (by cattle) which he outlined earlier in *Observations on the Theory and Practice of Landscape Gardening*: 'Whether trees be planted near the eye or at a great distance from it, and whether they be young plants or of the greatest stature, this browsing line will always be parallel to the surface of the ground, and being above the eye, if the heads of single trees do not rise above the outline of more distant woods, the stems will appear only like stakes of different sizes scattered about the plain . . . the browsing line will make a disagreeable parallel with the even surface of the ground; this can only be remedied by preventing cattle from browsing the under wood . . .. The browsing line is always at nearly the same distance of about (2m) six feet from the ground, it acts as a *scale*, by which theeye measures the comparative height of trees at any distance . . .'.[3]

For Repton the relationship between house and the surrounding landscape was paramount; he even argued that they should be considered as one. The style of the house, which in his eyes fell in simple terms into either classical or gothic, the latter becoming increasingly fashionable through his career, should be closely reflected in the style of its surroundings. Partly because of the circumstances and requirements of his clients, but also through his own inclination, Repton used his influence to reduce the scale of garden and landscape design at this time; it was rare that he ever carried out the kind of vast earthmoving that was regularly involved in the creation of a Brown landscape; streams were not dammed to make lakes and his planting did not often march over hundreds of acres. The grandest houses could happily be marooned within rolling parkland and hold their own, but Repton suggested that lesser edifices were better presented with the help of terracing, balustrades and, if necessary, formal flower gardens in the immediate surroundings. In all this he was thoroughly in tune with his public, for Repton's England – as has often been pointed out, not least because he was mentioned in person in *Mansfield Park* – was Jane Austen's England, soon to become Victorian England, full of squires and vicarages and the occasional exciting grandee.

Nothing pointed to Repton's awareness of his clients' tastes more clearly than his *Red Books*, for which he is almost as well known as for his actual gardens. In them, Repton devised a system of presenting his proposals which took advantage of his drawing and painting skills to clarify his suggestions to his clients in a manner that would be unfailingly attractive and flattering. Each *Red Book* followed a set pattern but was at the same time agreeably individual. An introduction and map would be followed by specific proposals explained in beguiling terms and accompanied by the famously ingenious illustrations with flaps which, when turned, revealed his alterations.

By the end of the 1790s a series of important commissions had virtually established Repton as the most fashionable garden designer of the day, in particular his work for Thomas Coke at Holkham, for the Duke of Portland at Welbeck Abbey and for Lord Darnley at Cobham Hall. Both Welbeck and Cobham were projects that lasted for ten years or more. The former involved three red books – although many suggestions in the last of them, drawn up for the Duke's son, were not carried out. At Cobham Repton was clearly satisfied with his efforts as he showed in *Fragments on the Theory and Practice of Landscape Gardening* in 1816 after the long project was complete: 'The house is no longer a huge pile standing naked on a vast grazing ground. Its walls are enriched with roses and jasmines; its apartments are perfumed with odours from flowers surrounding it on every side; and the animals which enliven the landscape are not admitted as an annoyance. All around is neatness, elegance and comfort; while the views of the park are improved by the rich foreground, over which they are seen from the terraces in the garden, or the elevated situation of the apartments.'[4]

In 1795 Repton was consulted by Paul Cobb Methuen, the owner of Corsham Court in Wiltshire, about a commission significant for two reasons: it was the start

Sheringham on the Norfolk coast was almost Repton's last commission and arguably his most assured.

of Repton's partnership with the architect John Nash, and it was also a place where Brown had worked extensively – he had made alterations to the house and had also done work in the park, but had died before the project was complete. When commissions had involved architectural work, in the early years of his career, Repton had consulted an old friend from Norwich, William Wilkins; the partnership with John Nash that started with the Corsham job was to last a number of years, and saw Repton's eldest son, John Adey – who had been completely deaf since his childhood – employed in Nash's office as an architectural draughtsman.

Repton's work in the park at Corsham demonstrated deference towards Brown's work and unexecuted plans, while the most interesting aspect was the quantity of tree-planting; in mixing native beech and oak with more unusual varieties he showed, as Edward Hyams points out, that he 'kept up with the process of acclimatization of exotic plants, for although *Quercus ilex*, Holm Oak, one of the species he planted at Corsham, had long been introduced to England, both *Q. coccinea* and *Q. phellos* were eighteenth-century introductions and still of very limited distribution in England. Both were what Sir William Chambers would have fulminated against as "American weeds".[5]

During the late 1790s, Repton's partnership with Nash produced one of his most outstanding pieces of landscape, at Luscombe Castle in Devon. They were working here for the banker Charles Hoare, half-brother of Richard Colt Hoare of Stourhead. Luscombe, while not large, was one of the most successful gothic houses of the period, and the setting that Repton created around it, with closely wooded hills and a long view south up the main valley, remains intensely romantic. What he and Nash achieved so emphatically was what Mark Girouard described as, 'a "natural" house in a "natural" setting'.[6]

By 1800, however, Repton no longer needed an architectural partner. The volume of work continued unabated, but as well as John Adey, Repton's third son, George, had also trained as an architect – as a pupil in Nash's office –

and between them the family were well able to cope with such architectural work that different projects demanded. With the publication of most of his major books in addition to constant travel, the first decade of the new century was the busiest of Repton's career, the output only curtailed by his carriage accident in 1811.

Despite the incapacity forced upon him by the accident for the last years of his life, Repton produced at Sheringham in Norfolk, perhaps the most complete design of his career, and one which he considered his favourite. The property had recently been bought by a Mr and Mrs Abbot Upcher, who determined to build a new house that would take maximum advantage of the natural surroundings. With the assistance of John Adey, Repton designed the house and its interiors and all the elements of the surrounding garden and landscape. Although situated on the coast near Cromer, Sheringham has no views to the sea. The house lies near the foot of a wooded hill – a position selected by Repton to protect it from wind – and its views are inland. One of Repton's most adventurous decisions was to retain the area of farmland in front of the house rather than put it all down to grass, and to concentrate the effect of his extensive new planting of woodland in different sites beyond. There are, however, views to the sea from many parts of the grounds, and a temple was erected on one hill from which to admire the elegant colonnaded front of the house and to look out to sea. There is no doubt that it gave Repton enormous satisfaction that one of the most enjoyable – and admired – commissions of his career was carried out in a county that he had known so well for most of his life.

Sheringham was probably the most important of Repton's later landscape work, but one later commission, at Ashridge, for the Duke of Bridgwater, showed Repton happy to create formal gardens between a house and its park setting – work which heralded the return of decorative and flower gardening through the 19th century. Ashridge already had a Brown park which the duke wanted to leave untouched, but around the house Repton designed a series of ornamental gardens, including a monk's garden and a circular rosarium. Only parts of these gardens survive today; at the time, they quickly became enormously influential.

Repton finally died of a seizure in 1818, having known for some time that he would not live long. If any evolutionary transition can be tied to a date, then his death set the final seal on the expansive landscape settings for country houses which had developed in all their variety through the 18th century and which had dominated garden philosophy. In future these landscapes might be retained, but usually as the framework to a more decorative and detailed style of gardening.

GEORGE WASHINGTON (1732-99)

MOUNT VERNON, *Virginia, USA*

GEORGE WASHINGTON combined his work as a soldier and statesman with a lifelong passion for horticulture and farming. The family property at Mount Vernon, first settled by a Washington in the mid 17th century and extending to some 3,200 ha/8,000 acres, gave him ample scope to indulge this passion. Over a period of some forty years Washington replanned the place to become a model homestead, with house, garden and farm closely bound together in a way that has provided a lasting influence. Coming from a well-to-do family himself, and marrying in 1759 a wealthy widow, Martha Dandridge Custis, Washington had all the necessary resources to implement his ideas to the highest standards.

Washington was a pragmatist; while maintaining a fiercely anti-English political stance for much of his life, he nevertheless appreciated their agricultural expertise to the extent of corresponding regularly with leading English farming figures. He appears to have been less influenced by English ideas on landscape and gardening, and although he admired the architect Batty Langley's book,

New Principles of Gardening, Washington's garden at Mount Vernon was clearly rooted in American culture. Trees and shrubs were Washington's especial interest, and he grew almost exclusively native American species. Throughout the garden an orderly neatness and geometry helped to balance the visual enjoyment of the larger landscape and the nearer, more small-scale detail of the flower garden and of individual specimens; to balance practical productivity and aesthetic pleasure.

The site of Mount Vernon, with the house positioned on a bluff overlooking the Potomac River, had enormous natural qualities; Washington rebuilt the house to his own design, producing a home that was classically dignified, with a central block flanked by two smaller wings at right-angles. The overall simplicity heightens the effect of the sparingly used decorative features – the lantern cupola, the verandah along the main front overlooking the river, and the curving arched colonnades linking the main block to the wings. On the river side he maximized the house's position and views by keeping the sloping ground down to the river as open park. The areas of garden were laid out on the other side of the house, beyond a circle of lawn enclosed by the central block and wings; here a large central bell-shaped lawn was bounded on each side by a drive, and outside these were symmetrical walled rectangles, their ends away from the house curving to a point. One of these walled areas contained the vegetable garden, the other the flower garden.

Along the curving drives, which divided from a central entrance gate, Washington carried out his most successful and innovative planting. Groves of ornamental and evergreen trees – carefully chosen native species and many transplanted from the wild – shrouded the approach to the house and concealed what lay ahead. Outside the trees were areas of shrubbery carefully filled with plants that Washington had collected, some in the wild, others from the leading plantsmen of the day such as John Bartram's (*q.v.* p. 61) son William, in Philadelphia. Bartram's nursery would also have supplied plants for the flower garden which appears to have been largely the domain of

Washington's wife Martha. Here and in the vegetable garden Washington added some of the most delightful features of the Mount Vernon garden: pairs of 'pepperpot' hexagonal gazebos with elegant hipped roofs, one in the corner closest to the house, the other in the far point of each area. However attractive the little buildings might be, it was typical of Washington's practical approach to gardening – so influential to future generations of Americans – that each had its own utilitarian purpose. The gazebo at the far end of the flower garden was a seed store, while the matching building in the vegetable garden was a tool shed.

Like Monticello (q.v. p. 77), Mount Vernon set a standard of garden design and plantsmanship which, given the status of their owners, was to have enormous impact on American gardens. While acknowledging the qualities of European gardens and reflecting some important influences, the emphasis on horticulture and natural landscape, with a minimum of architectural or other ornamental embellishment, confirmed a tradition that stretched back in very basic form to the early colonists and which became deeply entrenched in the development of American gardens.

RICHARD WOODS (1716-93)

BROCKET HALL, *Hertfordshire;* BUCKLAND HOUSE, *Oxfordshire;*
CANNON HALL, *Yorkshire;* WARDOUR CASTLE, *Wiltshire;*
WORMSLEY PARK, *Buckinghamshire*

RICHARD WOODS is the best example of the small group of landscape designers who were working at the same time as 'Capability' Brown (q.v. p. 62) and closely influenced by him, who never managed to escape fully from his considerable shadow. In Woods's case the comparison is particularly apt; he was born in the same year as Brown, and while the two men are known to have both worked at different times at Hartwell House, Oxfordshire, Belhus

Park and Thorndon Park, both in Essex, and Wardour Castle in Wiltshire – the only one of the four where Woods's work survives – it is understood that they never collaborated. The link between them is further cemented by their respectively partnerships with the architect James Paine, for five of whose houses Woods designed the surrounding landscape. In *Theory and Practice of Landscape Gardening* Humphry Repton wrote dismissively that, 'Brown followed Nature; his illiterate followers copied him.'[1] While this is a harshly exaggerated opinion of Woods's talent as a landscape designer, it confirmed the acceptance of Brown's supremacy which ensured that, in Woods's case, his commissions rarely broke out of geographical and social constraints as Hugh Prince has described. 'Employed by City merchants and prosperous Essex squires, Woods enjoyed local patronage but did not gain admission to the charmed circle of Whig aristocrats and *cognoscenti*.[2]

Woods was based in Essex for most of his career and the majority of his work was in Essex or the neighbouring counties. Cannon Hall in south Yorkshire, where he worked in 1761 for John Spencer, was one of the few exceptions; it was also one of his largest commissions – Spencer spent some £30,000 on Woods's improvements to the landscape. Woods took advantage of the natural terrain to create a series of three lakes linked by cascades along the bottom of the valley, to which the ground sloped gently from the house. He planted woodland beyond the far side of the lake where the ground rises up to Bentcliffe Hill but kept open the view to Cawthorne church. The south side of the garden was enclosed with a long ha-ha beyond which the picturesque feature of a 'ruined' church was erected alongside a small pool.

Brocket Park, where Woods was commissioned by Lord Melbourne, was his most successful design, notable for the fine serpentine lake that he created by damming and expanding the River Lea. It was spanned by a characteristic three-arched bridge by James Paine. Here, in particular, Woods proved himself a more than competent all-round designer and surveyor, with his blend of tree-

The garden at Mount Vernon has been largely replanted but is still as laid out by George Washington and retains his delightful gazebos.

planting, water and open spaces of parkland, and occasional architectural embellishment – but his work was never quite on the scale that Brown, with his far larger practice and wealthier clients, was able to achieve.

THOMAS WRIGHT (1711-86)

BADMINTON HOUSE, *Avon;* SHUGBOROUGH HALL, *Staffordshire;* STOKE PARK, *Avon*

THOMAS WRIGHT was a shadowy, eccentric figure, a mathematician and astronomer who charted the course of the Milky Way and an amateur architect and garden designer who was adopted by a number of aristocratic patrons to design their gardens and an extraordinary variety of architectural features for them. Born in County Durham, he eventually returned to live there.

Most of Wright's commissions were carried out during the 1750s and 1760s. He designed flower gardens as well as architectural features – Chinese, classical and gothic – but his work appears to have been the result of his own or his patrons' personal preference or whim rather than that of any prevailing style or fashion of the time. There was true originality and quality in his work, much of it recorded in charming drawings and sketches which he himself published and which were republished in 1979 in E. Harris's book, *Thomas Wright, Arbours and Grottoes.*

The eccentric Wright would appear to have forged an ideal partnership with Norborne Berkeley, created Lord Botetourt, once described as, 'a semi-fraudulent and bankrupt peer of winning manner',[1] for whom Wright's work at Stoke Park was the longest-lasting substantial commission of his career, and the most substantial other than his series of garden buildings for Sir Charles Sedley at Nuthall in Nottinghamshire, none of which survive. As opposed to most of the rest of his work Stoke Park involved a large amount of landscape design as well as the addition of

architectural embellishments – and, initially, alterations to the house itself, in particular adding tall bays which gave expansive views out over the parkland and woods which sloped away from the main sides. Wright replanned the park and woods to maximize the views both from the house and up to it, and to provide a series of circuitous walks for visitors. Wright obviously paid considerable attention to the decoration of the various woods with unusual plants, as well as the addition of architectural features which included an Ionic rotunda and a copy of the Monument to the Horatii at Albano. A number of his additions recorded his client's connection with the dukes of Beaufort, for his sister married the 4th duke and, following Lord Botetourt's death in 1770, she inherited Stoke. In one wood a tomb was built to the memory of the 4th duke who died in 1756, while an obelisk on a hilltop was a similar memorial to his daughter – Botetourt's niece – Elizabeth Somerset. Most of Wright's architectural additions at Stoke disappeared during the 20th century when the house was a hospital, but the quantity of surviving evidence and planting has encouraged an ambitious restoration project.

It was clearly the family ties which led Wright to work at Badminton and the link is illustrated by the rustic root houses or hermitages which he built at both places. The one at Stoke was called Bladud's Cell and hidden away in dense woodland, while at Badminton the Hermit's Cell or Root House was the best known of a highly idiosyncratic series of plans for naturalistic buildings, some thatched, others castellated and for wooded groves and decorative flower gardens – which Wright prepared for the 4th Duke and subsequently for his son. Most of the plans were never carried out but the Hermit's Cell survives as the most obviously bucolic example of this type of building from the period to be found anywhere in England.

Shugborough, where Wright worked for Thomas Anson, MP for Lichfield, has a remarkable collection of buildings and architectural ornaments, many of them celebrating the epic voyage round the world by Anson's brother George (who was made an admiral and a peer in recognition when he returned in 1744). Booty from a ship captured by Anson financed the decoration of the park, and the work was a collaboration between the two brothers, Wright and, later, the architect James 'Athenian' Stuart.

Wright's main contributions, in addition to general advice, were to design the domed pavilions that flank the central block of the house and some of the more unusual architectural features such as the ruins on one bank of the River Sow and the Shepherd's Monument, the design for which appeared in his book. The monument is a cave-like recess with a classical façade. Inside, a carved relief by Peter Scheemakers after a painting by Nicholas Poussin depicts shepherds in a classical landscape; and some inscrutable carved letters mysteriously suggest the signifi-

cance of the monument to one or other Anson brother.

Wright's work at Shugborough – and all his garden commissions – appear to have ended in 1762, the year of Admiral Lord Anson's death, and thereafter Thomas Anson commissioned James Stuart (whom he would have met through their mutual membership of the Dilettanti Society) to make further architectural additions of an Athenian nature to the park: a Triumphal Arch on a hilltop, a copy of the Arch of Hadrian in Athens; a Doric Temple; and the Lanthorn of Demosthenes, a copy of the Monument of Lysicrates. Wright was content to retire to his native Durham where he designed a modest house for himself and filled the small garden with unusual embellishments, and devoted himself to mathematics and astrology.

THE HIGH VICTORIAN ERA
1820-1880

REPTON'S INFLUENCE was immediate and far-reaching, not only in England but also in the United States where his most important admirer was Andrew Jackson Downing (*q.v.* p. 108). Downing became the first major American garden designer and writer. Once English gardens had abandoned the emphasis on spacious landscape and a reverence for ancient classicism they became a much more appealing source of inspiration to the New World. Repton had written on many occasions that houses should be either classical or gothic and should be built in whichever style was most suitable for the surroundings; Downing in turn maintained that houses should either be 'in the classical mode' or picturesque – gothic, or rustic cottages. Their gardens were to reflect the style: either smooth lawns, rounded deciduous trees and immaculate flower gardens, or dark conifers and a stream cascading through a woodland glade. The application of Downing's ideas was never as simplistic as these principles would imply; none the less, it was a fundamental step forward in the laying down of basic ground rules. Downing was killed before he had time to establish a widespread practice as a garden designer – which he would undoubtedly have done – but his influence lay in popularizing garden-making

Paxton's conservatory wall at Chatsworth survives
as evidence of the ingenuity of the various
glasshouses he designed for the garden.

95

around a set of principles and ideas outlined in his books, notably, *The Theory and Practice of Landscape Gardening,* published in 1841.

In England the figure who did most to popularize gardening, mainly through his writing, was an indefatigable Scot, John Claudius Loudon. He became a confirmed admirer of Repton while at the same time focusing his attention on more modest middle-class – and in many cases urban – audiences that had not existed in Repton's Regency England. His writing also influenced Downing, who urged his fellow Americans to read both Loudon and Loudon's wife Jane, a champion of women gardeners. Both men maintained that their principles of garden design and planting could be applied to any garden regardless of size by scaling down the features to fit. Loudon graded gardens in categories of one to four – of which the smallest were the suburban villas for whose owners he wrote extensively – while Downing argued that his principles could be applied to the smallest cottage garden. Both stressed the importance of maximizing the potential of individual trees or shrubs; part of Loudon's gardenesque theory was that everything in a garden should be displayed to its own individual best advantage.

Loudon's writing may have instructed the gardeners of England's burgeoning Victorian middle classes, but in other areas gardening was harnessed to increasingly fast-moving Victorian productivity. Just as aesthetics and philosophy had influenced garden design in the early 18th century and had played their part in the appearance of the 18th-century landscape, so a century later the technical ingenuity that accompanied industrial and commercial growth was applied to gardens and influenced their design. Coal furnaces heated glasshouses and the brick walls of kitchen gardens while steam engines were harnessed to throw fountain jets far into the air. Although, as in architecture and many other departments of the arts, garden style became essentially retrospective and derivative, progress lay in the application of newly-acquired techniques and materials. The removal of the glass tax in 1845 opened the way for the conservatories, hothouses and glasshouses that became such features of Victorian gardens; and the intricacies of their construction appealed hugely to the Victorian mind.

The other impetus for the conservatory was the ever increasing influx of plants from abroad. There had been a steady trade in plant collecting throughout the 18th century – especially from the United States, where the climate ensured that many varieties were well suited to English conditions. During the early decades of the 19th century, encouraged by the growing demand for plants, the trade mushroomed. Technically the single greatest boost to the trade was the Wardian Case, a specially designed glass box for transporting live plants, invented by Dr Nathaniel Ward and first used during the late 1830s, when it rapidly established an impressive success rate. Kew, the Royal Horticultural Society, other botanical groups and private individuals all became actively involved in dispatching collectors overseas, either to search for tender exotics from tropical regions that would be displayed under glass, or to build up collections of plants from temperate areas, that would grow happily in Britain. Often visiting virtually unknown and hostile territories, plant collectors were one of the few genuinely productive and non-aggressive aspects of 19th-century imperialism. The conifers that David Douglas introduced from the western United States and the rhododendrons introduced from the Himalayas alone serve to illustrate the extent to which 19th-century plant introductions revolutionized British gardens.

The emphasis in large Victorian gardens was on display and the revival of formal Italianate gardens such as those designed by Charles Barry, and the technical improvements in raising plants, ensured by the middle of the century that these displays would be at times overpowering. Formal terraced parterres, decorated with a rich array of statuary, urns, balustrading and fountains, provided the setting for intricate patterns of annual flowers produced by bedding systems perfected by leading head gardeners. John Fleming, the head gardener at Cliveden – designed by Barry for Duke of Sutherland – developed a biannual bedding system which enabled the Cliveden parterre to have an early and late summer display each year; it was a system that was soon adapted at grand gardens all over the country. Even more intricate were the scrollwork parterres designed by William Nesfield, in a style that harked back to early formal English knot gardens; often containing only box hedging and coloured gravels the effect was nevertheless far more brilliant than the Tudors or Stuarts would have known.

Many of these larger gardens had existing 18th-century parks which the Victorians were happy to retain as suitably spacious surroundings, while concentrating their efforts on the areas of formal decorative gardens that surrounded the house. Where tree planting was carried out, the most popular varieties were newly introduced species of conifers – mainly from America – which were planted in pinetums and arboretums, or occasionally in impressive but somewhat bizarre avenues such as the monkey-puzzle avenue planted at Bicton in Devon in 1842. The oppressive, at times gloomy atmosphere of pinetums matched the Victorians' enjoyment of dark gothic architecture and decoration. However, where a wider range of trees was planted with a view to their individual display – as in Robert Holford's outstanding arboretum at Westonbirt – the effect was something that native deciduous varieties could not rival.

Overleaf: At Westonbirt Robert Holford planted his collection of trees around a series of majestic open glades. His son George added the now renowned acers.

Gardening journalism became a major means of popularizing Victorian gardening ideas, and also provided a forum for the growing ranks of professional and amateur gardeners. Loudon's pioneering *Gardener's Magazine,* founded in 1826, was followed by the even more popular *Gardener's Chronicle,* founded in 1841 by Joseph Paxton. Paxton himself was the gardening figure who more than any other personified the age: hugely productive in a variety of fields, his work as a gardener ranged from one of the grandest private gardens in England, Chatsworth, to the increasingly significant area of public parks and gardens in urban areas with free access for local people. His public park at Birkenhead was the first to be open constantly and with no admission charge, and similar schemes by other designers, not least Paxton's assistant at Chatsworth and Birkenhead, Edward Kemp, soon followed. Kemp was curator of Birkenhead for many years, during which time he laid out similar parks for a number of major towns in the north of England. As well as providing public spaces for those with no gardens of their own Kemp also, in 1850, published his *How to Lay Out a Small Garden*, a book whose popularity confirmed the extent to which gardening was becoming increasingly popular.

One area of Victorian garden development which particularly appealed to Americans was that of public parks and gardens. The Americans A. J. Downing and F. L. Olmsted both visited England in 1850 and enthused over Paxton's Birkenhead Park far more than over any of the impressive private gardens that they visited. After Downing's death Olmsted became the central figure in the American garden scene and he established landscape architecture as a profession. The designs of Olmsted's parks, of which Central Park in New York was the first and perhaps the best known, owed much to what he had seen in England; his skill lay in successfully adapting what he had observed to the subtly different American conditions.

Markedly different social conditions as well as the established tradition that American gardens should tend towards productivity and not pure decoration, and should at the same time harmonize with the surrounding countryside, ensured that they did not indulge in the ornamental excesses of English private gardens. By the latter decades of the century, however, the situation on both sides of the Atlantic had changed dramatically. In America new industrial and commercial wealth was producing the great houses and gardens of the country place era, while in England reaction to the ostentations of the Victorian garden gave rise to the Arts and Crafts movement and a search for a more natural style of gardening.

SIR CHARLES BARRY (1795-1860)

CLIVEDEN, *Buckinghamshire*; DUNROBIN CASTLE, *Sutherland*;
HAREWOOD HOUSE, *Yorkshire*; SHRUBLAND PARK, *Suffolk*;
TRENTHAM PARK, *Staffordshire*

CHARLES BARRY, knighted in 1852 in recognition of his work for the new Houses of Parliament, was the most influential figure in the growing fashion for Italianate terraced gardens in mid-Victorian England. Often of enormous proportions, their ornamental features offset by intricate patterns of brilliantly coloured flower bedding, these gardens have come to be seen as the epitome of high-Victorian gardening. Today, most of Barry's major garden designs survive, but almost invariably their details have been simplified or their scale reduced.

Born in London, the son of a wealthy stationer, Barry trained as a surveyor before setting off in 1817 on an architectural tour of Europe, during which his admiration for Italian architecture was aroused. On returning to England in 1820, he set up in architectural practice and rapidly became widely respected as a designer of both country houses and of the metropolitan buildings that were soon to be the landmarks of prosperous Victorian cities.

In 1833 he was commissioned to rebuild Trentham Park in Staffordshire by the 2nd Duke of Sutherland, soon after he had inherited the title. On his father's death the 2nd duke had taken on one of the most impressive and enormous inheritances ever amassed; it combined both estates in Sutherland of some 400,000 million hectares/ 1 million acres and the fortune of the last Duke of Bridgewater, the foremost aristocratic grandee of the Industrial Revolution. The Duke of Sutherland was to be Barry's most munificent patron; in addition to the work at Trentham, he commissioned work at Dunrobin Castle – the ancient Sutherland seat on the north-east coast of Scotland – and at Cliveden in Buckinghamshire.

At Trentham Barry produced what was nothing short of a palace (demolished in 1910 after the family moved out in 1905, because the proximity of the polluted River Trent made it uninhabitable). The main front looked out towards 'Capability' Brown's (*q.v.* p. 62) expansive park, with a lake three-quarters of a mile long, and along this façade of the house Barry laid out the most ambitious of all his gardens. On a flat site he created a series of terraces, richly decorated with balustrading, statues, urns, pavilions, arcades and fountains, and containing elaborate parterres. William Nesfield (*q.v.* p. 116) may have collaborated in the design of the parterres, but the thousands of plants grown for the biannual displays were raised in glasshouses by Trentham's head gardener (it was head gardeners of this kind who were to rise to heights of power and prestige in the 19th century). Although the whole effect of house and terraced garden was unashamedly ornate, the great views out and the scale of Brown's lake and park in front kept it all in proportion – a memorable scene of Victorian grandeur. The terraces are still recognizable, but the garden has lost all its ornaments and is today a forlorn shadow of its former self.

While his work was continuing at Trentham, in 1835, Barry was commissioned by the duke to begin the transformation of Dunrobin into what became the most impressive house or castle in the Highlands. Barry planned the garden to complement the fantastic, pinnacled castle which he modelled perched on its steep cliff and looking out to the North Sea. A monumental stone terrace linked the castle and its almost sheer retaining walls with the slope below and double flights of stone steps were built descending towards the large open area where Barry laid out a series of three intricate parterres, the largest – central – one of which was circular. The scale of the garden as laid out by Barry is illustrated by the facts that one of the main borders, along the seaward wall of the parterres needed 15,000 annual plants each year and that the clipped box hedging extended to a total of two miles.

Back in England, in 1843, Barry was commissioned to provide the foreground to another of Brown's most impressive landscapes, at Harewood House in Yorkshire, a project which was if anything more successful that the similar one at Trentham. As well as making alterations to the house he laid out an architectural terrace garden in front of the south front, its parterre containing a pattern of box-hedged beds around three fountain pools, and commanding spectacular views across Brown's descending parkland to the lake at the bottom.

Shrubland Park in Suffolk, generally regarded as Barry's most successful garden design, was one of the last major commissions of his career. After altering the house he turned his attention to the steeply sloping ground in front, which dropped for some 23m/70ft – ideal terrain for his uninhibited Italianate essay. From the first terrace garden along the front of the house a central pedimented loggia led to a richly ornamented stone stairway of one hundred and thirty-seven steps descending to divide into two flights at right-angles and leading to a semi-circular balustraded parterre. From a larger loggia on the far side of the parterre further steps descended to the park beyond. When William Robinson (*q.v.* p. 157) was called in to simplify some of the planting he wrote that Shrubland was 'the great bedding-out garden, the "centre" of the system in England'.[1] Miles Hadfield, not an admirer of Barry's work, described Shrubland as, 'great yet depressingly mechanical architectural grandeur'.[2] None the less, even if it was impressive rather than original, and lacked the vigorous sense of movement and decorum of its Italian models, Shrubland was a true representative of gardens of the high-Victorian era, the culmination of a period style that was soon to suffer a reaction and to be denigrated for its architectural and horticultural opulence.

JAMES BATEMAN (1811-97)

BIDDULPH GRANGE, *Staffordshire*

BIDDULPH GRANGE, created by its owner James Bateman, encapsulates the mood of mid-Victorian England better than any other surviving garden. Built on the proceeds of coal-mining, its position in the industrial heartland of the 19th century, its complexity and strength of atmosphere, heterogeneous inspiration and quality of construction were all typical of the period. Equally important, Biddulph demonstrates the manner in which gardening was diversifying in style and the part that horticulture, especially newly-imported and exotic plants, was increasingly playing. From a youthful interest in orchids – about which he became an acknowledged authority, building up important collections of the plants – he developed a taste that was catholic and yet discerning, with especial interest in the exotics that, by the mid-century were beginning to flood into England; from China, North and South America, Africa and many other parts of the world. Bateman sponsored plant-collecting trips and plants were named after him, such as *Rhododendron batemani* collected by Dr Joseph Hooker and which first flowered at Biddulph in 1863. The architectural and horticultural eclecticism at Biddulph make it impressive, exciting and overpowering – rather than a place of beauty in the 18th-century sense of the word – and it illustrates in garden terms Geoffrey Jellicoe's argument that 'the practical and the romantic were the twin poles of nineteenth-century England.'[3]

Bateman was born in Lancashire, the son of a wealthy industrialist who moved to Knypersley Hall in Staffordshire when James was a child. He developed his interest in orchids while at Oxford and, in 1838 seemingly confirmed that gardening would be of primary importance in his life when he married Maria Egerton-Warburton. She was a knowledgeable and enthusiastic gardener; her brother created the mid-Victorian garden of Arley Hall in Cheshire and other Egerton-Warburton relations created the gardens of Tatton Park, also in Cheshire and Oulton Park in Yorkshire. A few years later Bateman was able to put his new horticultural interests in practise when he purchased a former vicarage and surrounding land on Biddulph Moor, some two miles from his parents' home at Knypersley. In 1846, having begun to rebuild the house in fashionable Italianate style and renamed it Biddulph Grange, Bateman began transforming the surroundings into a

Shrubland Park was Charles Barry's most theatrical Italianate garden.

garden. A year later, he first met Edward Cooke, the marine artist who also had a keen interest in plants, was a close friend of Dr Nathaniel Ward who had designed Wardian cases and conservatories for ferns and orchids. Cooke's involvement in the development of the garden at Biddulph – especially architecturally – was of decisive importance as Peter Hayden confirms, 'Edward Cooke probably designed all the architectural features in the garden at Biddulph. He frequently made models of what he designed and he also played an active part in building rock-work, planting trees and shrubs, and gathering ferns and other native plants in the wild for the garden.'[2]

The house stood in an elevated position and the garden was laid out on the sloping ground in front and beyond, and away to one side where the ground rose gently to the boundary of the property. In partnership with Maria and with advice from Cooke Bateman conceived the garden as a series of individual areas, all markedly different in character and appearance, concealed from one another to heighten the element of surprise and impact but linked by an intricate series of rock tunnels and pathways. The different geographical inspirations for some parts of the garden, such as Egypt and China, combined with the Batemans' known religious devotion, led Dr Brent Elliott to suggest that evangelical fervour was one of the influences on the garden's development: 'As a preliminary to the second coming, the world was once again bringing all its past history into light; and the garden at Biddulph Grange, by evoking vanished and alien civilizations, served as an affirmation that the millenium was coming.'[3]

As Bateman's house and garden developed simultaneously he and Maria were able to ensure that the two fused together to a remarkable degree. The unity was first suggested by the fernery through which one passed to reach the front door and within the house itself a series of different horticultural rooms were incorporated: huge windows joined the billiard-room and an adjacent fern house; the dining-room looked into a colonnaded court inspired by the peristyles of ancient Greek and Roman houses; there were also an orangery, a conservatory-corridor, and a

camellia-house between the drawing-room and the library. The integration was continued below the house's south-facing terrace where a series of individual formal gardens, divided by yew hedges and incorporating parterres and flights of steps, and including Maria Bateman's own garden, descended to the rhododendron ground around the lake where more informal treatment began. One of the garden's most famous features was the Dahlia Walk, its blocks of bold colour divided by buttresses of yew, which ascended parallel to the house in broad steps, from the fountain on an axis with the lake and araucaria parterre at the western end to the garden house whose flat balustraded roof formed part of a broad terrace.

Immediately to the west of the axis of the fountain and araucaria terrace the Italian Garden descended in formal, stepped levels to one side of the lake while in the other direction, beyond the dahlia walk from the house, an area called China lay concealed and enclosed by a series of stone walls and rockwork. Here a subterranean passage emerged in a Chinese temple overlooking a pond; a bridge in the same style crossed the pond; a Joss House stood perched on a promontory; to one side a gilded ox looked out from beneath a decorative canopy over a dragon parterre of coloured gravel; and a giant stone frog stared out over the water. All the architectural and ornamental features were vividly painted and stood out brilliantly against the surrounding evergreens and rocks. The plants originated from China or Japan and included many of the most important or exciting recent introductions and this element of horticultural novelty continued throughout the Biddulph garden, for instance in the pinetum reached via a tunnel from the rhododendron ground and which curved round to the east forming an effective boundary to the garden, and in the arboretum established along the long eastward axis stretching away from the main garden to an avenue of Wellingtonias – not surprisingly planted with some of the first specimens of the tree to be grown in Britain – where now only interplanted Deodar cedars remain.

Beyond the eastern terrace into which the roof of the

summer house was incorporated lay Egypt, a darkly mon-umental scene of stone sphinxes, yew clipped into obelisks and a pyramid, at the far end of which sat the Ape of Thoth, with coloured glass in the roof producing an eerie red glow. Back-to-back with the pyramid and connected to it was a Cheshire cottage no doubt inspired by Maria's family origins and creating one of Biddulph's most bizarre changes of mood. From its door the pinetum swept away enclosing the more placid quoit ground and bowling green.

As remarkable as the individuality of the component areas which were primarily responsible for Biddulph's strange eclecticism, and the variety of planting including a host of new introductions, was the extraordinary skill of the garden's technical construction. Cooke's influence was particularly strong in the creation of naturalistic rockwork – great walls, turrets, tunnels and covered archways were built with blocks of Millstone Grit from a local quarry, the stones individually chosen and positioned free of mortar. In the terraces along the main south front and to the east hedges were clipped to different widths to disguise dis-crepancies in space shapes – for instance in front of Egypt – and small 'ledge' hedges were planted in front of the main ones to disguise irregularities of slope.

The restlessness that is one of Biddulph's characteris-tics appears to have derived from Bateman himself; having effectively completed the garden by the mid-1850s, he made significant alterations throughout the 1860s, espe-cially to the terraces in front of the house, before finally selling the property in 1871. The house was destroyed by fire in 1896 and rebuilt in an Edwardian neo-classical style far less attractive than the Victorian original, and became a hospital in the 1920s. In 1988, by which time all architec-tural links between house and garden had been severed, the badly decayed garden was taken on by the National Trust, which has carried out its most ambitious and expensive restoration programme to date (prior to the work at Stowe). The work has included excavating and rebuilding the dahlia walk, which had been completely submerged by earth-levelling for hospital wards, restoring

and repainting the buildings and other features in China, and rebuilding collapsed rockwork. In the process the spirit of this extraordinary, complex, and historically important garden and its creator is being revived.

DAVID DOUGLAS (1799-1834)

ALTHOUGH DAVID DOUGLAS was not specifically respons-ible for any single garden, as one of the earliest and most intrepid of plant-collectors at the beginning of the golden period of collecting, he had an enormous impact upon British gardens by virtue of the species he discovered and introduced from America, as well as upon American's appreciation of their natural resources. In the short period of a decade Douglas introduced from America a large number of the most noble conifers that have subse-quently been grown in Britain and in the process under-went a series of perilous journeys to virtually unknown parts of the western United States. In 1824, having previously worked for four years at the Botanic Garden in Glasgow under W. J. Hooker (later Sir William and director of Kew), the twenty-three-year-old Douglas left Liverpool for the western seaboard of America as the Royal Horticultural Society's first officially appointed plant-collector.

His expedition lasted for three years in British Colum-bia and Oregon. He was the first European to reach the Blue Mountains of Oregon and much of his surveying work was extensively used by the United States govern-ment in charting previously unknown territories. Fore-most of the trees – and one of the most magnificent of any species – that the trip produced was the one that bears his name, *Pseudotsuga menziesii*, the Douglas Fir, but there were many others as he remarked with characteristic humour in a letter to Hooker, 'you will begin to think that I manufacture Pines at my pleasure'.[1] Whether threatened

Overleaf: At Biddulph Grange the Cheshire Cottage looks out to the pinetum; through the cottage is the garden known as Egypt.

by nature, as on one occasion when his canoe was swept away and with it his notes, instruments and hundreds of carefully collected specimens, or other humans such as unfriendly Red Indians, the invariably dishevelled Douglas remained relentlessly combative and indefatigable, travelling hundreds of miles on foot, in canoes or, occasionally, on horseback.

Returning to England in 1827 Douglas set out once again for the western United States in October 1929. He remained away for nearly five years collecting in California and in Hawaii. He saw the giant redwoods that were not introduced for another fifteen years and successfully collected and dispatched a whole range of plants including the conifers for which he is best known. His devotion to his work was demonstrated by one discovery in Hawaii shortly before he died, a fern, of which he wrote that it was, 'identical with *Asplenium verida* of my own native country, a circumstance which gave me inexpressible pleasure and recalled to my mind many of the happiest scenes of my life'.[2] It was in Hawaii on his way home to England in July 1834 that he met his death. Walking alone with his terrier Billy, he fell into a disguised pit made to catch wild cattle by the local natives and was gored to death by an enraged bullock that had fallen in previously.

Douglas was only thirty-four when he died, but as Miles Hadfield confirms, his work was of unique importance. 'The trees, shrubs and plants collected and first introduced by David Douglas in his short life have probably had a greater effect on the British landscape and its gardens than those collected by any other single individual'.[3] The garden plants that he introduced included the evergreen *Garrya elliptica*, the 'Oregon Grape' *Mahonia aquifolium*, the 'Flowering Currant' *Ribes sanguineum* and *Lupus polyphyllus*, the parent of most garden varieties in cultivation. Among his trees are some of the most magnificent and prized species and, in forestry terms, the most valuable: the 'Giant Fir' *Abies grandis*, the 'Noble Fir' *Abies procera*, the 'Sitka Spruce' *Picea sitchensis*, the 'Monterey Pine *Pinus radiata* and the 'Western Red Cedar' *Thuja plicata* – and, of course, his own 'Douglas Fir'.

ANDREW JACKSON DOWNING (1815-52)

NEWBURGH, *New York State, USA;* WHITE HOUSE, CAPITOL AND SMITHSONIAN INSTITUTE, *Washington, USA*

IN JULY 1852 ANDREW JACKSON DOWNING drowned in a steamship accident on the Hudson River aged only thirty-six. In 1841 he had published *Landscape Gardening: A Treatise on the Theory and Practice of Landscape Gardening,* the first definitive American book on the subject and as such a major landmark; in the remaining eleven years of his life he established himself as the foremost authority on gardens and landscape in the country. Born the son of a nurseryman, he was introduced to horticulture at an early age. He was the family's youngest child by many years, and a natural interest in learning was encouraged by the fact that he suffered from ill-health, with the result that he emerged well-educated and unusually widely read. A wide general knowledge and an absorbing interest in gardening were the basis of his contribution to the development of American gardens. By a process of distillation he used his assimilated information about European – primarily English – gardening to produce something specifically applicable, both geographically and culturally, to America.

Downing's book revealed how well acquainted he was with the leading English writing on the broad subject of landscape and gardens, notably Edmund Burke's *A Philosophical Enquiry into the Origin of our Ideas of the Sublime and Beautiful* (1757), *Three Essays on the Picturesque* (1810) by Sir Uvedale Price, and the work of Humphry Repton (*q.v.* p. 81) and J. C. Loudon (*q.v.* p. 112). He probably admired Repton most, although Loudon, being a contemporary, was the most immediate influence as Downing made clear: 'Mr Loudon's writings and labors in tasteful gardening are too well known to render it necessary that we should do more than allude to them here. Much of what is known of the art in this country undoubtedly is more or less directly to be referred to the influence of his published works. Although he is, as it seems to us, somewhat deficient as an artist in imagination, no previous author ever deduced, so clearly, sound artistic principles in Landscape Gardening and Rural Architecture; and fitness, good sense and beauty are combined with much unity of feeling in all his works.'[1]

Downing maintained that American gardens should aspire to be either beautiful or picturesque; each would require a different style of landscape and planting – as well as of architecture – and yet each would be equally adaptable to American conditions and to large or small-scale treatment. In a way that reflected the democratic ambitions of 19th-century Americans, and Downing was at pains to stress the importance of small gardens and how they could be created to best advantage; in 1842 he published his second book, *Cottage Residences*. An awareness of public as well as of private requirements also led him to promote the need for public parks. Downing's death deprived him of the chance to carry out any of this work himself but his initiative was forged into a major element of the American landscape tradition by his partner Calvert Vaux and by Frederick Law Olmsted (*q.v.* p. 120).

In 1845 Downing became editor of the publication *The Horticulturalist*, as well as publishing, with his brother Charles, *The Fruits and Fruit Trees of America*, which rapidly became the country's standard work on the subject. Two years earlier he had edited and introduced *Gardening for Ladies* by Loudon's wife, Jane. Just as he stressed the importance of small gardens and public gardens, so Downing believed that American women should play an active and integral role in gardening, and outlined his hopes in his introduction to the book: 'Mrs Loudon's works are intended especially for the benefit of lady gardeners – a class of amateurs which, in England, numbers many and zealous devotees, even among the highest ranks. It is to be hoped, that the dissemination in this country of works like the present volume, may increase, among our own fair countrywomen, the taste for these delightful occupations in the open air, which are so conducive to their own health and to the beauty and interest of our homes.'[2]

The scope of Downing's influence can be gauged immediately from the verdict of one contemporary writing about *The Horticulturalist*: 'Not a nook or corner of the West can be found that does not exhibit evidence that it has been affected by its influence. Every new tenement, every garden, lawn and group of ornamental and fruit trees shows about it the "Downing touch".'[3] Downing himself put his ideas into practice at his own home and garden, Newburgh, overlooking the Hudson River in countryside that was familiar to him all his life. He designed and built the house himself and the garden displayed the kind of variety that he advocated in his writing: a main lawn allowing for uninterrupted views out to the river and yet enlivened with beds of brightly coloured flowers; a formal flower garden; and placed in irregular groups or individually, a fine selection of ornamental and flowering trees, including many rare varieties.

Downing had absorbed much about English gardens through his reading, but in 1850 he left America for the first time and travelled extensively through England. The trip was a huge success and Downing was able to enjoy and evaluate the places and sights he had read about industriously for so many years. The size and openness of London's parks commanded his great admiration, and he determined to emulate them on his return to America – as he made clear in one of his 'letters' sent back for publication in *The Horticulturalist*: 'London parks are actually like districts of open country – meadows and fields . . . lakes and streams, gardens and shrubberies, with as much variety as if you were in the heart of Cambridgeshire and as much seclusion in some parts at certain hours as if you were on a farm in the interior of Pennsylvania.'[4]

Downing returned home with an architect assistant, Calvert Vaux, who would help him with the increasing quantity of commissions, mostly for houses and gardens for the prosperous estates that lined the Hudson river. The most 'prestigious of these commissions was the official request to landscape the grounds of the White House, the Capitol and the Smithsonian Institution in Washington, all of which he carried out with Vaux's assistance.

Downing was killed at a time when he was poised to

confirm his reputation as America's first great landscape designer in practice as well as print. Nonetheless his reputation was such by 1852 as to guarantee the spread of his ideas throughout America and through all levels of society. America now had a firm base for her own tradition of gardening, one that was to expand rapidly, and demonstrate that in some areas the country had already taken the lead in contemporary practice.

WILLIAM SAWREY GILPIN (1762-1843)

BALCASKIE, *Fife;* BICTON PARK, *Devon;* CLUMBER PARK, *Nottinghamshire;* NUNEHAM PARK, *Oxfordshire;* SCOTNEY CASTLE, *Kent;* SUDBURY HALL, *Derbyshire*

WILLIAM SAWREY GILPIN was the last major protagonist of the picturesque movement before it became absorbed by the Victorian garden; even Gilpin's work demonstrated an acceptance that picturesque features were often most successfully adapted to a garden landscape in conjunction with formal features. Gilpin's uncle, the clergyman William Gilpin, was a prominent figure in the picturesque movement of the 18th century; his *Essay on Prints,* published in 1768, predated Sir Uvedale Price and Richard Payne Knight by some twenty-five years and clearly defined certain natural and architectural features that showed picturesque qualities. Gilpin's father, Sawrey Gilpin, was a talented painter of animals, mainly horses; his son became an accomplished watercolourist before turning to landscape gardening.

By 1832, when he published his *Practical Hints for Landscape Gardeners,* illustrated with his own drawings, Gilpin had established a successful practice. At Nuneham Park, Lord Harcourt's seat in Oxfordshire, he was responsible for altering the immediate surroundings to the house, and planted judiciously positioned groups of conifers to vary the views out to 'Capability' Brown's superb parkland.

As well as rebuilding the old balustraded terrace along the house he redesigned the garden that had originally been made by the poet William Mason. Gilpin's work at Clumber Park in Nottinghamshire, for the Duke of Newcastle, was more extensive and included one of the most stately avenues in England: double rows of limes stretching for nearly three miles from one lodge entrance. Observers might question the use of such a clearly formal landscape feature by a disciple of the picturesque, but Gilpin explained his reasons in *Practical Hints*: 'Where the approach is of necessity to be carried through a length of uninteresting space, as at Clumber from Tuxford (a distance of three miles from the outer lodge to the park gate), passing between farms in various occupation, the best way of getting over such country is by an avenue, as it is there done; which not only avoids a multiplicity of gates but is in character with the magnitude of the domain through which it leads.'

At Clumber, too, he designed the series of ornamental terraces which certainly provided a foreground for the picturesque views across Clumber lake to a temple nestling in woods on the far side, but on the whole looked forward to the Italianate gardens of the Victorian period. Equally formal was the Lincoln terrace that he laid out along the lakeside to the east of the house, with flower beds and statues.

Clumber has suffered since Gilpin's day and in 1938 the house was demolished, but after a public appeal it became a National Trust property in 1946 and in recent years much restoration has been carried out, including replanting missing sections of the great avenue, restoring the Lincoln terrace (without the beds and statues), and the foundations of the terraces in front of the house.

If Gilpin's formality at Clumber looked forward to the Victorian garden, at Edward Hussey's Scotney Castle in Kent he produced one of the most acclaimed landscapes of the picturesque movement. On Gilpin's advice Hussey demolished the house which had been built onto the remains of the mediaeval moated castle at the foot of a slope and commissioned Anthony Salvin to build a new

The view from the terrace in front of Salvin's new house down to the old castle at Scotney; William Sawrey Gilpin's finest picturesque essay.

house on top of the hill looking down to the castle. The picturesque nature of the view was greatly enhanced by the quarry formed below the house, from which stones for the new house were taken. Today Gilpin would be well pleased with the effect as one looks down from the top of the closely planted quarry to the castle shrouded in trees and encircled by water.

ROBERT STAYNOR HOLFORD (*1808-92*)

WESTONBIRT, *Gloucestershire*

ROBERT HOLFORD'S arboretum at Westonbirt represented a new dimension for British gardens, by which the wealth of new varieties of trees and shrubs becoming available from overseas was grafted onto the best traditions of large-scale garden design. Holford determined from the start that Westonbirt would combine botanical importance in the range of trees planted with aesthetic pleasure in their arrangement and grouping. The success of this enterprise has arguably not been exceeded since. As the arboretum matured it was added to and developed by subsequent generations of his family, in particular by his son, Sir George Holford; in 1956 it was taken on by the Forestry Commission which has carried out extensive regeneration and replanting within Holford's original grand design.

Robert Holford inherited the Westonbirt estate and the fortune which financed his work in 1839, but had begun work on the arboretum ten years earlier. Between 1863 and 1870 the house was rebuilt for him in grand neo-Elizabethan style by Lewis Vulliamy who was almost certainly also responsible for the terraces and Italian garden around the house. The ownership of the house and its surrounding gardens and arboretum is now divided, but Holford originally designed the two to be linked by a pattern of majestic rides radiating out from a point opposite the house and along which he planted the initial areas of the arboretum. After establishing windbreaks of evergreens around the perimeter of the arboretum's proposed 60ha/150 acres the first major plantings were of the North American conifers introduced by David Douglas – such as the Douglas Fir and Giant Fir, of which Westonbirt had some of the first specimens to be planted in Britain.

Holford's success at Westonbirt lay in his judgement of scale and the manner in which he planted the arboretum with sufficient open space to ensure that trees would be presented to best advantage and in unconfined harmony with their neighbours, even when grown to maturity decades later. Groups of the same variety were planted together to emphasize their effect, while elsewhere the juxtaposition of American conifers and native deciduous varieties highlighted contrasting characteristics and qualities.

For the last twenty years of his life Holford worked at Westonbirt in partnership with his son George, who continued the planting after his father's death. By this time many of the original trees were beginning to approach their full size. As well as expanding the overall area, George Holford was able to make his own contribution with the planting of smaller ornamental varieties, notably Japanese maples, to enrich the rides and vistas and give Westonbirt its unrivalled display of autumn foliage.

JOHN CLAUDIUS LOUDON (*1783-1843*)

DERBY ARBORETUM, *Derbyshire*

AS THE ERA OF THE 18TH-CENTURY LANDSCAPE came to an end and the steady emergence of a wealthy middle class in England brought gardening out of the exclusive domain of a landowning oligarchy, John Claudius Loudon's prolific writings became the spearhead of the popularization of gardening; they also laid the foundations of the 'modern' garden of today. Loudon's influence was not limited to Britain; his ideas and writing were widely disseminated in America by an admiring Andrew Jackson Downing (*q.v.* p. 108). By the 1820s it was clear that gardening was no longer something that could be categorized simplistically but was becoming increasingly heterogeneous – both socially and horticulturally – and this was to continue throughout the 19th century.

There was a recurring note of melancholy throughout Loudon's career; he was dogged by ill-health and periods of frenetic productivity were attempts to stave off financial disaster. It is inconceivable that he would have been able to sustain his massive writing output without the assistance of his wife Jane, whom he married in 1830. They met after he wrote a review of her novel *The Mummy*, and their marriage was a close-knit partnership. Miles Hadfield writes: 'Despite failing health and the rise of rival publications, Loudon continued his writing, seeking to stave off creditors. In December 1843, whilst dictating to Jane at midnight, he stumbled, collapsed and died.'[1]

Loudon was born in Scotland, the son of a Lanarkshire farmer, and retained an interest in agriculture and the potential improvement of its techniques throughout his life. He soon showed, however, that his primary interest lay in horticulture, and leaving school at the age of fourteen began working for an Edinburgh nursery. In 1803, aged twenty, he left Scotland for London where he set himself up as a freelance writer and quickly produced the first batch of publications that established his reputation. They ranged from discussing the laying-out of public parks to the setting-up of hothouses. He was only twenty-three when elected a member of the horticulturally élite Linnean Society.

Shortly afterwards Loudon suffered the first of the serious bouts of illness that were to continue throughout the rest of his life: an attack of rheumatic fever that left him with one arm shortened and a permanent limp. In order to recuperate he took up farming, first in Middlesex and subsequently on a larger scale at Great Tew in Oxfordshire, where he was so successful that by 1812 he was able to give up the farm and invest a substantial sum of money. He left England and for the next few years travelled extensively on the continent, even venturing into Russia; he returned to find that his investments had been a disaster and that he was effectively bankrupt. Loudon responded in the only way he knew: he set out to re-establish himself by sheer hard work – a gruelling pattern that was to repeat itself for the rest of his life.

By the 1820s, thanks to rigorous self-education and extensive travel, Loudon's gardening knowledge was prodigious; his strongly held convictions and aspirations gave it also a sharp social edge and relevance, and it was this that substantially accounted for his enormous influence through the Victorian era. Ironically, the only private garden in England where Loudon's work survives is stately Ditchley Park in Oxfordshire (he redesigned the shape of the lake), but he was principally interested in gardening for a far broader social spectrum than his predecessors had ever envisaged – both in terms of private gardens and public parks. By the 1820s London and the industrial towns of the north were expanding rapidly and yet there were no provisions of open spaces for working people to be able to enjoy relatively clean air or somewhere to walk. Loudon was probably the first vociferous advocate of public parks or gardens, arguing that continental countries were far ahead of England; 'our continental neighbours have hitherto excelled us in this department of gardening; almost every town of consequence having its promenades for citizens *en cheval* and also *au pied*.'[1] The campaign by Loudon and others to make the provision of public parks an issue of social reform achieved an important success when parliament set up a Select Committee on Public Walks in 1833.

Loudon's earliest writing promoted the natural or irregular style of gardening that had formed the foundation of Sir Uvedale Price's picturesque style, but over the years Loudon shifted his ground and in the process found himself more in sympathy with the ideas and work of Humphry Repton – especially from the latter part of Repton's career. By 1840 Loudon was editing and republishing Repton's complete garden writing, a move of considerable importance in perpetuating the latter's reputation. While aiming for a far wider audience than Repton ever worked for, Loudon appeared to acknowledge the latter's influence in that his approach to gardening style was essentially broad-minded and he was one of the first to advocate different types of garden for different situations. He actually drew up socially based categories of gardens: fourth-grade gardens for small semi-detached houses in an essentially urban setting; first-grade ones for larger suburban or even rural properties that might extend to 40ha/100 acres. From earlier, accepted styles of gardening he created a new one: the gardenesque. He describes it thus: 'By the gardenesque style is to be understood the production of that kind of scenery which is best calculated to display the individual beauty of trees, shrubs and plants in a state of nature, the smoothness and greenness of lawns; and the smooth surfaces, curved directions, dryness and firmness of gravel walks; in short, it is calculated for displaying the art of the gardener.'[2]

Loudon's first major publication came in 1822 with his *Encyclopaedia of Gardening*, whose sheer size and popularity – eight editions within the next twelve years – set the tone for all his future writing. The first issue of the *Gardener's Magazine* appeared in 1826, and its significance is clearly defined by Brent Elliott: 'For the first time there was a forum in which gardeners could discuss their work, both technical and artistic; campaign for better wages and improved working conditions; and debate the political questions of the day, and the merits of cooperatives, allotments, and cottage gardens. A heavy proportion of the text was written by Loudon himself, largely in the form of tours, both in Britain and on the Continent, describing and criticizing the gardens he visited. Through these discussions, he was able to put forward in a concrete way his opinions on garden style.'[3] The *Gardener's Magazine* ran as a monthly from shortly after its appearance, and although it ceased publication with Loudon's death in 1843, was the prototype of all subsequent popular gardening journals and magazines.

1838 witnessed the productive zenith of his writing career; during that year he published both *The Suburban Gardener and Villa Companion* and the eight volumes of his monumental, scholarly *Arboretum et Fruticetum Britannicum (The Trees and Shrubs of Britain, Native and Foreign)*. The first was addressed to the swelling ranks of Loudon's middle-class readers; the second, which had taken over three years to compile, was the greatest testimony to the industry of his marital partnership with Jane and has never been surpassed for the scope and accuracy of its descriptions and illustrations.

In 1830 Loudon had been invited to design a botanical garden for Birmingham but to his intense disappointment the project foundered. Another opportunity arose, however, in 1839 when he was asked to design the Derby Arboretum. This was opened the following year on a site donated by Joseph Strutt, a local textile magnate and philanthropist. The arboretum gave Loudon the opportunity to put his ideas about landscape and public parks into practice. Around a broad central path and a peripheral path individual trees and shrubs were planted so as to appear to best advantage. Lesser paths in a regular pattern led through the rest of the park and a series of mounds were created to give the site topographical variety and a sense of enclosure. Virtually none of Loudon's original planting of over a thousand different specimens survives today but his plan of paths and series of mounds still provide the arboretum's essential framework.

Unlike his contemporary Joseph Paxton (*q.v.* p. 122), whose weekly *Gardener's Chronicle* first appeared in 1841 and replaced the *Gardener's Magazine* as the most popular gardening journal when Loudon's magazine ceased publication in 1843, Loudon conspicuously failed to achieve fortune and status during his lifetime. After his death his wife Jane continued their work, reissuing much of his writing and adding to it with books of her own which especially encouraged ladies to take up gardening. In 1872 recognition finally came from one of the leading gardening writers of the next generation, William Robinson (*q.v.* p. 157), who dedicated his weekly journal *The Garden* to Loudon's memory. Although little evidence of his work survived it was just acknowledgement of his abiding influence.

William Nesfield's intricate main parterre at Broughton Hall.

WILLIAM ANDREWS NESFIELD (1793-1881)

BLICKLING HALL, *Norfolk*; BROUGHTON HALL, *Yorkshire*; CASTLE HOWARD, *Yorkshire*; CREWE HALL, *Cheshire*; DORFOLD HALL, *Cheshire*; HOLKHAM HALL, *Norfolk*; RODE HALL, *Cheshire*; ROYAL BOTANIC GARDENS, KEW, *Surrey*; SOMERLEYTON HALL, *Suffolk*; WITLEY COURT, *Worcestershire*

WILLIAM NESFIELD became the leading practitioner of 'parterre' gardening in mid-Victorian England, but his often highly detailed and ornamental designs have suffered at the hands of future generations who have either greatly simplified them or swept them away. All the gardens listed above have been simplified; at none are Nesfield's complex patterns preserved.

The son of a Durham parson, Nesfield was educated at Winchester and Trinity College, Cambridge, but left aged only sixteen to begin a career as a soldier, which saw him fight in the Peninsular War and in Canada. Retiring on half pay he took up landscape painting and garden design. His sister married Anthony Salvin, the architect of two of the most individual Victorian houses, Harlaxton Manor in Lincolnshire and Peckforton Castle in Cheshire, and responsible for innumerable alterations to houses and castles throughout the country. He also designed Nesfield's home, one of a pair of villas in North London, where he carried out his first garden designs. This architectural connection played a significant part in Nesfield's career; as well as working with Salvin, he also worked with the other two major Elizabethan and Jacobean revival architects, William Burn and Edward Blore.

No evidence of Nesfield's early work remains, but by the mid 1840s his reputation for garden design had clearly been established, for in 1844 he was asked to supply plans to landscape a newly acquired area of some 20 ha/50 acres at the Royal Botanic Garden at Kew. Ownership of the Royal Botanic Garden had been transferred to the government in 1840 and Sir William Hooker had been appointed the first director in 1841. Nesfield's plans, radiating from the garden's most magnificent new addition, Decimus

Burton's Palm House, were for the adjacent pleasure grounds (still royal property). His work at Kew is particularly interesting because it is the only example of his landscape design as such, and because his *patte d'oie* of vistas survive virtually as he laid them out: from the main door of the Palm House one leads towards the Brentford ferry gate on the river, the central one, the Syon vista, to Syon House on the far bank, the third to Sir William Chambers's Pagoda. From the Pagoda, the Cedar vista to the river completed a triangle with the Syon vista. Nesfield also supplied designs for the arboretum whose planting was begun towards the end of the 1840s, and laid out the Broad Walk running from the Palm House lake towards Kew Palace on the north-west edge of the gardens.

The contractor who built the foundations of the Palm House was Sir Samuel Morton Peto, and it was he who gave Nesfield one of his next major commissions. Peto was a remarkable Victorian magnate who began life as a bricklayer and became a millionaire through his building work (which included the Houses of Parliament) and by constructing railways. Nesfield was asked to lay out new ornamental gardens for Sir Morton's recently acquired home, Somerleyton Hall on the Suffolk coast. John Thomas, the sculptor who produced most of the decorative details of the Houses of Parliament, was employed to transform the existing house into something more substantial and fashionable, with the eclectic result described by Olive Cook: 'As an image it astonishes by the diversity of the elements which the architect has managed to assemble under one roof.'[1]

Nesfield laid out a parterre to the west of the house and designed and planted the yew maze to the north-east, while Joseph Paxton (*q.v.* p. 122), a friend of Peto's through their mutual enthusiasm for railways, carried out other work. Peto overreached himself with the lavish winter garden that Thomas built, and by 1863, in debt to the tune of £4 million, sold Somerleyton to another self-made magnate, Sir Francis Crossley, a carpet millionaire from Halifax. (Peto's most important contribution to gardening was his son, Harold *q.v.* p. 154.) During World War II

Nesfield's parterre was grassed over, but a pattern of rose-beds – simpler than his original design – has been restored, with architectural domes of clipped golden and green yew which he planted, and the yew maze survives healthily, its paths leading to a central pagoda.

Towards the end of the 1850s Nesfield was commissioned to design major parts of the Royal Horticultural Society's gardens in Kensington, where he carried his enthusiasm for revived Tudor-style gardens to an extreme, producing patterns of coloured gravel and clipped box representing the British national plants of the rose, thistle, leek and shamrock, as well as a maze. The highly publicized gardens marked the most obvious extreme of High Victorian gardens, against which a reaction soon began and steadily gathered pace. Nesfield's work at the Kensington gardens introduced him to the sculptor John Thomas who had exhibited a model for a monumental fountain and shortly afterwards Nesfield recommended to the Earl of Carlisle, for whom he was working at Castle Howard, that Thomas should be commissioned to make a fountain group for the parterre that Nesfield was laying out; to provide, as Nesfield wrote to his patron, 'a stability of character in accordance with that splendid fellow Vanbrugh![2] Today the patterns of Nesfield's parterre have been grassed over, but Thomas's magnificent over-lifesize fountain group of Atlas supporting the globe, surrounded by four stone Tritons blowing shell trumpets, remains a suitable centrepiece of lawns and yew hedges in front of Castle Howard's south façade. At another of the great early 18th-century houses, Holkham Hall in Norfolk, Nesfield – working with William Burn – laid out a similar scroll-work parterre enclosed by elegant balustrading and decorated with urns and clipped evergreen pyramids and domes. Beyond the parterre the balustraded terrace extends outwards in a semi-circle to accommodate a round pond with a fountain decorated by a similarly monumental group of St George slaying the Dragon by Charles Smith.

At Broughton Hall in Yorkshire Nesfield created perhaps his most successful garden, which is today well preserved. The main feature at Broughton was the parterre that Nesfield designed for a new walled terrace, a pattern containing an intricate scroll and feather design in dwarf green and golden box, infilled with areas of coloured gravel and surrounded by paths of more gravel. Architectural alterations to the house included a conservatory, in front of which he made another parterre of beds; he also designed the Dolphin fountain and sited the various statues around the more distant and informal areas of the garden. During the 1870s the main parterre was grassed over but restored to Nesfield's design at the turn of the century – without the coloured gravel.

The type of *broderie* parterres that Nesfield created at Broughton was the work for which he became best known, and as his career progressed they became more intricate and decorative; in some cases he incorporated a family's initials or crests into the design. All this led to an appearance of artificiality which, if fashionable for a time, was soon to be highly criticized. And the coloured gravel that he so favoured occasionally brought problems of its own: at Stoke Edith in Hertfordshire he used a variety of blue spar that contained lead and killed all the box hedging – much to the owner, Lady Emily Foley's fury.

For the last ten years or so of his career Nesfield relied increasingly upon supporting work from his two sons – Markham, who became a landscape gardener in his own right, and William Eden who was an architect. By then the most highly regarded designer in the country, Nesfield was called in on what proved to be his last major commission – to design the most monumental garden of the period at Witley Court in Worcestershire. The house was destroyed by fire in 1938 and the garden (never in fact completed) left to decay, but enough survives in a quintessentially picturesque and mournful state to give an idea of the project's scale – a gardening equivalent of Brunel's steamship 'The Great Eastern'. For the south parterre Nesfield designed a gigantic fountain group of Perseus slaying the dragon with Andromeda, carved by James Forsyth. Weighing twenty tons it was the largest sculpture group in Europe and a coal-fired steam engine propelled the water nearly a hundred feet into the air.

Overleaf: the monumental Atlas fountain at Castle Howard, now surrounded by lawn and yew hedges but once the centrepiece of Nesfield's grand parterre.

Nesfield died aged eighty-eight at his home in Regents Park. He was one of the oldest surviving veterans of Wellington's campaign in the Peninsular and the most successful exponent of the part-Italian, part-French, part-Elizabethan/Jacobean formality that produced the High Victorian garden for the Italianate, Jacobean or gothic houses of the time. Highly skilful and well planned in their intricate detail and overall formality, and appropriate to the houses they were intended to adorn, Nesfield's stylized and to many eyes unnatural gardens were soon to be criticized.

FREDERICK LAW OLMSTED (1822-1903)

BILTMORE HOUSE, *North Carolina USA*; BOSTON PARKS, *Massachusetts USA*; CAPITOL, *Washington USA*; CENTRAL PARK, *Manhattan USA*; PROSPECT PARK, *Brooklyn USA*; STANFORD UNIVERSITY, *California USA*

EVEN DURING HIS OWN LIFETIME Frederick Law Olmsted was hailed as 'the father of landscape architecture' in the United States, and it is on this that his immense reputation rests. He designed a series of public parks, beginning with Central Park in New York, many of them in partnership with Calvert Vaux, the former assistant and partner of Andrew Jackson Downing (*q.v.* p. 108). The result was that by the end of the 19th century America had urban parks to rival any country in the world, and corrected what Olmsted had considered in the middle years of the century to be a glaring and deplorable social shortcoming. His major private commission, Biltmore House, came near the end of his long career, in 1888, and so properly belongs to the next section, with the country estates of other industrial and commercial magnates. But it too was on such a scale as to make it landscape rather than garden design.

Biltmore demonstrated Olmsted's knowledge, skill and imagination in the detailed designing and planting of a large-scale landscape – talents not perhaps so immediately obvious in his earlier urban works where, as his biographer Laura Roper rightly emphasizes, his major contribution was social: 'Under the impact of Olmsted's thought and practice, landscape design shifted its focus from decorative to social aims; land was to be arranged not only for scenic effect but also to serve the health, comfort, convenience, and good cheer of everyone who used it. In a country rapidly being urbanized, Olmsted's far-sighted moves to humanize the physical environment of cities and secure precious scenic regions for the use and enjoyment of all the people constituted a heroic undertaking.'[1]

Born in Hartford, Connecticut, Olmsted could claim descent from one of the oldest colonial families; James Olmsted and his family were among a group of Puritans who sailed from Essex to Massachusetts in 1632, only twelve years after the arrival of the *Mayflower*. A few years later he was one of the chief founders and builders of Hartford. Piety remained a strong family characteristic through ensuing generations, accounting in part for Frederick Law Olmsted's fiercely democratic views and social conscience. In circumstances curiously comparable to Andrew Jackson Downing's early life (*q.v.* p. 108), Olmsted's youth and education were interrupted by ill-health and he emerged with no set pattern for his future. At the age of twenty-one he sailed to China on a trip that lasted a year, and on his return, after a period when the most significant event for his future was a chance meeting with Downing in Newburgh, he embarked on a farming career.

The meeting with Downing aroused an interest that farming was not to satisfy and in 1850 he travelled to England for a tour of six months that had a profound effect on his future. He enjoyed the English countryside, but the visit also sharpened his appreciation of the differences between the great private parks and gardens of the aristocracy – which his American democratic sensibilities made it difficult for him to admire – and the single most stimulating discovery of his trip, Paxton's recently laid out public park in Birkenhead. On returning to the United States he recorded his impressions of England in *Walks and Talks of an American Farmer in England*, published in 1852. His close interest in the Birkenhead Park is clearly shown in the detail that he recorded: the width of the carriage-roads and borders; the mechanics of excavating the lakes and draining the ground, the surfacing of paths and the details of planting – all preserved to be consulted in the future. Overriding all his impressions was the central social issue for which his enthusiasm and admiration were unreserved: 'And all this magnificent pleasure-ground is entirely, unreservedly, and for ever the people's own. The poorest British peasant is as free to enjoy it in all its parts as the British queen.'[2]

Olmsted had given up farming shortly after returning from England, in order to devote more time to writing and publishing, and following the publication of his first book, he undertook a series of journeys through the southern states, writing articles on social and economic conditions, in particular on the problem of slavery.

In retrospect, Olmsted's life can be seen to have moved fitfully in the same direction: the initial excitement of Birkenhead Park was followed by a second meeting with Downing in 1851, where he also met Downing's new partner, Calvert Vaux. Five years later, after a financially disastrous period as a publisher, another chance meeting led Olmsted to apply for and be appointed to the position of Superintendant of New York's Central Park, at the time a source of constant local political bickering and almost completely unimproved. The major step came at the end of 1857 when the commissioners of the park decided to drop the existing controversial plan and hold a competition for the design contract. Downing, who would have been involved in the park's development, had died only months earlier, and Vaux invited Olmsted to become his partner in a joint application; in April 1858 they won the competition.

The Central Park project was to continue for many years, and involved so many problems and arguments that on more than one occasion Olmsted resigned in protest,

only to be reinstated. Nevertheless, it was the watershed in his career from which he never looked back. Olmsted and Vaux's design combined social priorities with quality of landscape and a thorough understanding of the practical requirements of a big city. In sinking the essential arterial roads out of sight, they enabled commercial traffic to cross unimpeded by slower park traffic on the smaller surface roads, and in this way emphasized the park's status as the city's focal point while retaining its atmosphere and looking to the future of greatly increased traffic volume. The overall plan for the park was clearly influenced by the natural style of gardening that both Vaux and Olmsted had studied in England, but the varied design and planting for the different areas was also carefully worked out so as to make the best of the extremely poor terrain with rocky outcrops and hollows; the result, with its reservoirs, tree-planting and wide spaces of open lawn, was – in America – as innovative a piece of town planning as landscape design.

Perhaps most surprising was Olmsted's unshakeable self-assurance and confidence in this his first essay into landscape design. It demonstrated that he had, at last, found his true vocation. He wrote that the park would 'not only be more convenient for exercise than any existing metropolitan pleasure-ground, its details more studied, more varied and substantial in character, but that there will be greater unity of composition, details being subordinate to general effects, than in any other.'[3]

Olmsted's self-confidence was proved to be well placed for, with the exception of lengthy interruptions during the years of the Civil War – to which he committed himself actively with characteristic fervour – his practice with Vaux was to assume a position of busy and unchallenged supremacy in America. For a time during the war years Olmsted was based in California, but, encouraged by Vaux, returned east at the end of 1865 to work on a major commission for Prospect Park in Brooklyn – a far more attractive natural site than Central Park and as a result an arguable more attractive landscape design.

The frank and at times volatile nature of Olmsted's

relationship with Vaux meant inevitable friction and in 1872 they dissolved the partnership and went their separate ways. During a period of some fifteen years they had not only set standards for landscape design in America but demonstrated how best the profession of landscape architecture could be organized and expanded in a receptive society. The break brought no reduction in Olmsted's workload. By 1890 he had laid out a series of parks for Boston, often referred to as the 'Emerald Necklace', had designed the grounds of the Capitol in Washington and had begun work at Stanford University in California, as well as undertaking many other projects. Around this time – he wrote characteristically: 'My office is much better equipped and has more momentum than ever before. I am at this time (with my partners) the landscape architect of some twenty works of considerable importance, that is to say, I do not include in that ordinary private grounds. Nine of these twenty are large public parks of cities; two, government works; three, works of commercial corporations; one of a benevolent corporation, and six, private undertakings of such character as to make them matters of public interest, operation on them being systematically reported in the newspaper'.[4] In 1888 Olmsted became involved in the commission that took him through to retirement in 1895: the Biltmore estate that George Washington Vanderbilt had recently purchased in the mountainous countryside around Asheville in North Carolina. Biltmore became the first and grandest of America's great country estates, a vast French château-style house looking over formal gardens to thousands of acres of landscaped woodland all around. Olmsted designed the formal gardens, including an Italian garden, an enormous walled garden, and the sweeping vista reminiscent of Vaux-le-Vicomte that ran from the east front of the house to a statue of Diana on raised ground in the distance. He derived greater satisfaction from planting an arboretum, laying out the approach to the house to run through acres of woodland until the chateau was suddenly revealed, and encouraging Vanderbilt to establish the estate as primarily an area of scientifically managed forestry. As with most of

Olmsted's projects, progress was not completely smooth; yet although the arboretum was never completed to his wishes, the major area of forest, in excess of 40,000 ha/100,000 acres, eventually became the United States's first national forest.

While working at Biltmore Olmsted became an increasingly sick man and in 1895 he retired from practice as a landscape architect. The end of that year saw his memory fading rapidly, and with it his mental faculties, and the last eight years of his life witnessed a relentless decline. Some years before his death, Olmsted brought his two sons into the firm, and in 1899 they were among eleven landscape architects who formalized recognition of the profession by founding the American Society of Landscape Architects. It was a landmark that would have given more satisfaction to Olmsted than the public admiration for his own pioneering work and the landscapes that he designed over a period of some forty years.

SIR JOSEPH PAXTON (1803-65)

BIRKENHEAD PARK, *Merseyside*; CHATSWORTH, *Derbyshire*; SOMERLEYTON HALL, *Suffolk*

JOSEPH PAXTON brought to the world of horticulture the dynamism, engineering skills and enjoyment of size that were all integral characteristics of mid-Victorian England. Probably only the great bridge, boat and railway builder, Isambard Kingdom Brunel, excelled Paxton in typifying the period, although Paxton had the edge as an all-rounder: gardener, architect and engineer, town planner, railway director and Member of Parliament. Most famous as the architect of the glass and iron building for the 1851 Great Exhibition in Hyde Park – later erected in Sydenham as the Crystal Palace – his most lasting contribution was as a gardener, both in his influence on those who followed and for his work at Chatsworth in Derbyshire. Shortly

Looking across one of the lakes in Birkenhead Park to Paxton's boat house.

after his death the 7th Duke of Devonshire, son of Paxton's main patron, wrote in his diary: 'There is no one whose name will be so permanently associated with Chatsworth.'[1]

Paxton was born into the large family of a Bedfordshire farmer and his first job was as a gardener to the squire of the next village. There he obviously received a good basic training, for in 1823, aged twenty, he moved to the newly created gardens of the Royal Horticultural Society in Chiswick, on land leased to the society by the 6th Duke of Devonshire, part of his estate at nearby Chiswick House. Three years later, when the duke needed a new head gardener at Chatsworth, Paxton was offered the job. It marked the beginning of a remarkably close and fruitful relationship, and Paxton soon became, not simply a gardener, but effectively agent of the Chatsworth estate as well as personal attendant and travelling companion for the duke – as Miles Hadfield described, the duke's 'Admirable Crichton'.[2]

When Paxton arrived at Chatsworth the place had been undergoing architectural alterations at the hand of Jeffrey Wyatville, but the gardens were in no comparable state to the 18th century – the time of the cascade and Thomas Archer's pavilion and 'Capability' Brown's park. Paxton went immediately and energetically to work, as his own description of his first few hours at Chatsworth describes: 'I left London by the Comet Coach for Chesterfield and arrived at Chatsworth at half-past four in the morning of the ninth of May, 1826. As no person was to be seen at that early hour, I got over the green-house gate by the old covered way, explored the pleasure grounds and looked round the outside of the house. I then went down to the kitchen gardens, scaled the outside wall and saw the whole of the place, set the men to work at six o'clock; then returned to Chatsworth and got Thomas Weldon to play me the water works and afterwards went to breakfast with poor dear Mrs Gregory and her niece, the latter fell in love with me and I with her, and thus completed my first morning's work at Chatsworth, before nine o'clock'.[3] (After falling in love in 1827, Paxton did marry

Mrs Gregory's niece Sarah Brown, the daughter of a millowner in Matlock.)

Paxton remained at Chatsworth until the 6th Duke's death in 1858. The scale and scope of his activity there during the 1830s and 1840s was enormous, and for two decades the estate was as much his domain as that of its owner. After the Great Exhibition of 1851, when he was awarded his knighthood, he became something of a national celebrity and had many commitments away from Chatsworth – not least as a director of the Midland Railway and a Member of Parliament from 1854 until the year of his death.

Paxton's work at Chatsworth was a steady programme of planting, engineering and architectural schemes. Considering his activity, one remarkable and commendable factor was the extent to which he worked round the major existing features rather than sweeping them away in the name of progress: the cascade was retained, partially extended, and re-aligned to be at an exact right-angle to the south façade of the house. Nonetheless, by the time Paxton had finished it could certainly no longer claim to be the most magnificent water feature at Chatsworth, for high on the hill to the east of the house he built an aqueduct with arches of roughly hewn blocks of stone, from the end of which an enormous waterfall dropped to naturalistic rockeries below. The aqueduct also provided sufficient water and power for the gravity-fed fountains in the formal water gardens beyond the south façade of Chatsworth: the Sea Horse fountain closest to the house, and beyond, in the canal, the Emperor fountain that Paxton constructed in honour of a proposed visit from the Emperor of Russia in 1844 (the visit did not eventually take place), its 27m/80ft jet making it at the time the highest fountain in the world.

Before the construction of the water features, Paxton had carried out extensive tree-planting programmes at Chatsworth, creating the pinetum and arboretum on the great wooded bank that lies to the east of the house and of the garden proper. He perfected the technique of glasshouse construction, and the work at Chatsworth for which he is most famous was the construction of two glasshouses that were to become wonders of the Victorian age. The first was the Great Stove, or Conservatory, built between 1836 and 1840 and the largest glasshouse in the world. It survived until shortly after the World War I, when it was demolished, hopelessly uneconomic. A few years later another, smaller, conservatory was built to celebrate one of the feats of Victorian horticulture, the first flowering in England of the exotic giant waterlily, *Victoria amazonica*.

Like the Great Stove, the Lily House has not survived, but its design provided the pattern for the Great Exhibition building: an ingenious ridge-and-furrow pattern in glass with a central glazing-bar known as 'the Paxton gutter' had major structural supports of iron, and the lighter panel-work of wood. Both buildings were constructed from prefabricated panels, which allowed the exhibition building to be erected in an impressively short time. Paxton's glasshouse construction does survive at Chatsworth in the Conservatory Wall, a series of conservatory cases, taller and more architectural than traditional cold frames, extending up a gentle slope from James Paine's stables to William Talman's Temple of Flora. At Somerleyton Hall in Suffolk, Paxton built a range of camellia houses with ridge-and-furrow pattern roofs for his railways friend, Sir Morton Peto.

While at Chatsworth Paxton turned his attention to another department of gardening in which he was first in the field and which had enormous and laudable social importance. For some years a number of influential people – not least J. C. Loudon (*q.v.* p. 112) – had been campaigning for public parks for England's increasingly industrial and urban society, and in 1843 Paxton designed Birkenhead Park in Liverpool, the first specifically designed town park with free access for local people. Birkenhead not only laid the foundations of public gardens in Britain, but also provided an inspiration to Europeans and Americans, in particular to F. L. Olmsted (*q.v.* p. 120) who wrote after visiting Birkenhead in 1850: 'The baker of Birkenhead has the pride of an OWNER in it.'[5]

The site at Birkenhead of just over 40 ha/100 acres was low-lying and swampy with no natural features of any interest. The challenge provoked/inspired Paxton to combine his engineering skill with a highly original design. The whole area was drained and two lakes with irregular sinuous arms were formed in the east and west halves, both with islands. The spoil and rocks from the lakes' excavation were thrown up into mounds for planting and rockeries, and around these a system of paths wound, to reveal only limited views and areas being viewed at any one time. At one end of the larger lake Paxton designed an elegant boat house. As well as giving pedestrian visitors to the park constant surprises and different vantage-points to enjoy, Paxton produced an ingenious traffic plan that maintained the park's links with the surrounding town by means of a peripheral circulation system for commercial traffic, while providing limited access for park traffic through the middle of the park. Birkenhead was a radically forward-looking piece of urban planning, of a kind that did not become commonplace until much later in the century.

In typically Victorian manner, Paxton's whole career was held up as a shining example; at a time when the status of gardeners – especially of head gardeners – was enjoying rapid elevation as their skills were increasingly recognized and relied on, Paxton became the key figure in demonstrating what could be achieved: Chatsworth; Birkenhead and the Crystal Palace; the editorship of more than one gardening journal, including the *Horticultural Register* started in 1831; architect of, among other things, one of the most magnificent of mid-Victorian houses, Mentmore Towers in Buckinghamshire; Member of Parliament and railway magnate . . . Brent Elliott sums it up: 'From beginning his career as an under-gardener he ended his days as Sir Joseph Paxton MP and railway millionaire. Few could emulate Paxton's career, but all could aspire, and while none ever quite scaled the heights that he did, some came reasonably close.'[6]

INTERNATIONAL INFLUENCES
1880–1920

THE PERIOD THAT USHERED IN THE 20TH CENTURY laid the foundations of the contemporary garden; while today virtually no one creates or looks after a garden in the Victorian manner, plenty still follow the principles and guidelines that were being laid down around the turn of the century. The widespread reaction against Victorian gardens accused them of lacking taste or a sense of scale, of showing little or no relationship between house and garden, and of having a formality that was only superficially classical or Italianate.

The reaction took not one form but several. William Robinson (*q.v.* p. 157) forcefully advocated informality and native perennial plants rather than ranks of glasshouse-raised annuals; while architects such as Reginald Blomfield (*q.v.* p. 133) were advocating formality of an overall architectural character, with a far greater fusion between house and garden. In between were Thomas Mawson (*q.v.* p. 150) and the partnership of Edwin Lutyens (*q.v.* p. 146) and Gertrude Jekyll (*q.v.* p. 138) demonstrating that the most satisfactory garden balanced architecture and horticulture in a manner that was founded on attention to detail and which could be adapted to any scale.

The quality and ingenuity of Italian Renaissance gardens
so admired in the United States around the turn of
the century were masterfully recreated at Vizcaya.

Equally important were the wider changes which greatly encouraged these stylistic developments. In the face of Victorian urbanization and industrialization, the countryside and rural life became increasingly revered – by the intellectuals of the Arts and Crafts movement in a studied, carefully considered manner; by others simply as an escape, either real or imagined. The role of the garden as the domestic manifestation of this ideal took on immense importance and, to a greater extent than had been the case at any time since the 17th century, the garden became social – a place for activity rather than purely a display to be admired. David Ottewill describes this in his definitive book on Edwardian gardens: 'Owners became active gardeners themselves; garden parties and garden fêtes increased in popularity; and the British propensity for sport was displayed by the bowling green and by tennis, which took the place of croquet on the lawn: tea was taken on the terrace; the loggia replaced the conservatory; rose-clad pergolas formed long corridors of shade leading from arbour or summer-house. The garden was conceived less as a spectacle to be viewed from the house than as a succession of outdoor rooms, each one affording fresh delights to the visitor.'[1]

While the great wealth possessed by many Edwardians led to an ostentatiously unproductive, if socially active way of life, they were unstinting admirers of quality and spent their money to achieve it. Their houses were often architecturally derivative but were usually built to the highest standards of craftsmanship and were as far as possible historically accurate. This appreciation of quality extended to their gardens and for garden designers the pursuit of technical excellence became a primary goal. For many architects, notably Reginald Blomfield (*q.v.* p. 133), Harold Peto (*q.v.* p. 154) and Edwin Lutyens (*q.v.* p. 146), garden design was a natural and important extension of their house building – or alteration – and in many cases this greatly increased the unity of house and garden. However, within this architectural framework, variety was seen to be important, which led in turn to an emphasis on quality of planting; different areas of the garden were each given their own distinctive character in a manner that has continued to be admired to this day.

Country house gardens created for those with sufficient money had a wide range of features: paved terraces around the house; herbaceous borders and rose gardens; often a formal water garden; yew hedges used extensively to make enclosures or vistas; and around the garden's perimeter areas of woodland that were opened up with winding paths and, if the soil was suitable, planted with the flowering trees and shrubs such as magnolias, rhododendrons and camellias being introduced from overseas. Further variation was provided by fashionable oddities: Japanese gardens enjoyed a widespread vogue as knowledge of that hitherto mysterious country began to filter back to the west towards the end of the 19th century; rock gardens, often constructed on a massive naturalistic scale, were championed by plant collectors such as Reginald Farrer, who wrote *My Rock Garden* in 1909 and followed it with his *The English Rock Garden*, published in 1919. Tender exotics were now usually confined to greenhouses and cultivated – along with sumptuous fruit – for bringing into the house as decoration for that most Edwardian of inventions, the house party. At Sandringham King Edward VII, the original inspiration of the house party, constructed a vast range of teak glasshouses for this purpose; they stretched for 270m/300yds along one side of the main walled garden and were paid for by the profits from his Derby-winning horse, Persimmon.

Much has been made of the running argument of the time, as to the relative qualities of natural and formal gardens, and in particular of the personal differences between their two most vociferous protagonists – William Robinson and Reginald Blomfield. In the event neither man was as extreme in his practical gardening as in his written opinions. Robinson, whose indignation was originally aroused by what he referred to as the 'pastry-cook' style of High Victorian gardening, had many formal elements in the garden he created at Gravetye Manor. Blomfield's primary objective was to establish that garden design was the rightful domain of architects, his main priority being that the immediate surroundings of a house should be formally architectural and that the garden should have a well-structured framework. Most observers appreciated that the extreme positions on either side were neither practical nor desirable and applied one or other according to personal taste.

For those creating purely formal gardens the only truly acceptable models were Italian. Moving away from the Victorian Italianate/French hybrids of highly ornamental terraces containing elaborate parterres, the Edwardians looked far more closely at the originals of the Italian Renaissance and aspired to the same balance of architecture and landscape. Men like Harold Peto (*q.v.* p. 154) and Sir George Sitwell (*q.v.* p. 160) steeped themselves in knowledge of Italian gardens and yet at the same time adapted their enthusiasm with enormous skill to the particular qualities of an English landscape, producing some of the most evocative and successful gardens of the period.

The Italian quality was achieved not by the application of geometry and rich ornamentation, but by far more subtle spatial arrangement of enclosures, descending levels and large vistas, and the judicious positioning of statuary and architectural features of the highest quality.

If Italian gardens became a feature of Edwardian England, they enjoyed an arguably even more extensive revival in the United States. At a time of newly created commercial and industrial fortunes, Americans looked to continental Europe for the models of taste in all forms of art, architecture and decoration; where gardens were concerned the Italian examples unquestionably achieved the highest regard. By the 1890s the Beaux Arts tradition of decorative classicism was being encouraged by American enthusiasm for Paris and French taste, and was already influential in the United States. It was focused on gardens by the appearance of two widely read books: Charles A. Platt's *Italian Gardens*, published in 1894, and Edith Wharton's *Italian Villas and their Gardens*, published in 1903. These Italian models quickly led to huge sums of American money being spent on building houses and laying out surrounding gardens in a sumptuous, fashionable and historically admired style.

Assisted by the Italian-trained garden designer Diego Suarez, James Deering, the heir to a fortune built on agricultural machinery, created the most impressive Italian garden of the period at his Villa Vizcaya overlooking Biscayne Bay on the coast of Florida. The new house was built in the style of a Venetian palace, and Deering laid out the main area of garden beyond the loggia on the south front, with a series of grand formal vistas stretching away across terraces of clipped evergreens and formal expanses of water. The garden was highly architectural, with sweeping flights of steps, 17th- and 18th-century Italian statues and a *casino*, standing on a mound surrounded by live oaks, as the focus of the central vista and looking out over the bay in the other direction. The garden's quality lies in the fact that the inspiration of the Italian originals was followed with the strictest accuracy and nowhere was the level of ornament allowed to overreach itself.

The formal Italian gardens in both England and America were often designed and laid out with extraordinarily skill, which spoke both of the knowledge of their designers and the technical standards of the time; but they were essentially period pieces which would become a rarity after World War I and thereafter almost extinct. A more lasting garden style was established in England by Jekyll and Lutyens because their work focused on the qualities of vernacular architecture, of local traditions and materials, and on fastidious plantsmanship. Held together by a firm structural framework, and intensely detailed, their gardens did not require expansive acres and settings to achieve their effect. Indeed many of the most ingenious, such as the Deanery garden in Berkshire, were made in limited and potentially awkward sites. Their work also demonstrated how gardens could display a succession of different appearances throughout the year. Their sources were numerous:

At Renishaw Sir George Sitwell introduced the Italian
ideal to an English garden and landscape.

the principles of the Arts and Crafts movement; the championing of 'natural gardening' by Robinson; Jekyll's artist's eye and Lutyens's architectural feel for materials and their texture; the suitability of native plants often seen in humble cottage gardens; the need for scale rather than size. The garden could look out to a landscape beyond or lead into the countryside, but such expansive qualities were not a pre-requisite for success – a good garden could equally well be made in a suburban setting. In all this, and the adaptability that it incorporated, their example and guidelines were to be the most widely followed by future generations in both England and America.

SIR REGINALD BLOMFIELD (1856-1942)

CHEQUERS, *Buckinghamshire;* GODINTON PARK, *Kent;* MELLER-
STAIN, *Berwickshire;* MOUNDSMERE MANOR, *Hampshire;*
SULGRAVE MANOR, *Northamptonshire*

A S AN ARCHITECT AND GARDEN DESIGNER there was no figure more representative of the Edwardian period than
Sir Reginald Blomfield. In an age of domestic luxury and
magnificence for those who could afford it, he designed
some of the most magnificent houses, such as the 'neo-
Wren' Moundsmere Manor in Hampshire. He was also a
leading protagonist of the principle that the garden – or at
least those areas that surrounded a house – were first and
foremost the domain of the architect not the gardener, in
order to ensure the necessary sense of order and unity
with a house. The gardens he designed, with expansive
terraces, clipped yew hedges and judiciously positioned
buildings or ornaments; were in part an early 20th-century
evocation of 17th-century formality. Blomfield was also
keenly aware of the social ethos that lay at the heart of
Edwardian country house life, and whenever possible par-
took of that life himself – hunting and shooting, and playing golf and cricket from the house he owned at Rye.

In his architecture Blomfield married an early loyalty
to the Arts and Crafts movement with a neo-classical style
that appealed to his clients, and whether he was adapting
an existing house or building a new one his work demonstrated all the quality of design and craftsmanship that
became hallmarks of Edwardian building. At the same
time he emerged as a leading figure in the major gardening
controversy of the turn of the century, advocating formal,
architectural gardens as opposed to those with a more natural, horticulturally orientated style, which were equally
vociferously promoted by William Robinson (*q.v.* p. 157).
But for every country house garden where horticulture
was the major priority there were more where garden and
house were required to provide a setting of impressive formality for gardening display and social entertainment; for
these, Blomfield's ideas and designs were ideally suited.

Born the son of a Devon clergyman who subsequently
moved to livings in Kent, Blomfield gained a scholarship
to Exeter College, Oxford, from where he went in 1881 to
join the architectural practice of his uncle, Sir Arthur
Blomfield. Young Blomfield devoted the first part of his
career to his work as an architect but was obviously for-
mulating strongly held views on garden design, which he
revealed in 1892 with the publication of *The Formal Garden in England.*

The book was greatly enhanced by the quality of illustrations drawn by F. Inigo Thomas (*q.v.* p. 162), while its
text spelt out Blomfield's advocacy of architectural gardens
in an uncompromising – if not always strictly accurate –
manner clearly designed to oppose the views of William
Robinson. 'It is evident that to plan out a garden the
knowledge necessary is that of design, not of the best
method of growing a giant gooseberry'[1]; it also showed
early signs of the pompous self-confidence that he
retained for the rest of his life. In his memoirs, published
in 1932, he wrote: '*The Formal Garden* did in fact knock
out the landscape gardener and all his wicked ways, and
though many mistakes have been made in scale, and in
attempts to do a great deal too much with pergolas, water-
pieces, temples and other devices, an advance has been
made in garden design in the last forty years as marked as
that in the designing of buildings.'[2]

Blomfield's book rapidly achieved a reputation, going
into three editions, much to the author's satisfaction. It
appeared almost simultaneously with J. D. Sedding's
Garden Craft Old and New, which similarly championed
architectural formality in garden design – although in
more moderate tones than Blomfield's – and the two books
were seen to line up on the side of the argument promoting formality against the naturalism advocated by William
Robinson. In fact, as Clive Aslet has pointed out, the real
differences between the two sides were not as great as the
argument suggested, but the situation served to present
opposite poles in garden style, which were brought
together in the later Edwardian garden, principally by
Gertrude Jekyll and Edwin Lutyens.[3]

Overleaf: *Mellerstain was Reginald Blomfield's grandest*
commission, even though his full scheme of terraces leading
to the lake and view of the Cheviot Hills was not completed.

The principles put forward in *The Formal Garden In England* set out his conviction that an architect's brief should include the design of the garden, which became increasingly evident in Blomfield's major country house commissions. The earliest that still survives to his original plan – and arguably the most attractive – is Godinton Park in Kent, where he worked for a banker, Mr Ashley Dodd, who had recently purchased the property. Blomfield built a new wing on to the romantically gabled brick Jacobean house and laid out gardens that blended exceptionally well with the house and the surrounding park. His design contained a number of features that he was to repeat in most of his later gardens, in particular clipped yew hedges which at Godinton were given the distinctive appearance of gables to match those of the house, and a satisfying balance of straight lines and formal curves.

The main axis of the garden was planned roughly north-south from an enclosed garden of clipped box pyramids around a statue of Pan – one of a number of figures which were already in the garden and repositioned by Blomfield to enhance his design – then across lawn to descending steps and a formal lily pool which he made out of an existing pond. The geometric rectangular shape of the pool was softened by curving the far end, and the curve was repeated in the balustraded belvedere which gave views out across the park. The rest of the main area of Blomfield's garden runs parallel to this main axis from the house's south front, through a rose garden to lawn with formally arranged planting and statues, where he retained the mature trees which formed the boundary to the west. He also replanned the large walled garden and later – in 1916 – added the intimate Italian Garden inserted between one end of the walled garden and the stable courtyard beside the house.

Blomfield's work at Godinton was closely attuned to the house's scale and character, and this is equally evident in his far grander work at Mellerstain in Berwickshire where he was commissioned by Lord and Lady Binning in 1909. Along the main front of the Adam mansion Blomfield laid out a series of three balustraded terraces beyond which a great sweep of lawn descended to a lake with the Cheviot Hills in the distance. From the top terrace of lawn and clipped yews flights of steps divide over the roof of a pillared arbour – Blomfield called it a '*crypto-porticus*' and lead down to the central, largest, terrace with intricate parterres. Further steps divide around a lily pool and descend to the third terrace. Blomfield's ambitions went far beyond the completed work, but his client called a halt – not unreasonably – as Blomfield accepted in his autobiography: 'My scheme was to have been carried onto an immense grass hemicycle overlooking the lake at the foot of the hill, in the best manner of le Nôtre, but we had to abandon this; indeed it would have required the resources of Louis XIV to carry out the whole of my design'.[4]

Blomfield's last country house commission, Sulgrave Manor in Northamptonshire, involved the restoration of an old house rather than an extension or complete new house and this presented a contrasting architectural brief to most of his previous work, while the garden that he laid out bore many distinct hallmarks of his style. Sulgrave, built in 1558, was the ancestral home of the American president George Washington (*q.v.* p. 89) and had been lived in by the family for one hundred and fifty years. In 1914, in a state of sad disrepair, the manor was bought by a trust set up to further Anglo-American friendship; it called in Blomfield, embarked upon a comprehensive restoration, and has retained ownership ever since. As well as being a place of pilgrimage for Americans and a haven of international friendship, Sulgrave today retains close contact with George Washington's home, Mount Vernon, in Virginia.

Blomfield restored Sulgrave's appearance as an Elizabethan manor and laid out new gardens in place of run-down farm buildings. Small formal flower gardens, such as the rose garden on the east side of the house, and a bowling green, blend with more architectural features carefully scaled to the manor's relatively modest overall proportions, while Blomfield's favoured yew hedges provide divisions and axes, most effectively next to the entrance courtyard where he made a circular enclosure. Today – as at his other gardens – Blomfield's work has achieved a maturity which serves to increase the quality of his design. Characteristically, Blomfield himself had no illusions about his achievement at Sulgrave: 'Sulgrave Manor in its completed state, with its bowling green, its yew hedges, its orchard and its garden of old English flowers, gives a very good idea of what the place might have been when it was occupied by the first Washington who owned it, a mayor of Northampton.'[5] Most relevant about this turn-of-the-century comment is the emphasis on historical accuracy – in both style and atmosphere; an emphasis that was becoming of increasing importance in garden design. More and more 20th-century gardens would be designed around established houses from earlier periods, and a balance between the varying degrees of formality and informality, architecture and nature, could be struck accordingly.

ACHILLE DUCHÊNE (1866-1947)

BLENHEIM PALACE, *Oxfordshire*

BLENHEIM WAS THE ONLY BRITISH COMMISSION for Achille Duchêne who was arguably the first garden designer to enjoy an international career. The quality and success of his work in his native France, where he initially joined the existing practice of his father, Henri, restoring historic formal gardens such as Vaux-le-Vicomte and Courances, and creating new ones such as Voisins in a style that evoked the golden age of French gardening during the time of André le Nôtre, encouraged the Duke of Marlborough to choose him rather than a British designer to work at Blenheim – probably the most prestigious commission in a career which otherwise saw work in Germany, the United States, Argentina, Russia and Australia. And yet, perhaps the most intriguing aspect of Duchêne's career was his uncanny perception about the future of his profession; even before World War I, when he first worked at

Blenheim, he suspected that economic and social factors would ensure that these would be amongst the last privately commissioned grand gardens and that large schemes of the future would be communal and recreational, in the form of urban public parks. In the aftermath of the war his suspicions were vindicated and, as Monique Mosser has written, 'only urban planning and public schemes could henceforth provide commissions of the scale he required.'[1]

The work at Blenheim was commissioned by 'Sunny', 9th Duke of Marlborough, who was determined to restore Blenheim to its early 18th-century glory and repair the neglect and damage of his immediate predecessors; it was paid for by the railway fortune of his American wife, Consuelo Vanderbilt. (By the time Duchêne was employed the duke and duchess had separated but the necessary finances were fortunately still available.)

Before the war Duchêne's first task was architectural – restoring to Vanbrugh's original plan the stone paving of the enormous north court that had been grassed over by 'Capability' Brown. His first chance of garden work came when the duke removed an uninspiring Victorian shrubbery on the east side of the palace and commissioned a formal parterre. Duchêne laid out an intricate pattern of box-hedging and gravel around a circular pool, with the American Waldo Story's gilded Mermaid fountain as a lavish centrepiece, and the whole enclosed by yew. Although called the Italian garden, and with a long vista continuing beyond the garden opposite the palace façade, Duchêne's parterre is both far more French in character and reminiscent of the early 18th-century work of Henry Wise at Blenheim.

After World War I Duchêne returned to Blenheim to create his most spectacular addition, the water terraces between the west façade of the house and 'Capability' Brown's lake. By this time the duke had married for the second time, another American, Gladys Deacon, whose likeness was to be immortalized in Duchêne's garden on the faces of two lead sphinxes carved by H. Ward Willis. In the creation of this garden Duchêne came up against his client's overbearing manner on a number of occasions, not least when he presented his initial proposal for the water garden: 'You are the architect, I am the Duke' . . . and he continued by addressing Duchêne in the third person: 'The problem for Monsieur Duchêne is to make a liaison . . . between the façade of Vanbrugh and the water line of the lake made by Brown. To reconcile these conflicting ideas is difficult. The difficulty is not diminished when you remember that the façade of the house is not limitless and the line of the lake is limitless. As an example, if you turn your back to the lake and look at the façade, your parterre basin etc. is in scale to the façade, but if you look at the same parterre from the rotunda to the lake it is out of scale with the panorama.'[2]

Thus admonished, Duchêne was despatched to try again – this time with success. His revised design, as carried out, was for two terraces linked (in a manner reminiscent of Vaux-le-Vicomte) by two flights of steps in a retaining wall with five central arches: the upper terrace square and much the larger, with a formal pattern of *bassins* and scrollwork hedges; the lower terrace rectangular with two rectangular pools. The centrepiece of one pool was Bernini's fountain modelled on the River God's fountain in Rome (moved from the grand cascade where it had stood since the time of the 1st duke), of the other, a more modest obelisk.

Further ornamented by statues and urns, Duchêne's water garden was a superb design for the situation. The duke was pleased, but could not resist, rather ungraciously, having the last word; on Duchêne's main drawing of his layout he added a large note saying, 'If you study this picture and compare it with the finished work on the terraces you will realise the immense influence I had over the architect in making the effect of the terrace classical in appearance, and how I succeeded in destroying the French middle-class view of a formal garden.'[3] He originally resisted Duchêne's desire for fountains but these were added later and by the time the work was virtually complete he was prepared to be more magnanimous, writing to Duchêne that, 'the ensemble of terraces is magnificent and in my judgement far superior to the work done by le Nôtre at Versailles.'[5]

The duke never managed to carry out his most ambitious garden project, the restoration of Henry Wise's great south parterre, which would almost without question have involved Duchêne again; and the water terraces at Blenheim were effectively Duchêne's last major private commission. Despite all the vicissitudes of his relations with the duke the project was a triumph and the equal of his earlier commissions in France. In a rare manner it was a revival garden that managed a high degree of architectural originality and panache and it remains one of the most distinguished additions in the long history of Blenheim's landscape.

GERTRUDE JEKYLL (1843-1932)

AMPORT HOUSE, *Hampshire;* AMMERDOWN PARK, *Somerset;* ASHBY ST LEGERS, *Northamptonshire;* BARRINGTON COURT, *Somerset;* BARTON ST MARY, *Sussex;* CHINTHURST HILL, *Surrey;* DEANERY GARDEN, *Berkshire;* FOLLY FARM, *Berkshire;* GODDARDS, *Surrey;* GREY WALLS, *Lothian;* HESTERCOMBE, *Somerset;* HAZELHATCH, *Surrey;* THE HOO, *Sussex;* KING EDWARD VII SANATORIUM, *Sussex;* LAMBAY CASTLE, *Eire;* LINDISFARNE CASTLE, *Northumberland;* MELLS PARK, *Somerset;* MARSH COURT, *Hampshire;* MILLMEAD, *Surrey;* MUNSTEAD WOOD, *Surrey;* ORCHARDS, *Surrey;* PASTUREWOOD HOUSE (**Now Beatrice Webb House**), *Surrey;* PUTTERIDGE PARK, *Bedfordshire;* SULLINGSTEAD, *Surrey;* TIGBOURNE COURT, *Surrey;* WINKWORTH FARM, *Surrey;* WITTERSHAM HOUSE, *Kent;* WOODSIDE, *Buckinghamshire*

IN RECENT YEARS the republication of Gertrude Jekyll's own books, her treatment by a number of writers and a revival of interest in unusual perennial plants have conspired to elevate her to the position of fairy godmother of 20th-century gardening. In this we are encouraged by a collage of images; Sir William Nicholson's painting of her

Achille Duchêne's water terrace at Blenheim with Brown's lake and park beyond.

stout leather boots and his portrait of her bearing a similarity to Queen Victoria; her fondness for the simple qualities of rural and domestic life; her training as a painter and her work as a craftswoman; her quiet education of the brilliant but inexperienced young architect 'Ned' Lutyens to the virtues of vernacular craftsmanship and local materials; and her encyclopaedic knowledge of both wild and cultivated plants. It is a position fraught with the danger of absurd sentimentalization to present this most practical, at times awkward lady as a paragon; equally important in the expansion of the Jekyll myth is the element of nostalgia – because most of her work consisted of specific planting schemes of perennial or annual plants, little survives in its original detail.

However, neither the disappearance of her work, nor the romanticizing of her reputation should be allowed to detract from her remarkable contribution, both individually and in partnership with Lutyens, in laying the foundations of the garden as we know it today. Her importance lies not so much in her actual planting schemes – subsequent generations have often found them too demanding and highly detailed – as in the principles she laid down about the overall conception and design of a garden, as well as its detailed composition. These principles have been readily understood and identified with in this century because they were born out of a practical experience that preferred the small and intimate to the large and expansive. Size to Gertrude Jekyll was not a prerequisite for gardening success and as if to emphasize the point she was seldom involved in Lutyens's more grandiose projects. Her forte was attention to detail, horticulturally in terms of colour and plant form, architecturally in terms of materials used and in her sensitive response to laying out even the most awkward of sites.

Gertrude Jekyll was born in London but her family moved to Surrey when she was a small child and rented Bramley Park, a country house between Guildford and Horsham. Her parents were well off, progressive, upper-middle class Victorians who, when Gertrude was seventeen and had been educated at home by governesses,

decided that their daughter should be given the chance to develop her obvious artistic talent and took the avant-garde step of sending her to the South Kensington School of Art. Two year's experience at art college combined with her natural talent and intelligence, helped to launch her into leading Victorian artistic circles. She also travelled extensively on the continent at this time. She was naturally drawn towards the Arts and Crafts movement, whose aspirations were closely attuned to her own, not least in the desire to emphasize the qualities of rural life, be it a simple cottage garden, a blacksmith's forge, or modest vernacular architecture. Her interest in the arts was wide; in addition to painting and drawing she took up embroidery, inlay work, and a variety of other crafts, coming across as a formidably talented young woman.

In 1868 Gertrude and her family moved from Surrey to a house in Berkshire that her father inherited, but when he died in 1876 her mother decided to return to Surrey with the five children, bought a plot of land at Munstead, close to their old home at Bramley, and commissioned the architect J. J. Stevenson to build a house. It was at Munstead that Gertrude Jekyll's gardening began, first around the family's new house and subsequently, from the early 1880s, on an adjacent plot of some 6 ha/15 acres which she bought with the long-term view to establishing her own independent home there. As Jane Brown wrote: 'She was well-equipped for making her undoubted masterpiece – she had been learning about plants all her life, she had made careful notes about all the flowers and gardens she had seen all over Europe and while visiting her friends in England, and through her painting and embroidery she had developed her taste and understanding of colour and design. She had her new gardening friends at the Royal Horticultural Society who would keep her in touch with all that was going on, and she had plenty of friends around her too, both other "gentle" gardeners and the tougher kind who would work to her instructions. Her old friends among the Bramley villagers down the road would see to that.'[1]

In the 1870s Gertrude Jekyll had also embarked upon

the second pillar of her career – garden writing. William Robinson (*q.v.* p. 157) had published his *The Wild Garden* in 1870, in which he expressed his rumbustiously denunciations of Victorian parterre gardens and led the call for a more natural and subdued style of gardening. The following year he published the first issue of *The Garden*, to which Gertrude Jekyll was an early subscriber, and in 1875 the first of her many articles appeared in the magazine; she was later briefly to edit it. Just as she was becoming steadily more immersed in the gardening world, so increasing short-sightedness was limiting her other artistic activities, and by the late 1880s gardening and garden writing were established as the major outlets for her ideas and talents. As important as anything was her role in bridging for the first time the division between professional and amateur gardeners, and in promoting by example the full involvement of women in gardening.

In 1889 she was invited to tea by a local friend and rhododendron grower, Harry Mangles, where she met the twenty-year-old Edwin Lutyens (*q.v.* p. 146), recently established in his own architectural practice in Gray's Inn Square in London. Lutyens himelf later described – in a manner tailor-made to promote nostalgia – the meeting that heralded so much for both of them, and for the future of garden design: 'We met at a tea-table, the silver kettle and the conversation reflecting rhododendrons . . .. She was dressed in what I learnt later to be her Go-To-Meeting Frock – a bunch of cloaked propriety topped by a black felt hat, turned down in front and up behind, from which sprang alert black cock's tail feathers, curving and ever prancing forwards.'[2] As she left in her pony cart she invited him to Munstead Wood. The friendship between the middle-aged gardening spinster and the ambitious young architect was cemented over the next few years by his regular visits to Munstead Wood. Gertrude Jekyll took Lutyens all over the Surrey countryside in her pony cart, awakening him to the possibilities of creating houses and gardens in vernacular style and using local materials, and of putting into practice her gardening principles.

The partnership was first tested at Munstead itself, where Lutyens initially designed a modest cottage for Miss Jekyll and subsequently in 1895, Munstead Wood house itself. David Ottewill writes: 'In the opening chapter of *Home and Garden*, Miss Jekyll described how the house was built in the spirit of the local traditions with Bargate stone walls, hand-made tiles, mullioned windows and joinery of locally grown oak, an early and enthusiastic example of the application of Arts and Crafts principles inspired by the writings of Ruskin and Morris and the work of Philip Webb.'[3] The garden was already well established so to some extent the house had to fit in. Although the garden disappeared some years ago, it is important to describe the major features since they, and their relationship with the house, provided the basis for all Jekyll and Lutyens's future work.

The house was positioned near the centre of the triangular piece of ground, facing north-south. The more formal connected areas, including the nut walk flanked by mixed borders, the pergola and the main flower border, lay in front of the north courtyard, with the walled kitchen garden beyond. The 'Hut' (Lutyens's original cottage) was to the south-west of the house, with its own small areas of garden, while the large area to the south and east beyond the stone terrace and lawn in front of the house, was the woodland garden. There is a current campaign to organize the restoration of the Munstead Wood garden to some resemblance of the original.

Munstead became the central focus for Gertrude Jekyll's gardening, a microcosm of her ideas and practice, where new colour schemes were tried, new plants first used, and all the details meticulously recorded; as she grew older and travelled less, her life increasingly fused with the surroundings of her home. It provided much of the material for her succession of books, in particular the second, *Home and Garden*, published in 1900. The first book, *Wood and Garden*, published in 1899, immediately widened her reputation, and others followed in a regular flow during the next few years; after *Home and Garden* came *Lilies for English Gardens* (1901), *Wall and Water Gardens* (1901), *Roses for English Gardens* (1902), *Old*

Overleaf: Harmony of architecture and planting as here at Hestercombe was at the heart of Gertrude Jekyll and Edwin Lutyens' partnership.

West Surrey (1904), *Flower Decoration in the House* (1907), *Children and Gardens* (1908), *Colour in the Flower Garden* (1908) and *Garden Ornament* (1918). She also collaborated with architectural writers to produce two influential books on English houses and gardens: *Some English Gardens* with G. S. Elgood (1904), and *Gardens for Small Country Houses* with Lawrence Weaver (1912) which, like her own books, became an acknowledged classic.

If Gertrude Jekyll's writing output was impressive during these years, her partnership with Lutyens was equally prolific. Her nephew and biographer, Francis Jekyll, estimated that she was commissioned to supply designs or advice for a total of nearly three hundred and fifty gardens, although the involvement, particularly latterly was often limited to supplying a suggested planting scheme, without actually visiting the garden in question. Over a hundred of these gardens, among them her major commissions, were with Lutyens, the most fruitful years of the partnership being from 1897, the year that the house at Munstead was complete, until 1907 or 1908. Thereafter, as Gertrude Jekyll became older, both her desire to leave Munstead and her output diminished, while Lutyens's architectural interests shifted away from the style in which they had worked together most happily, as the nature of many of his commissions changed.

The years that saw the most successful and lastingly influential 'Lutyens house and Jekyll garden' commissions began with Orchards in Surrey and included Le Bois des Moutiers in Normandy, Deanery garden in Berkshire (for Edward Hudson, founder of *Country Life*), Marsh Court in Hampshire, Folly Farm in Berkshire, The Hoo in Sussex, Lambay Castle in the Bay of Dublin and Hestercombe in Somerset. Although all the gardens were different there was continuity in the application of certain principles, guidelines and stylistic techniques. The major constant was unity; unity between house and garden, between planting and architectural features, between different areas, between plants within a border or an area of woodland and – relatively new to the Edwardian age but increasingly a priority – unity between the garden as a place of horticulture and ornament and as a place for social activity.

The overall result was the creation of what can only be described as a house and garden ideal. Lutyens's near-photographic memory and architect's eye and training produced the parameters within which Jekyll's knowledge and skill could be applied. His designs provided outlets for her ideas on the use of water, on the decoration of paths and doorways, or the right pattern for a flight of steps in a certain situation. Both partners paid attention to detail to an extraordinarily high degree; when married to a firm overall plan, this produced a picture of often great complexity in its component parts, yet held together with natural ease. In each case Jekyll's major contribution was the plants, individually and in association. Although William Robinson had begun the move towards using old-fashioned and native perennial plants in preference to arrays of annuals, it was Gertrude Jekyll who demonstrated how this should be done, and as a result hers was the more lasting influence.

For her no cottage garden flower that she spied from a Surrey lane was too humble so long as it was suitable for a given situation, while the hosts of new varieties from overseas were judged equally on their merits. In *Home and Garden* she outlined the simple priority by which she was guided: 'Often when I have had to do with other people's gardens they have said "I have bought a quantity of shrubs and plants, show me where to place them" – to which I can only answer, that is not the way in which I can help you – show me your spaces and I will tell you what plants to get for them.'[4]

In addition to her work with Lutyens Miss Jekyll carried out other garden designs on her own – most often for local friends or acquaintances in Surrey – and with other architects. Today there are a number of Surrey gardens which still maintain a small element of planting which she advised on – perhaps one border or a woodland walk. Most substantial of her other garden designs was Barrington Court in Somerset. The property had been acquired by the National Trust in 1907, and as part of the restoration some ten years later the architects, Forbes and Tate, asked Miss Jekyll – by this time nearly seventy-five – to supply designs for a series of enclosed gardens which were fitted in around existing old farm walls and buildings.

Although the productivity of Miss Jekyll's partnership with Lutyens had waned by the last years before World War I, she did have one major contribution left to make: the planting schemes for the first of Lutyens's war cemeteries and his subsequent work for the War Graves Commission. Miss Jekyll suggested to Lutyens that the cemeteries should be planted to combine a sense of dignity with warmth and an evocation of home; the simple lines of low clipped hedges, symbolic individual trees, spring bulbs, roses and other identifiably English plants, became the guidelines for all future War Graves Commission planting, and was poignant evidence of how her gardening philosophy was always inextricably bound to people.

After World War I the number of potential clients with the financial resources declined and the way of life that had existed in Edwardian England hardly survived. Nonetheless, the influence of Lutyens's and Jekyll's work can be seen to this day – not only in general terms but through the host of productive 20th-century gardeners that followed, both English and American. Beatrix Farrand (q.v. p. 174) in particular comes to mind. Miss Farrand made an historically decisive contribution when she purchased the great majority of Gertrude Jekyll's garden plans, housing them at her own home at Reef Point, Maine and later passing them to the University of California, Berkeley. The survival of Miss Jekyll's plans preserves a vital treasure-trove of her work and, for instance, enabled the garden at Hestercombe in Somerset to be replanted with great accuracy according to her original design. Out of the gardening kaleidoscope of the latter decades of the 19th century and the early 20th, Gertrude Jekyll's most telling contribution was to advocate and demonstrate how gardening could best be scaled down and popularized in any modest home without compromising on quality or interest.

MAJOR LAWRENCE WATERBURY JOHNSTON (1871-1958)

HIDCOTE MANOR, *Gloucestershire*

IT IS A SURPRISE FOR MANY PEOPLE to discover that Hidcote Manor, celebrated as one of the most 'English' gardens of the 20th century, was created by an American, Lawrence Johnston – although, it has to be admitted, an ex-patriot one. Edward Hyams, among the most knowledgeable commentators on gardens and their history, sums up Lawrence Johnston's achievement at Hidcote, describing it as 'the master work of the twentieth century; and, as such, bringing together in itself an expression of all the principle styles and traditions of English gardening in a brilliantly successful combination.'[1]

Lawrence Johnston was born in Paris, the only child of wealthy American parents who, like other of their contemporaries, went to Europe during the latter years of the 19th century attracted by its culture and sophistication. Lawrence was brought up and educated in Paris before going to Trinity College, Cambridge. England evidently made an enormous impact upon the cultured young man, for in 1900 he decided to become a naturalized British subject, and as if to emphasize his loyalty to his adopted country, he joined the British army and left England for the war in South Africa.

The major step in Johnston's life came in 1907, after his return from Africa, when his mother purchased for him a 110 ha/280 acre farm at Hidcote, an exposed bluff on the northern edge of the Cotswolds, looking west towards the Vale of Evesham and the Malvern Hills. Its windswept nature might have seemed unwelcoming, but the bracing air suited Johnston who suffered from weak lungs. It was not long, however, before farming took second place to gardening, and this rapidly became a consuming interest for the rest of Johnston's life. He had no practical experience or training behind him, but obviously had a clear idea of how his garden would evolve, an old cedar of Lebanon on one side of the house and, at a distance, a stand of beech trees, providing the initial anchors for his design.

The fundamental balance of the garden is between the intimacy of the succession of enclosures and the theatrical beckoning of the three main vistas: the first across the open theatre lawn to the stand of beeches (now only one tree) on a raised mound; the second, parallel, from the cedar in the 'old garden' closest to the house and rising through the red borders to the stilt garden and a wrought-iron gateway at the top; the third, at right-angles, leading off from one of the pair of gazebos at the top of the red borders, dipping down to cross the stream valley before rising up between beech hedges to another gateway on the garden's boundary. Although formal in design, the structure of the garden is softened by the use of hedges rather than walls. Johnston's Hidcote was very different in concept from the Edwardian gardens that Jekyll and Lutyens or Thomas Mawson were laying out at the same time; it seems to come from a later, less stylized, period. Its influences are catholic but always restrained: the immaculate 'stilt' garden of pleached hornbeams that continue the main axis of the red borders, clearly inspired by Johnston's French upbringing, contrasting with the natural informality of the stream garden.

Critics have commented on the scale and construction at Hidcote – paths and steps too narrow, for example; a lack of coherance between the different areas – but most would agree that any such faults are more than adequately disguised by the planting throughout the garden. The different enclosures, hedged in a mixture of holly, yew, beech, copper beech and hornbeam lead one to another and their varying identities enabled Johnston to indulge his rapidly acquired skills and knowledge as a plantsman to the full. Native plants filled some areas, such as the nostalgic old garden closest to the house, while more choice and unusual varieties were collected for other areas through his widening circle of gardening friends. Between the wars Johnston's interest led him to join two plant-collecting expeditions, the first to southern Africa (when, as Alvilde Lees-Milne has described, Johnston, 'who liked his comforts, brought along his Italian cook and chauffeur valet[2]), the second and more adventurous with the plant collector George Forrest to Yunnan in China, although illness forced Johnston to retire early.

Hidcote developed uninterrupted until 1914, when Johnston rejoined the army and was away until the end of the war. The ensuring years saw necessary repair work and regeneration carried out, a steady expansion of the garden's range of plants, and the creation of the last new areas; and it was at this time that the garden's reputation began to make itself known. From the 1920s Johnston divided his time between Hidcote and a second home he had bought in the south of France, where he was creating another garden and where he died in 1958. Some ten years earlier the National Trust had agreed that Hidcote should be the first garden to be accepted on its own merits as a property for the Trust.

Johnston was an intensely shy, fastidious man who remained a bachelor all his life and allowed only two of the many new varieties of plants that he raised to be named after himself. While there is no doubt that he was fortunate to be able to finance the creation of his garden as he wished, there was never the sense of great sums of money having been spent, in the way that was immediately noticeable in many of the gardens of his contemporaries. This gives it an appealing air of understatement, which has played an important part in its attraction. John Sales writes: 'The immense influence of Hidcote on gardens of this century is manifest both here and abroad . . . indeed it is difficult to find a country house garden where his ideas have not been used, consciously or unconsciously.'[3]

SIR EDWIN LUTYENS (1869-1944)

ABBOTSWOOD, *Gloucestershire*; AMMERDOWN PARK, *Somerset*; AMPORT HOUSE, *Hampshire*; ASHY ST LEGERS, *Northamptonshire*; BARTON ST MARY, *Somerset*; BUCKHURST PARK, *Sussex*; DEANERY GARDEN, *Berkshire*; EATON HALL, *Cheshire*; EDNASTON MANOR, *Derbyshire*; FOLLY FARM, *Berkshire*; GLEDSTONE PARK,

In the areas surrounding the house, the garden at Abbotswood contains a
series of skilful architectural features by Edwin Lutyens.

Yorkshire; GODDARDS, *Surrey;* GREAT DIXTER, *Sussex;* GREAT MAYTHAM, *Kent;* GREY WALLS, *Lothian;* HAZELHATCH, *Surrey;* HEATHCOTE, *Yorkshire;* HESTERCOMBE, *Somerset;* HEYWOOD, *Eire;* THE HOO, *Sussex;* LAMBAY CASTLE, *Eire;* LINDISFARNE CASTLE, *Northumberland;* LITTLE THAKEHAM, *Sussex;* LONG BARN, *Kent;* MARSH COURT, *Hampshire;* MELLS PARK, *Somerset;* MUNSTEAD WOOD, *Surrey;* NASHDOM, *Buckinghamshire;* ORCHARDS, *Surrey;* OVERSTRAND HALL, *Norfolk;* THE PLEASAUNCE, *Norfolk;* PUTTERIDGE PARK, *Bedfordshire;* ST PETER'S HOME, *Suffolk;* THE SALUTATION, *Kent;* TEMPLE DINSLEY, *Hertfordshire;* TIGBOURNE COURT, *Surrey;* TYRINGHAM, *Buckinghamshire;* WITTERSHAM HOUSE, *Kent;* WOODWIDE, *Buckinghamshire*

THERE IS NO PARTNERSHIP in garden history comparable to the one between the architect Edwin Lutyens and the gardener Gertrude Jekyll. At a time when garden design was feeling its way towards greater harmony between house and garden, towards reconciling a sense of orderliness with a natural, uncontrived informality, and extolling the virtues of intimate detail, both horticultural and architectural, their combined response appeared to have had all the answers. Today, of all gardening and landscape achievements, only the description 'a house with a 'Capability' Brown park, can conjure up as immediate and vivid an image as 'a Lutyens house with a Jekyll garden'.

Like Brown's exhaustive popularity up and down the country, their partnership emerged from a period of fundamental readjustment in the evolution of gardens to respond to a seemingly limitless demand. As prosperity spread beyond the confined social areas of mercantile or landed grandees, a major preoccupation of the upper middle classes became the tasteful and fashionable improvement of their homes; by the turn of the century this almost always involved the garden as well.

For Edwin Lutyens the early and most productive years of the partnership with Gertrude Jekyll ensured his position as one of the most original and sought-after architects of the period. Lutyens was very much the junior in age and experience, initially learning far more from Miss Jekyll than he would ever teach her, but soon Gertrude Jekyll's designs were to take second place in Lutyens's development as an architect. While her priorities and taste remained constant – though the nature of her contribution varied with each commission – for Lutyens the process involved subtle but constant change; from the vernacular intimacy of Munstead and Orchards he progressed at the height of his career to the impressive but always human-scaled ingenuity of the Deanery at Sonning. At Ammerdown Park, Lutyens was already demonstrating an increasing feel for the purely classical, which was to produce in the immediate pre-war years the relatively small scale of the Salutations and Ednaston Manor, but after the war extended to the austere grandeur of Tyringham and Gledstone Hall – both light years away from his earlier work with Gertrude Jekyll.

Lutyens was born in London, the tenth of thirteen children, nine of them boys. His father had initially followed family tradition by becoming a soldier but left to take up painting; he enjoyed more than a measure of success in this field, and through painting became a close friend of Sir Edwin Landseer, after whom his son was named. Like the Jekylls, the Lutyens moved from London to the country, to Thursley in the south-west corner of Surrey, where Edwin was brought up. Childhood illness kept him from school and he was mainly educated at home. In later life the limitations he felt this imposed upon him showed in self-defensive humorous banter, but it is arguable that deprivation in some areas was compensated for by his extraordinarily retentive memory and ability to commit scenes and ideas to paper in instantaneous but accurate drawings. His years at home also gave him ample time to take in the surrounding countryside and its buildings, a grounding for his future forays with Gertrude Jekyll.

Lutyens grew up determined to become an architect and to follow the Arts and Crafts and Domestic Revival style of Philip Webb. Anxious to get on, and full of nervous energy, he did not complete the architecture course at the South Kensington School of Art (which Jekyll had attended some twenty years earlier) but still managed to get accepted as a pupil in the fashionable architectural practice of Ernest George and Harold Peto (*q.v.* p. 154) where he made a telling impression on his fellow-pupil and lifetime friend and architectural contemporary, Herbert Baker: 'I first met Lutyens there, who, though joking through his short pupilage, quickly absorbed all that was best worth learning; he puzzled us at first, but we soon found that he seemed to know by intuition some great truths of our art that were not learnt there.'[1]

In 1889, on the strength of a commission from an acquaintance in Surrey and after two years' pupilage, Lutyens left and set up practice on his own in Grays Inn in London; he was still only twenty. Later that year he met Gertrude Jekyll and his education as an architect was influenced in a manner that would set him apart from his contemporaries; Jekyll's architect godson, Harold Falkner, says she gave Lutyens the 'sense of material that made him different from all other architects of his time.'[2]

As their early tentative friendship blossomed, fostered by the compatability of two highly gifted but emotionally solitary characters, Lutyens's first architectural priority became the successful and complete fusion of a house and garden. At Munstead he was limited by the fact that much of the garden already existed, but Orchards, the next major commission, was a blank canvas and an opportunity seized, as David Ottewill has described: 'Orchards was the first masterpiece of garden design to spring from the partnership and is especially notable for its unity with the house. A new-found confidence was apparent, and materials, both plants and paving, were treated with restraint. Already the main formal characteristics of their style were established: the projection of the lines of the house outwards along routes and vistas; the multiplication of the forms and materials of the house thereby increasing its apparent size; and the subsequent breaking down of these forms by clothing them with luxuriant, informal planting.'[3]

Orchards was begun in 1897 and for the next ten

years he developed and applied his architectural skills and techniques with unfailing ingenuity and originality to suit the demands of clients and their different situations. The houses bore many similar hallmarks: asymmetrical plans allowing for courtyards and variety; steep gables and deeply pitched tiled roofs; tall, patterned chimney stacks reminiscent of grand Tudor houses. Most telling, however, was the continuation of stylistic features from house to garden, the arch of a doorway repeated in a loggia and extended in a flight of semi-circular steps or a curving garden seat, intricate brickwork repeated in a herringbone-pattern path or a garden wall, varying falls in roof-pitch continued in descending levels in the garden.

In 1897 Lutyens married Lady Emily Lytton, the youngest child of the Earl of Lytton, Viceroy of India during the late 1870s. The countess was a member of both Queen Victoria's and Queen Alexandra's households, and she made clear to Lutyens that he was expected to maintain Emily in suitable style. Once established in practice and in his partnership with Gertrude Jekyll, Lutyens worked unstintingly hard, but his marriage was to add a new edge of ambition as he strove to attain the necessary success that would enable him to indulge his wife. And yet they never managed to move out of London to the more peaceful existence of a house in the country that at times they both fervently hankered for; despite the huge sums involved in many of his projects and his often enormous workload, Lutyens never became a wealthy man.

By 1908 Lutyens's partnership with Gertrude Jekyll had become less important; his architectural practice was increasingly busy (the massive New Delhi commission, for example, was to begin in 1912) and Miss Jekyll, now in her mid sixties and busy with her own books, lacked appetite to leave Munstead. Lutyens's style of garden architecture was also becoming more individual and classical in inspiration. Early signs can be seen in the Italian garden of Ammerdown Park and the Great Plat and pergola at Hestercombe, both in Somerset, but the clearest examples came after the war with the grand formal canal gardens of Gledstone Hall in Yorkshire and Tyringham in

Buckinghamshire. In his earlier gardens Lutyens's preferred treatment of water had always been formal, as in the sunken pool garden at Marsh Court in Hampshire, the tank garden at Deanery Garden and the tank court and canal garden at Folly Farm, but now he was working to an altogether larger scale.

At Gledstone, Lutyens laid out a massive canal in a rectangle between enclosing walls, stretching away from the austerely classical south front of the house he had built for the Lancashire cotton magnate, Amos Nelson. At Tyringham a house by Sir John Soane already existed and Lutyens responded to its imposing façade with his most unequivocally Italianate design: a long canal extending from the house to the full limit of the garden area, its length broken at a cross-axis by a small circular pool with columns surmounted by lead figures. Beside the opposite arms of the cross path Lutyens built a pair of magnificent domed temples echoing the dome in the façade of Soane's house. The garden also answered the recreational demands of its owners in that the first, largest area of the canal was a swimming-pool with broad flights of steps down at both ends, and one of the temples was a changing-house.

In these later commissions Lutyens moved away from the style of garden architecture that he had perfected with Gertrude Jekyll and which was to prove of most lasting influence and importance. Few people of any period could afford to commission gardens on the scale of Gledstone or Tyringham and such clients were to become increasingly rare. By contrast, huge numbers of people were to be imbued with the spirit of a Lutyens house with a Jekyll garden and, if they could not perhaps achieve the standards or intricacy of detail found in the originals, they nevertheless aspired towards it. Lutyens-Jekyll commissions involved a complete interrelation of house and garden; they created places for living in, for relaxation and enjoyment; despite their horticultural and architectural quality, their work was not designed for show or to be admired. This balance that they sought has formed a cornerstone of the 20th-century garden, whether in England,

America or anywhere else in the world, and Lutyens encapsulated his ideals as a garden architect in a letter to his wife: 'A garden scheme should have a backbone – a central idea beautifully phrased. Thus the house wall should spring out of a briar bush – with always the best effect, and every wall, path, stone and flower bed has its similar problem and a relative value to the central idea.'[4]

THOMAS HAYTON MAWSON (1861-1933)

BURTON MANOR, *Cheshire;* DYFFRYN, *Glamorgan;* GRAYTHWAITE HALL, *Cumbria;* THE HILL, *Hampstead, London;* HOLKER HALL, *Cumbria;* LITTLE ONN HALL, *Staffordshire;* MADRESFIELD COURT, *Worcestershire;* MEADOWLANDS, *Cheshire;* ROYNTON COTTAGE, *Lancashire;* RYDAL HALL, *Cumbria;* THORNTON MANOR, *Cheshire;* TIRLEY GARTH, *Cheshire;* WIGHTWICK MANOR, *Staffordshire*

THOMAS MAWSON'S highly industrious career encapsulated much of the steady progress of professional garden-making from the 19th into the 20th century. From humble beginnings as a nurseryman, he ended his career as the first president of the Institute of Landscape Architects, in the process playing a central part in the linking together of garden design with the newly emerging profession of landscape architecture. Mawson demonstrated that it was possible – and professionally highly desirable, given evolving social conditions and demands – to be a garden designer, landscape architect and town planner. With established success came opportunities to make his career international, demonstrating the potential breadth of work that would become increasingly available through the 20th century. Successful entries in international competitions, notably in 1908 when he won the competition to design the gardens of the Palace of Peace in The Hague, initiated much of his work overseas which extended from Greece to Canada.

Much of Mawson's success as a garden designer, over

*Thornton Manor was the most varied design that
Thomas Mawson carried out for his munificent and
sympathetic patron William Lever.*

and above his technical ability, stemmed from the degree to which he was attuned to the demands of clients and the prevalent gardening tastes and priorities of his period. He designed in a manner comparable in general terms – albeit quite different in detail – to the partnership of his contemporaries, Edwin Lutyens (*q.v.* p. 146) and Gertrude Jekyll (*q.v.* p. 138), with a progression from formality immediately around a house, usually in the form of a raised terrace, through intermediate areas to a degree of informality around the perimeters of a garden. Like them, too, his strong admiration for the Arts and Crafts movement was often borne out in the detail of his features such as the stonework in terraces and balustrading.

Mawson's early career was spurred on by intense determination. Born in Lancashire, his childhood was dominated by his father's impecuniousness and young Thomas was forced to leave school at the age of twelve to start earning a living.

His first job was with a builder uncle in Lancaster, where he was able to gain some rudimentary experience in draughtsmanship and was strongly influenced by his uncle's interest in gardening. After his father's death, partly brought about by the business problems by which he had always been plagued, Mawson's mother moved the family to London. Here Thomas worked first for Wills and Seger, a prominent firm of nurserymen and garden designers, and subsequently for another nursery before eventually taking the decision to move back to the north-west of England where, in partnership with his two brothers, he set up the Lakeland Nurseries at Windermere. Mawson's previous experience and hard work kept the business going through its infancy until the plant trade could be supplemented with garden design work that was his exclusive domain.

Inevitably his first commissions were all local, and the most important, which happily survives today, was the garden at Graythwaite Hall, only a few miles from the Lakeland Nurseries on the west side of Lake Windermere, where Mawson worked from 1889 to 1895. For a first major project Graythwaite was admirably ambitious and

illustrated the tenacious confidence that helped Mawson throughout his life. Writing later, he himself recorded what he aspired to achieve at Graythwaite, and gave an interesting insight into his priorities at this early stage in his career: 'The design of these grounds, which is entirely new, is arranged so as to obtain as much of the picturesque as possible.'[1]

His design contained the blend of architecture and planting that was to become a hallmark of his work: formal terraces around the house and neat lawns leading to woodland and water gardens. The terraces that Mawson laid along the south and west fronts of the Graythwaite required extensive excavation but unquestionably improved the presentation of the house, while flights of steps down to the main south lawn sloping away to a battlemented yew hedge along its far boundary. Areas of woodland that originally bounded the garden were thinned to open up vistas and for replanting with more ornamental evergreen species, and a stream was landscaped into a series of bends and cascades with an arched stone bridge. Cowsheds, barns and a smithy were all removed to make way for tree planting, as were the old stables to the east of the house where Mawson laid out a small enclosed Dutch garden. Her yew hedges with low wrought-iron gates on opposite sides surrounded a pattern of box-edged beds, and two rows of domed yew topiary, the top half golden yew, the lower green. The Dutch garden completed the varied composition of the Graythwaite garden that Mawson was to repeat in different ways in many of his future commissions.

In 1900 Mawson dedicated the first edition of his book, *The Art and Craft of Garden Making*, to his client at Graythwaite, Colonel Sandys. Illustrated with watercolours, plans and sketches, the book was an immediate success and ran into five editions; it also enabled Mawson to open an office in London in the following year. However, the event that was to alter the future of Mawson's career most unequivocally was his meeting with a man from his own part of the country, William Hesketh Lever, later to become baronet, baron and finally Viscount

Leverhulme. Lever, a legendary merchandizing philanthropist, had built a model village, Port Sunlight, for his employees in the Wirral in 1888, and three years later bought Thornton Manor three miles away, which became his home. In his book on Edwardian gardens David Ottewill gives an enjoyable insight into Lever's character and his relationship with Mawson: 'In Mawson he had found the ideal person to aid him in his humorous landscaping campaigns. Possessed alike with inexhaustible energy, they shared a similar "High Church Nonconformist", Lancashire background and, as an architect manqué with definite ideas of his own and the ability to transfer them to paper, Lever was likely to find someone of Mawson's down-to-earth approach, and horticultural rather than architectural background, more accommodating than any of the leading garden architects.'[1]

The meeting took place in 1905, after Mawson had written to Lever asking for a donation towards work he had carried out in a local church. Lever had replied, 'Now that you have had the courage to ask me for a subscription, may I be so bold as to ask you to come and advise me upon the improvement of my garden at Thornton Manor? I have wanted to consult you for the last two years, but all my friends have warned me that it would be useless, as you never worked for anyone holding less social rank than a Duke, whereas I am only a poor and indigent soapmaker. Let me know if you can come.'[2] Lever had already amassed a pile of requisites for his garden at Thornton and it was these that formed the basis of their joint design. Lever explained to Mawson the purpose of his garden: 'I am afraid I do not want a garden so much for rest as for promenades and walks. I have tried sitting down in the retreats and garden shelters, but I cannot rest in them two minutes, but on the contrary I can walk about for a couple of hours at a time along the long stretch of walk I have made in the centre.'[3]

The 'long stretch of walk' Lever refers to was to a path extending away from the house right through the centre of the garden, descending in successive flights of steps to a sunken circular rose garden at the far end. Mawson described Thornton as, 'a formal garden of heroic proportions'[4] and although not exclusively formal it was certainly heroic. Mawson made a rectangular area parallel to the main path into a garden forum, with two rose pergolas 70m/105yds long, their Tuscan pillars made of concrete (one of Lever's innovations), and a parallel walk between pleached limes and clipped holly hedges. Mawson also built an impressive fernery next to the house, which had its own stream cascading from a rockery and leading to a conservatory.

Beyond the rose garden and garden forum he satisfied Lever's need for exercise with a series of walks through the surrounding woods, lined with clipped hedges or banks of shrubs. The walks take in many of Mawson's features, such as the lake of some 8 ha/20 acres that was formed out of a formal canal that Mawson had made earlier and the dell.

Mawson continued to work at Thornton until 1914, and also turned his attention to Lever's other gardens, at the remote estate on Rivington moor outside Lever's native Bolton, and at his London home. The Hill, in Hampstead. Although neither of these gardens survive in comparable condition to Thornton they do still give a good impression of the scope of Mawson's work. Rivington Pike was a superbly romantic site with hillsides dropping steeply away from Lever's Roynton Cottage. By the time Mawson had finished landscaping the surroundings with winding paths, flights of steps, a long arcaded pergola built of local millstone, rockeries, a selection of architectural features and extensive planting of ericaceous plants in the inhospitable surroundings, he was able to write with satisfaction that, 'of all the gardens which have administered to my professional enjoyment, none comes into competition with Roynton.'[5]

The garden at The Hill was planned for entertainment and was the most ornately decorative of all three. Mawson demonstrated canny acquisitiveness when he acquired the spoil from the excavation of Hampstead tube station and used it to build up the terraces from which a double flight of curving steps descended to a formal pool.

As one can still see today in the part of the garden accessible to the public, the pergola layout at The Hill, with its elaborate latticed framework supported by magnificent Tuscan columns in Portland stone, was certainly remarkable. The main pergola enclosed two sides of the formal garden but beyond, further extensions were added, in particular an arm extending via a bridge over the public footpath bordering the heath, and out into the west heath. From a temple a further line of pergola extended away again.

Lord Leverhulme's philanthropic leanings undoubtedly influenced Mawson's interest in town planning and public parks, and one of his most extensive schemes was carried out in Leverhulme's home town of Bolton. By the early 1920s Mawson was acknowledged as the senior figure in the profession, and the presidency of the Town-Planning Institute in 1923 was followed six years later by the presidency of the newly formed Institute of Landscape Architects. During the last few years of his life ill-health gradually forced him into retirement but, as David Ottewill writes, this only came at the end of a remarkably prolific career: 'Mawson's output was prodigious and owed much to his business acumen, professional competence and the firm foundation of his experience with Lakeland Nurseries. An ingenious scheme like The Hill, for instance, depended for its realization on a high degree of technical knowledge for landscaping. While he could turn his hand to many styles . . . most of his designs were monumental in character, Italianate in style, with Beaux-Arts discipline in layout, befitting the life-style of his Edwardian clients. At times his work appears rather hard and mechanical, lacking the warmth, human scale and exuberant planting of the typical Lutyens and Jekyll garden. But more often than not this was the logical outcome of a different regional context, and to some extent reflected Mawson's personal background. It is not difficult to see why he felt so much more at home with a kindred spirit like Lever and a rugged, windswept site like Rivington, than in the more protected and comfortable world of the "Surrey School".'[6]

HAROLD AINSWORTH PETO (1854-1933)

BUSCOT PARK, *Oxfordshire;* GARINISH ISLAND, *Eire;* HEALE HOUSE, *Wiltshire;* IFORD MANOR, *Wiltshire;* WAYFORD MANOR, *Somerset*

HAROLD PETO was born into the large family of the building and railway magnate Sir Samuel Morton Peto, the eighth of his father's fourteen children. When Harold was aged only nine huge mounting debts forced Sir Samuel to sell Somerleyton Hall, the lavish Italianate house he had built on the Suffolk coast, surrounded by gardens designed by William Nesfield and Joseph Paxton. The young child must have absorbed more than a fleeting memory of Nesfield's parterre and maze, Paxton's glasshouses and the fantastic winter garden built by his father's architect, John Thomas, for his future work as architect and garden designer gives the impression of being a clear reaction against the opulent style of his childhood. However, his mother's personal finances ensured that the family were brought up comfortably. Harold was sent to Harrow where one of his friends was the American Willie James, for whom he later built a superb Italian pergola at West Dean, James's celebrated home in Sussex.

In 1876 Peto established an architectural partnership with Ernest George; it was to become one of the most respected practices of the late Victorian and Edwardian periods, and in 1886 took on Edwin Lutyens (*q.v.* p. 146) as a pupil. Peto's architectural work was rooted in his admiration for renaissance Italy, and this primary source of inspiration also encouraged his growing interest in the links between house and garden. By the 1890s he was keen to get away from the restrictions of an architectural practice and partnership and, in 1892, parted company with George and set up on his own, offering garden and interior design as well as garden architecture. Peto's garden work demonstrated a feel for plants, though his use of plants was always controlled by his highly tuned architectural principles: 'The entirely subordinate place in the scheme that flowers occupy gives a breadth and quietude

The formal water garden at Buscot Park was Harold Peto's outstanding creation.

to the whole which is sympathetic, the picture being painted with hedges, canals and water tanks, broad walks with seats and statues and tall cypresses. If more of our English gardens could have an increase of this influence it would be well instead of their running riot in masses of colour irrespective of form.'[1] Such emphasis on horticultural form would have especially appealed to Gertrude Jekyll (*q.v.* p. 138), who included a flattering number of descriptions of Peto's gardens in her *Garden Ornament*.

Throughout his life Peto was an avid collector of classical artefacts and these were displayed in his own garden at Iford Manor which he bought in 1899 and where he remained for the rest of his life. After leaving the partnership, Peto worked extensively in the south of France, which was becoming fashionable for English people towards the end of the 19th century, and Iford combines the spirit of renaissance Italy with a feel for the warm Mediterranean coast. The house overlooks the steep valley of the River Frome, an ideal natural setting for the garden Peto was to create in a series of irregular terraces behind and to one side of the house. No doubt because it was his own, he was able to indulge in an uninhibited – although carefully ordered – eclecticism in the garden's decoration (something that was always subdued in his work elsewhere), with the result that the garden presents a treasure-trove of architectural features and classical remains.

At one end of the largest terrace, lined with statues, busts, urns, vases, columns and sarcophagi, an octagonal summerhouse, dating from the 18th century, was restored by Peto to become the focal point of the garden's main axis. In the centre is one of Peto's most successful and theatrical areas of the garden: an open colonnade with in front an urn set on a small balustraded terrace, overlooking broad stone steps that lead down to an oval pool and open grass terrace. Elsewhere steep flights of stone steps are decorated or flanked with urns and figures. As well as a *casita* with ancient pillars of Verona marble, Peto created the Cloister inside a simple stone building. Arcaded cloister walks extend around all four sides and it was here that Peto arranged most of his smaller antiquities and artefacts.

Throughout the garden the shades and textures of the different stone work were enhanced by planting, and evergreen cypress and juniper trees added to the Italian atmosphere. Today the garden survives in an admirable state – an ideal memorial to Peto's work.

Iford became the centre from which Peto worked on his most successful garden commissions before the outbreak of World War I; his three best preserved gardens are all within easy reach of his home. Without question his most masterly design was the water garden at Buscot Park in Oxfordshire, created for Lord Faringdon around 1904. Buscot already had impressive surroundings, including a large walled garden and two lakes set at a distance, as well as an extensive park. Peto's water garden was cut through trees to the east of the house, one of three vistas extending from the east terrace. This one had views to the lake and a glimpse of a temple on the far side; the other two looked along avenues. Peto's design encloses the long narrow water garden with clipped box hedging that projects and curves inside the flanking woodland, and the water drops gently through a system of formal canals and pools decorated with fountains and a small bridge, and flanked by classical statues; it shows a brilliant combination of architectural restraint and variation, depending, in true renaissance garden tradition, upon maximizing a simple theme by achieving spacial and material proportion.

At Heale House in Wiltshire Peto was employed by the Hon Louis Greville who had bought the beautiful Carolean house in 1890 and commissioned Detmar Blow to add a wing in matching style. (Peto's commission probably came through Greville's sister-in-law, Daisy, Countess of Warwick, whose garden at Easton Lodge in Essex – since disappeared – Peto had transformed.) Heale's setting is formed by the River Avon curving lazily around the south and east sides and it was here that Peto made his major contribution, linking the house to the river on two angles in an elegant design of broad terraces with balustraded retaining walls and steps. On the opposite, west, side of house, Peto also planned the vista which rises gently in three levels from a broad paved terrace in front of the house, along a central path to an old copper planter on the top cross terrace. His plans for the garden were never completely implemented, but today his architectural design provides an ideal framework for the replanting that has been carried out by the present owners.

Peto's third garden at Wayford Manor on the borders of Somerset and Dorset was laid out on a very similar hillside slope to that of Iford; it belonged to his sister Helen and her husband Lawrence Baker. If the decoration was more restrained than at Iford, the architectural framework was equally fundamental to Peto's concept of the garden. The Bakers had added to the Elizabethan house to restore its original E-shape, and in the forecourt between the house and farm buildings Peto laid out a simple formal pattern of yew-hedged enclosures. The main terrace below shows the strongest Italian influence. Built between the house and the slope of the garden below, it leads from ancient horse chestnuts at one end to an arched loggia that Peto added onto the house at the other. In the centre the terrace's balustrade is broken by steps leading to the garden's main path which descends to a lower grass terrace and down a slope to a water garden at the bottom. Below the horse chestnuts Peto gave the garden its most delightful feature – a small formal lily pool partially enclosed by walls and shaded by acers. Its presence only betrayed by its fountain, it is a true evocation of a *giardino segreto* of the Italian Renaissance.

Peto's last major commission before the war, which effectively ended his garden design work, was neither in England nor the south of France – where he carried out many commissions during the early 1900s – but on the romantic Irish island of Garinish, just off the coast of County Cork. In this remote but sheltered spot he created his most assured garden, combining classical inspiration with an evocation of Moorish gardens – especially in the small pool garden – and using plants that revelled in the island's exceptionally mild maritime conditions. The island's owner, John Annan Bryce, used the house and garden as a retreat, Peto displayed enormous sensitivity in the atmosphere that he created.

WILLIAM ROBINSON (1838-1935)

GRAVETYE MANOR, *Sussex*

WILLIAM ROBINSON, an Irishman, worked for many years as a practical gardener; later, he was to have a dramatic influence on the development of gardens through his forthright writing in which he castigated Victorian formal Italianate and parterre gardening, advocating a more natural style. He was a man of many complexities, about whom opinion was always divided: Gertrude Jekyll was unstinting in her admiration for his gardening ideas and was undoubtedly influenced by him in her own work, whereas Edwin Lutyens once described him as a 'foozle-headed old bore'.[1] Certainly his irascibility and vehement manner were not universally popular and, at a time when appearances were deemed important, he was undoubtedly less socially acceptable than Jekyll, Lutyens or his main antagonist, Sir Reginald Blomfield (*q.v.* p. 133). Nonetheless, there is no doubting the importance to his contemporaries of his writing. At a time when the shortcomings of Victorian gardens were mainfestly obvious and alternatives were being searched for, Robinson spelt out in battling terms what was wrong and what was to be done.

Throughout his life Robinson was reticent about his Irish upbringing and it is probable that a passionate desire to prove himself capable of escaping from this background fired the ambition that eventually brought him both reputation and a considerable fortune. We do know that he became a gardener at a young age and had a number of years' experience behind him when he began work at the Irish National Botanic Garden at Glasnevin. In 1861 he left Ireland for London and a job at the Royal Botanic Gardens in Regent's Park, and it was here that his gardening future was largely formulated. In England he was brought into direct contact with the excesses of Victorian gardening that he was soon to condemn, while in his work at Regent's Park his particular domain was the collection of hardy herbaceous plants – which led him to study and form a fierce affection for native perennials. His status was still relatively lowly, but appreciation of his ability was demonstrated in 1866 when he was elected a fellow of the Linnean Society at the age of twenty-nine. Shortly afterwards he left Regent's Park to embark on a full-time career as a freelance garden writer.

Robinson had already contributed articles to various gardening journals and his main work for the first few years was as horticultural correspondent to *The Times*, though he also wrote for *The Gardener's Chronicle* and *The Field*. His first two books, *Gleanings from French Gardens* (1868) and *The Parks, Promenades and Gardens of Paris* (1869) came as a result of some months spent in France, initially to write about the Paris Exhibition. His experience of the French gardening world evoked a characteristically extreme and mixed response, dislike of French gardens being matched conversely by unstinting admiration for their gardening techniques and tools. It was not until his third book, *Alpine Flowers for English Gardens* (1870), that his specific ideas about the potential improvements to English gardens began to be put into words, and his next book, *The Wild Garden*, published in the same year, mounted the campaign in earnest. The key to the book's arguments was Robinson's advocacy of planting native species – usually only seen in the wild – in a natural and uncontrived setting. The book had its detractors, many of them qualified and highly respected such as Theresa Earle, who wrote: 'In spite of all the charming things Mr Robinson says about it "wild gardening" is, I am sure, a delusion and a snare and must be taken with a great many pinches of salt.'[2] The book, however, was an instant success and had continued to be read ever since – the last edition was in 1983.

In 1871 Robinson took the decisive step of his career when he founded the weekly publication, *The Garden*, which soon became the most widely read gardening journal of the period. It gave him a regular outlet for his ideas, for his criticism of those he saw to be his opponents, and for the dissemination of an enormous quantity of information to the ranks of middle-class would-be gardeners. In 1883 he collected together much of this material, with

additions, into *The English Flower Garden*, the book which proved to be the cornerstone of his reputation. Hugely successful – fifteen editions appeared before his death, many of them reprinted more than once – the book was divided into two sections, the first describing Robinson's suggested gardening methods and appropriate plants, citing individual gardens as examples; the second and larger being a comprehensive catalogue of plants, shrubs and trees grown in Britain at the time. *The English Flower Garden* became something of a text book for Robinson's most ardent disciples, and naturalized bulbs, mixed borders and areas of natural woodland garden among his most treasured garden features – became as fashionable as neat rows of bright summer annuals had been earlier in century.

His journals and books, which continued to appear after *The English Flower Garden*, brought Robinson both reputation and material reward, and in 1885 he purchased the property of Gravetye Manor in Sussex, which he was to expand to nearly a thousand acres before his death. Some of his contemporaries were amused by Robinson's seigneurial attitude to his property and by the elements of formality that he incorporated into the garden, including terracing and a bowling green, pergolas and trellis, and neat plots for different varieties of plants, divided by symmetrical paved paths. But despite these apparent concessions to the opposition, Gravetye was true to many of his principles in its planting, perhaps especially in the extensive areas of woodland where he mixed native and exotic trees with flowering shrubs, and in the Alpine meadow of naturalized bulbs that sloped away from one side of the main garden down to the lake. Although the garden fell into decline after his death and the largest areas of woodland became Forestry Commission property in 1935, the main parts of the garden have recently been restored around a country house hotel.

When Robinson died, unmarried, aged ninety-seven, his horticultural battles were long over – the evidence of his influence could be found in gardens all over the country; but a glance at the foreword to one of the editions of *The English Flower Garden* gives a flavour of his writing

The planting in William Robinson's garden at Gravetye Manor is mainly restored, but in the style he advocated so vehemently.

and an indication of the crusade that he considered he had waged: 'This book is the muster of various once forlorn hopes and skirmishing parties now united with better arms and larger aims, and its beginnings may have an interest for others. I came to London just when the Royal Horticultural Society's garden at Kensington was being laid out, a series of elaborate patterns set at different levels, and the Crystal Palace, in its glory, was described by the Press of the day to be the most wonderful instance of modern gardening – water-temples, water-paths, vast stone basins and all the theatrical gardening of Versailles reproduced in Surrey.

'There was little or no reason admitted into garden design; the same poor imitation of the Italian garden being set down in all sorts of positions. If the place did not suit the style, the ground had to be bolstered up in some way so that the plan might be carried out – a costly way to get an often ridiculous result . . .. The flower garden planting was made up of a few kinds of flowers which people were proud to put out in thousands and tens of thousands, and with these, patterns, more or less elaborate, were carried out in every garden save the very poorest cottage garden. It was not easy to get away from all this false and hideous "art", but I was then in the Botanic Gardens, Regent's Park, where there was at the time a small garden of British plants, which had to be kept up, and this led me into the varied country round London, from the orchid-flecked meadows of Bucks to the tumbled down undercliffs on the Essex coast, untroubled by the plough; and so I began to get all idea (which should be taught to every boy at school) that there was (for gardens even) much beauty in our native flowers and trees, and then came the thought that if there was so much in our own island flora, what might we not look for from the hills and valleys of the countries of the northern and temperate world?

'From thoughts of this kind I turned to actual things, I saw the flower-gardener meanly trying to rival the tile or wallpaper men, and throwing aside with contempt all the lovely things that through their height or form did not conform to this idea (so stupid as to life), and this too the

rule, not only in the villa garden, but in our own great public and private gardens. There was, happily, always the beauty of the woods and lanes and the lovely cottage gardens in the country round London, and here and there, though rare, a quiet garden with things as the great mother made them and grouped them. And so I began to see clearly that the common way was a great error and the greatest obstacle of true gardening or artistic efforts of any kind in the flower-garden or home landscape, and then made up my mind to fight the thing out in any way open to me.'[3]

SIR GEORGE RERESBY SITWELL, Bt (1860-1943)

RENISHAW HALL, *Derbyshire*

SIR GEORGE SITWELL was an important figure in the tradition of patrician, landowning and gifted amateurs who have been making gardens since the 16th century. Using his love and deep knowledge of Italian gardens, Sir George created at the family seat, Renishaw Hall in Derbyshire, the most satisfying Italianate garden of the period, a place true to its renaissance inspiration and yet which fitted perfectly into its English surroundings. Sir George was a man of obsessive interests, likes and dislikes, and though few of his passions ever produced anything worthwhile, his devotion to Italian gardens produced both the garden at Renishaw and – later – his small book, *On the Making of Gardens*, published in 1909.

Sir George was highly strung all his life, and after suffering a nervous breakdown in 1900 he spent increasing amounts of time in Italy, initially collecting material for his book. He had been MP for Scarborough, the home town of his wife, Lady Ida, daughter of the Earl of Londesborough, but he gave up his seat and most of his other activities in England after his illness. In 1906 he bought the Castello di Montegufoni outside Florence, and in 1925 left England to live there permanently. Sir George's idiosyncracies and the creation of his garden at Renishaw are wonderfully evoked in the autobiography of Osbert, the eldest of his three literary children; the garden in Renishaw's inauspicious surroundings ('an oasis in an industrial desert', as one visitor described it) was also described by the youngest, Sacheverell, late in his life. 'How well I remember walking with my father in the gardens at Renishaw, which he designed and made. Indeed he landscaped the entire view for nearly as far as one could see, down to and beyond the lake at the bottom of the hill . . . It is perhaps typical of him and his fraternity that it was garden design that interested him, and he was himself uninterested in flowers – almost to the point of disliking them. I cannot remember his ever admiring one and I even believe that he rather resented flowers because they took the attention away from garden design. My old home at Renishaw, where I lived as a child, had no garden on its south side. There was just a sloping lawn and my father – if I may be allowed to use the expression – "masterminded" – the terraces that now stretch down the hill. The lake he made with the help of a number of unemployed from Scarborough, his other home and at that time his constituency.'[1]

These terraces, geometric but varying in size, and linked by paths and vistas, descended from the long battlemented façade of the house. Structure was provided by yew hedges, by whose size the young Osbert gauged his early progress: 'He made the great garden lay-out at Renishaw just before I was born, and I grew up, year by year, with its yew hedges. I never remember a time between the ages of three and seventeen when we were not the same height . . ..'[2] In true Italian tradition the garden was flanked by *bosci*, on one side woodland, on the other a lime avenue on a raised terrace which looked down onto the lower terraces of the garden. The central cross-axis of the garden ran from this terrace along a retaining wall to a gateway into the wood on the far side. On the lower terraces the central vista was across a circular pool with four symmetrical square recesses and, in enclosures on either side, a bowling-lawn and a secret formal water garden, access to which was gained over a small iron bridge. The yew hedges terminating in pyramids are comparable to Athelhampton, designed by Sir George's cousin, Francis Inigo Thomas (*q.v.* p. 162), but there is no evidence that Thomas was consulted at Renishaw. Despite Sir George's reservations about flowers, Gertrude Jekyll was consulted for advice about the planting of certain borders and the rose garden to one side of the main lawn on the upper terrace.

The construction of the garden was an absorbing and at times tortuous task for Sir George, which for weeks on end kept him busy from early in the morning until dusk. 'He walks up and down, surveying his work, which will never be finished, his head full of new projects of sun and shade, but never of flowers, measuring the various views with a stick to his eye or a pair of binoculars. Sometimes he is planning a boat of stone upon the lake, or a dragon in lead . . . for projects such as these, though most of them never materialized, he would cause wooden towers, built up of planks and joists and beams – like an early machine for seige warfare or a drawing by Piranese – to be erected here and there at the right points of vantage. In the summer he would spend many hours aloft on these platforms, with a large grey hat or grey umbrella to shield his light-coloured skin and eyes from the sun . . .'[3].

Despite all the day-to-day complications of the garden's creation Sir George never lost sight of his primary principle, learnt from Italian gardens, that a garden should never be made or considered in isolation, but as part of the larger landscape – a principle to which he returned regularly in *On the Making of Gardens*: 'We should abandon the struggle to make nature beautiful round the house and should rather move the house to where nature is beautiful.'[4]

The finishing touch to the Renishaw garden which gave it its abiding Italian flavour were the series of over-life-size statues, notably two outstanding pairs, which Sir George brought back from Italy. Initially the central steps down from the first main lawn to the lower terrace were flanked by modest obelisks but eventually these were banished to a less prominent part of the garden and their place taken by superb white marble figures of Diana and Neptune, reputed to be by Caligari. Beyond the main pool, on the garden's furthest retaining wall and flanking the semi-circular flight of steps that lead to the descending hillside, were placed a second similar pair – the Giants (Samson and Hercules). Once these figures were in position, looking outwards away from the house to the landscape beyond, Sir George's central vista was complete. Today the Renishaw gardens are maintained by Sir George's descendants exactly as he left them, save for the simplification of planting in most areas and the removal of some borders.

FRANCIS INIGO THOMAS (1866-1950)

ATHELHAMPTON MANOR, *Dorset;* BARROW COURT, *Avon;*
CHANTMARLE, *Dorset*

FRANCIS INIGO THOMAS was a well connected and versatile artist, an architect, garden-designer and painter who designed some of the most evocative revivalist formal gardens of the turn of the century. The son of a Yorkshire parson, he was a first cousin of Sir George Sitwell (*q.v.* p. 160), but unlike Sir George, who took his inspiration for his garden at Renshaw from renaissance Italy, Thomas's inspiration was rooted in 17th-century England. In 1903, shortly after returning from fighting in the Boer War, Thomas painted an elegant self-portrait in full hunting gear that has a comparable period air to Sargent's celebrated portrait of Lord Ribblesdale in similar attire. Thomas lived a bachelor life in Chelsea until his death, and, never driven by necessity, combined the life of a gentleman of leisure with architecture, painting and garden design.

Ten years younger than Reginald Blomfield (*q.v.* p. 133), Thomas also went to Haileybury and it was possibly this connection that brought about their collaboration in *The Formal Garden in England* (1892), Thomas providing the illustrations which gave the book so much of its quality. After Haileybury he went on to Pembroke College, Oxford where he decided to become an architect. On leaving university he joined the practice of the Gothic revivalists Bodley and Garner, where he remained until 1880, after which he travelled extensively on the continent, studying buildings and gardens, and painting and sketching. His first commission when he returned was for a cousin, the future Marquess of Willingdon, Viceroy of India, but largely due to Willington's forthright wife – whose taste was so questionable that Lutyens was later to write about her, 'if she possessed the Parthenon she would add bay windows to it'[1] – the project was not a success, and an invitation to work at the 16th-century Athelhampton Manor in Dorset must have come as an agreeable contrast. The house had been bought by Alfred Cart de Lafontaine in 1891 in a state of disrepair, and by the time he approached Thomas Lafontaine had already carried out some sensitive restoration. He commissioned Thomas to complete work on the house and, more importantly, to design gardens that would evoke the house's Tudor and Stuart past. It was a project to which Thomas was ideally suited. He laid out the gardens to the south and east of the house, planning a series of geometric enclosures and vistas who stemmed from the combination of simplicity and subtlety, notably in the change of levels and scale of enclosures. The main axis extends from the large Great Court to the south, descending via steps and through a narrow wrought-iron gateway to the contrastingly intimate circular Corona and on through a further gateway to the rectangular Private garden in front of a balustraded terrace along the house's east façade.

The small Corona is the hub of Thomas's design in that as well as the main axis another extends at right-angles towards the house's forecourt and in the opposite direction eastward. In the Corona a pool and fountain is surrounded by walls of warm Ham stone surmounted by a coronet pattern of curves and obelisks. Behind the walls clipped yew hedges enhance the sense of enclosure.

*Francis Inigo Thomas's garden at Athelhampton
Manor was designed to complement the Tudor
period of the house's architecture.*

In the Great Court a square sunken lawn was originally decorated with a pattern of flowerbeds around another formal pool and fountain. On the outer corners of each group of flowerbeds were clipped yew pyramids, which have subsequently grown to over 6m/20ft high, their size enhanced by the removal of the flowerbeds. Around the sunken lawn raised walks lead to a raised terrace where Thomas built a matching pair of pavilions. From this raised terrace the central view back across the descending levels of the garden, between yew pyramids and from one pool and fountain to the next, best captures the quality of Thomas's work. Subsequent extensions to the garden and alterations to the planting have done nothing to impair his design.

The Formal Garden In England was published while Thomas was working at Athelhampton, and though Blomfield as author benefited more from the book's success, Thomas's reputation was undoubtedly enhanced by the knowledge of gardens and artistic skill that were shown in the illustrations.

In the same year that the book appeared Thomas began work on his next major surviving garden – although one that is little known compared to Athelhampton – Barrow Court just outside Bristol. Thomas found an existing garden not ideally related to the Jacobean house and adjoining church which formed an L-shape. Rather than attempting to integrate the house more fully by developing the garden around it, he concentrated on making strong formal vistas that extended the garden outwards to take advantage of the view to the north-west over descending parkland. He then replanned the existing formal garden into a pattern of yew-hedged flowerbeds around a central pool, overlooked from one side by a long grass terrace with intimate walled enclosures at either end. Steps in the centre of the terrace led to Thomas's new main vista which began as a broad tennis lawn and led, at its park boundary, to his most dramatic addition to the whole garden: a semicircular wrought-iron screen, its sections divided by stone piers supporting busts representing the twelve months and broken in the centre by highly decorative wrought-iron

gates between monumental stone piers supporting finials. From here the central vista continued beyond the lawn through shrubberies and a lime walk to a smaller curving recess at the far end. In the curving screen and enormous lawn Thomas was creating something far more theatrical and Italianate than the more enclosed formal garden nearer the house, or, indeed, than his work at Athelhampton.

During the years immediately before World War I Thomas began work on his last major garden design, at Chantmarle, a Jacobean house in the Dorset village of Frome St Quentin. To one side of the house the ground dropped in a steady slope, and in a pattern similar to those of his previous gardens Thomas linked this area to the house's forecourt with a design around two major axes at right-angles. Beyond the forecourt he built a long canal under a high stone wall, with a parallel grass walk bounded by a yew hedge on the far side, The canal extended beyond the limit of the forecourt and where it crossed the axis at right-angles Thomas placed a pair of obelisks on the retaining wall. Between them the vista extended across a circular balustraded lily pond shrouded by four Irish yews and up successive flights of stone steps. These led first to a croquet lawn surrounded by clipped box hedging, and then on to a higher grass walk to the boundary, which was marked by wrought-iron gates between stone piers.

Thomas carried out no further garden designs after World War I although he lived to be well over eighty and in spite of the fact that his architectural style was still widely fashionable in the 1920s, and the quality of his work well known. Because of the small number surviving commissions, Thomas is little known today: he deserves better recognition.

ERNEST HENRY WILSON (*1876-1930*)

AS DAVID DOUGLAS was the most celebrated and important plant-collector to work in the United States, so

E. H. Wilson was among the collectors who went east, to China and the Himalayas. On the quantity of plants that he discovered during this career – some 3,000 and, more decisive, the 1,000 or so of these that were successfully introduced into western gardens he was the single most productive plant-collector in history. For the first half of his career he worked for the Veitch nursery, throughout the 19th-century a leading force in plant-collecting. As Veitch began to decline during the early 1900s and as a result of contact made during his early career, Wilson subsequently worked for the Arnold Arboretum which was part of Harvard University and, by the turn of the century, the most active and prestigious horticultural institution in the United States. For the Arnold Arboretum he expanded his field of activity from China to Japan, Australia, New Zealand and Africa and eventually became the institution's resident director.

Wilson typified all the best qualities of plant-collectors through the ages; great knowledge combined with an unending zest for new discoveries and enormous tenacity and powers of endurance. Having worked in a nursery in Solihull he joined the Royal Botanic Garden at Kew as a student aged twenty-one and two years later was recommended by the director to the Veitch nursery who were looking for a suitable candidate to send to China. In 1899 the twenty-three-year-old Wilson sailed for China via the United States, having never left England before in his life. The main purpose of his trip was to find the *Davidia involucrata*, the 'Pocket-Handkerchief Tree' reports of which had been sent to Veitch by a resident contact in China, an Irishman called Augustine Henry. Wilson spent three years in China at the height of the Boxer Uprising, when Europeans were regularly violently attacked. Wilson met up with Henry who directed him to the remote valley where – twelve years earlier – he had seen the davidia. When Wilson eventually arrived the tree had been cut down by a local tribesman who had used it to build his cabin. Undaunted, Wilson pressed on to other areas convinced that he would find the tree. After travelling for over a thousand miles, often on foot, he was eventually rewarded and returned to England in 1902 with the valuable davidia seed, as well as quantities of plants.

He returned to China for Veitch a year later, again with the commission to find one specific plant, *Meconopsis integrifolia*, the yellow-flowered 'Lampshade' poppy. In a trip lasting only a year Wilson again returned successful and laden with a variety of new species. Wilson had stopped at the Arnold Arboretum en route to China on his first trip and it was for them that he made his last two trips to China, in 1907 and 1910. On the second of these trips he enjoyed possibly his most celebrated success when he returned with quantities of Regale lily bulbs which became one of the most popular of all garden plants. It was a trip when he nearly died of starvation was attacked by bandits and when his leg was crushed in a landslide, but the discovery was the most rewarding of his whole career. Having travelled 1,800 miles up the River Yangtze from Shanghai and a further 250 miles up the small tributary of the River Min he came into a small valley where thousands of lilies were in flower; 'for a brief season this lily transforms a lonely semi-desert into a veritable fairyland.'

Wilson had earned himself the epithet 'Chinese' Wilson before the age of thirty-five and when he subsequently visited Japan he was equally successful. For many years the Japanese had jealously guarded the evergreen Kurume azaleas, one of their horticultural prizes, but Wilson demonstrated similar tact as he had done with the Chinese when James Veitch commented, 'he was unusually sympathetic to the Chinese temperament', and was rewarded with double aspect group of azaleas which became known as 'Wilson's fifty' and have proved hugely popular in gardens in both America and Europe. Eventually he succeeded C. S. Sargeant, who had been director when Wilson first visited the Arnold Arboretum in 1899, as director of the institute but having escaped countless numerous brushes with death on his expeditions he was killed in a motor accident while visiting England in 1930 aged only 45.

BRITISH AND AMERICAN STYLE
1920-1950

IN 1920 GERTRUDE JEKYLL (*q.v.* p. 138) was an old lady of seventy-seven who virtually never left her home at Munstead Wood while Edwin Lutyens (*q.v.* p. 146), the most admired architect of his generation, was doing very different work from their joint commissions. Nevertheless, the influence of their early work together was to be all-pervading during the inter-war years and indeed on into the period after World War II. The partnership would not in any event have survived in the post-World War I conditions. The economic and social security of the Edwardian era had all but disappeared and many people were to look to gardens to provide an alternative form of security and tranquillity – havens in an uncertain world.

As the availability of cheap labour shrunk dramatically, more people gardened themselves and the architecture/garden design commissions that had flowed during the Edwardian years diminished. There continued to be grandiose flourishes: Lutyens's design at Gledstone Hall and Tyringham; Sir Philip Sassoon's Port Lympne; Achille Duchêne's water terraces at Blenheim Palace; but they were the exception. The tendency was for gardens to become more thoughtful and understated, their display seasonal and horticultural, rather

The small-scale harmony of formally enclosed
areas of varied planting created by Lawrence Johnston at Hidcote has
become a twentieth-century ideal.

than the conspicuous permanent ornamental statements of earlier times which had become prohibitively expensive for most people.

It is fair to say that the majority of interesting new designs of this period were carried out by Americans, and, in the United States Gertrude Jekyll's greatest admirer was Beatrix Farrand (*q.v.* p. 174), who became the most important garden designer of the inter-war years on both sides of the Atlantic. Like Lutyens and Jekyll, Farrand demonstrated an extraordinary ability to maintain the minutest attention to detail throughout a large and complex garden design. Although her gardens were sometimes of impressive size, grandiose effect was never a priority. Instead, historical gardening traditions were interpreted to suit, and the overriding consideration, whether in England or America, was for the qualities of an individual site (especially relevant at Dartington Hall in England), and of its surrounding landscape (as at Dumbarton Oaks in America). Farrand's successful work, like that of A. J. Downing (*q.v.* p. 108) exactly a hundred years earlier, demonstrated that national gardening traditions could be adopted to a specific site and the requirements of individual clients in either country.

Farrand's work contained formal characteristics but was not traditionally classical; rather it interpreted these traditions and applied them in a contemporary manner. This approach to garden design was taken further by another American, Fletcher Steele (*q.v.* p. 181), who moved on from designing formal architectural gardens fashionable among his wealthy clients in the 1920s, to applying modernist principles to classical traditions in the 1930s. An admirer of le Corbusier, Steele demonstrated that modernism could be applied to garden design through attention to texture and spatial arrangements and through strong unity with surrounding landscape.

For another American, Jans Jensen, the use of trees and plants native to a particular area – in his case the mid-West – was of paramount importance and his work represented an important affirmation of the naturalism that had long been an American gardening tradition. Jensen's contemporary Frank Lloyd Wright was the prime mover in what became known as the 'Prairie school' of modern architects and Jensen's design became known correspondingly as the 'Prairie style'. His open informal designs led to commissions for a number of public parks but his major private work was for the Ford family in Michigan, in particular for Edsell Ford, son of the founder of the motor car empire. Jensen's Edsell Ford Estate is dominated by his planting of native hardwood trees, especially oaks and maples, spaced and planted in groups on open lawn to maximize individual features such as autumn foliage.

After World War II Thomas Church and other leading figures of the California School whose careers had begun during the 1930s, were applying modernism to garden design in a style that was both radical and highly suitable to the Californian surroundings in which they worked. In England, gardening tradition was sufficiently deeply entrenched to resist a widespread application of modernist principles; pure modernism, as advocated by Christopher Tunnard (*q.v.* p. 182), had made little headway in England before 1939 when Tunnard emigrated to the United States. What did emerge, however, was that modernist and abstract ideas and features could be integrated into garden and landscape design far more readily than into either architecture or the decorative arts – where the obvious stylistic differences made the achievement of common ground difficult to attain. During the early years of his long career, for example, Geoffrey Jellicoe (*q.v.* p. 206) combined an unreserved admiration for the gardens of the Italian Renaissance with a strong commitment to modernism, as is shown in his contrasting designs for the Italian garden at Ditchley Park in Oxfordshire and the modern restaurant and garden for visitors to Cheddar Gorge in Somerset.

The major outlet for modernism in English garden and landscape design was to be provided by the newly emerging profession of landscape architecture, formalized in 1929 when the Institute of Landscape Architecture was founded – exactly thirty years after the establishment of an equivalent body in the United States. It was clear from the earliest days that as commissions for private gardens declined it was in the field of public landscape that professional garden designers could find new openings and be able to work on a large scale. However, although it was immediately able to respond to demands from the well-established tradition of public parks and gardens, landscape architecture really came into its own after World War II.

In 1929 it was Thomas Mawson (*q.v.* p. 150) who was elected, only four years before his death, the first President of the Institute of Landscape Architects – a clear reflection of the strength of the garden designing establishment. As a result, a number of younger members of the profession turned for example and inspiration to the United States where the senior professional organization had been firmly rooted in the public landscape tradition of F. L. Olmsted (*q.v.* p. 120).

In England by the 1930s the interests of most gardeners were increasingly focused upon planting rather than garden architecture, and a desire for informality was often expressed successfully in the creation of natural woodland gardens. Here, mature native trees provided the setting for winding paths and glades planted with flowering and ornamental trees and shrubs underplanted with spring bulbs. A major attraction of such woodland gardens was that they extended a garden's life throughout most of the year, from early-spring to late-autumn. This style of gardening could also be adapted to available space, from the smallest glade to acres of woodland, and some of the most ambitious gardens of the period were created in this style.

A number of woodland gardens had been begun before World War I, often by men who had financed plant-collecting expeditions and subsequently built up extensive collections of plants such as rhododendrons and camellias; between the wars these gardens had reached maturity and their reputation had spread. At Bodnant in North Wales Henry McLaren (later the 2nd Lord Aberconway) developed the more natural woodland areas of the garden below the typically Edwardian Italianate terraces that descend from the house; in Sussex the Loder family's two gardens at Leonardslee and Wakehurst Place became renowned for their collections of woodland plants, in particular rhododendrons; while in Cornwall gardeners such as J. C. Williams at Caerhays Castle, took advantage of the area's mild conditions to create gardens filled with rhododendrons, camellias and magnolias, raising many new varieties themselves. In 1925, Williams raised at Caerhays the first of his williamsii hybrid camellias, which is described in *Hilliers Manuals of Trees and Shrubs* as 'one of the most valuable hybrid shrubs ever produced.' To these were added new gardens, some of them on an even grander scale: at Exbury in Hampshire Lionel Rothschild planted some two hundred acres of woodland with rhododendrons and azaleas, building up a collection of international renown in particular of hybrid azaleas; in Windsor Great Park Eric Savill added the outstanding Savill and Valley gardens to the existing royal gardens, his ornamental woodland, also of some two hundred acres, filled with trees and shrubs from many temperate areas of the world, and natural water gardens, created around lakes and streams.

For most people, however, size was not a priority, and it was rather the garden of 'compartments' that was emerging as typical of 20th-century garden style, in which each area could be given its own identity and relate in mood to the rooms of a house. These gardens were to some extent inspired by the Jekyll and Lutyens example, but Lawrence Johnston (*q.v.* p. 145) had already shown at Hidcote – largely created before World War I and completed during the 1920s – that they could be less obviously architectural, with divisions provided by hedges rather than walls, and paths and terraces simplified. The impressive planting schemes of Edwardian gardens were being continued by a few designers, like Norah Lindsay, and some owners, like Major Edward Compton in his spectacular

*Vita Sackville-West's Sissinghurst: romantic,
evocative and universally admired.*

double herbaceous border at Newby Hall in Yorkshire, but the general tendency was towards a reduction in scale balanced by an effusive style of planting. Examples of this can be seen in the garden at Tintinhull created by Phyllis Reiss and, most famously, in the garden at Sissinghurst Castle created by Vita Sackville-West and her husband Harold Nicolson.

THOMAS CHURCH (1902-78)

EL NOVILLERO, *California, USA*; PHILLIPS HOUSE, *California, USA*

THOMAS CHURCH was one of the founders of the contemporary private garden. Although his practice did not extend outside California and his style was developed to respond to the specific landscape and climate conditions of America's west coast, his ideas have spread world-wide. In England the modern movement and abstract art struggled to have any real impact upon garden design, so entrenched were the historical traditions of ornamental and flower gardening. In the United States the situation was different: the very size of the country and the range of landscape and climatic conditions were far more conducive to a break away from traditional attitudes and styles.

Church himself was educated at Berkeley and Harvard universities in the Beaux Arts tradition that had produced the grandly formal gardens and landscapes of the late 19th and early 20th centuries.

Beaux Arts splendour and those who could afford it were devastated by the depression that followed 1929, just at the moment when the modern movement was making an impression upon architecture with the work of men such as Frank Lloyd Wright.

Church returned to California in 1930 and established his practice as a landscape architect at the same time as three other well-known contemporaries from Harvard, who also rejected the established traditions: Garrett Eckbo, Daniel Kiley and James Rose.

Church determined that his work should follow principles that answered both human and landscape demands, responding closely to each specific site. Garden design had been steadily developing in answer to the demand that gardens should be closely unified more with the house, that they should be places for living in addition to providing visual enjoyment. Church's work showed a direct reponse to new lifestyles in a manner especially relevant to California: gardens became outdoor rooms, their adjoining boundaries sharply defined by stone – or more often concrete – and plants were used functionally but strikingly in contained beds.

Much of Church's early work was in small gardens where he employed a variety of novel techniques to balance an illusion or greater space with intricate detail on a small scale. In 1947 he was commissioned to design the garden at El Novillero at Sonoma, which has proved to be his most influential work. The house and garden were in a setting of salt marshes with sinuous channels and enclosed by live oaks – these became for Church symbolic Californian trees that he incorporated into his designs wherever possible.

The garden's central synthesis is between sharply linear concrete and decking composed of redwood planks laid in the fashion of a parquet floor, and the curving lines of the kidney-shaped swimming pool with its abstract sculpted island – in itself a departure from conventional design shapes. Beyond the pool the garden flows naturally into the rocky landscape and distant mountains. Michael Lancaster summed up the impact of the El Novillero garden when he wrote: 'Informed by the Cubist idea that a scene may be seen simultaneously from a number of viewpoints, and by his feeling that a garden should have no beginning and no end, Church, typically, has placed the rounded V-shaped pool so that it cuts across the pattern of concrete and redwood squares, each stressing the rhythm of the other. Line plays against line, form against form, the whole uniting with admirable restraint, into a composition which has its own unique identity and at the same time belongs essentially to the site.'[1]

While Church's contemporaries, Eckbo and Kiley, and his assistant at El Novillero, Lawrence Halprin, established practices that concentrated primarily on larger-scale landscape architecture and on public rather than private commissions, Church himself remained primarily a designer of smaller private gardens. In 1955 he published *Gardens for People*, a book which encapsulated his beliefs and principles and helped to disseminate them to a wide audience; it also confirmed Church's reputation as one of the pioneers of modernism in garden and landscape design.

BEATRIX (JONES) FARRAND (1872-1959)

DARTINGTON HALL, *Devon*; DUMBARTON OAKS, *Washington DC, USA*; ABBEY ALDRICH ROCKEFELLER GARDEN, *Maine, USA*; PRINCETON UNIVERSITY, *New Jersey, USA*; YALE UNIVERSITY, *Connecticut, USA*

BEATRIX FARRAND is a figure of immense significance in 20th-century garden design, not least as the first professional to be involved in the creation of major gardens in both the United States and England. Dumbarton Oaks, Washington DC and Dartington Hall, Devon, stand at the pinnacle of gardens made in either country between the wars and Farrand's work demonstrates a uniquely successful fusion of Anglo-American gardening traditions and ideas. As well as her talent as a designer and knowledge as a plantswoman, she also brought to her work a warmly sympathetic personality and approach to gardens. At Dumbarton Oaks she was commissioned by Mildred Barnes Bliss and at Dartington by Dorothy Elmhirst; both were acquaintances who, during the progress of the work, became Farrand's close friends.

Beatrix Farrand was adamant that the success of professional garden design depended on a close partnership between designer and client, and in this she was a model to her colleagues. When she died, aged eighty-seven, Dorothy Elmhirst wrote in an article published in the United States: 'No one who worked with Beatrix Farrand could fail to be impressed by her professional attitude to her job. Always the first to go out in the morning she was the last to come in at night. Her energy seemed able to surmount any obstacle – even the worst onslaughts of rain and cold. In her tweeds and mackintosh we could see her tall, erect figure conversing – in all weathers – with architects, builders, gardeners – tactfully collaborating with them all and slowly winning them to her ideas . . .. Her finely chiselled face and dignified bearing seemed indeed the personification of royalty. Her clear incisive mind was greatly enriched by her cultural background. Both in her professional capacity and as a friend she was in every way a remarkable woman.'[1]

The daughter of a well-off New York family, Beatrix Farrand's upbringing was cultural and artistic, and included a number of formative trips to Europe. Her love of gardening was confirmed when she studied at the Arnold Arboretum, part of Harvard University and, by the end of the 19th century, establishing itself as one of the foremost horticultural institutions in the world. Her earliest and abiding gardening influences were her aunt, the novelist Edith Wharton, and, more importantly, Gertrude Jekyll. Edith Wharton was a central figure in the revival of Italianate gardens in America during the late 19th and early 20th centuries, not least through her book, *Italian Villas and Gardens*, first published in 1903.

In the early 1890s, at the time that Gertrude Jekyll was making the garden at Munstead, Beatrix Farrand, still in her early twenties, was setting up a modest practice based in New York, working mainly for friends and acquaintances. When she travelled to England in 1895 the highlight of her trip was a visit to Munstead where the building of Lutyens's new house was in progress. For the rest of her career Beatrix Farrand acknowledged the influence of Gertrude Jekyll's principles upon her own work and it was she who disseminated knowledge and admiration of Gertrude Jekyll's gardens and ideas throughout the United States. Her most significant contribution in this field was the purchase in 1948 of the majority of Gertrude Jekyll's plans and drawings. Initially these were housed at her own home at Reef Point, Bar Harbor, in Maine, where it was Beatrix Farrand's life-long ambition to establish a horticultural foundation, to maintain her garden and library; in this she was disappointed, due to lack of funds, and in 1955 her library, including the Jekyll plans and drawings, went to the University of California at Berkeley.

The esteem in which Beatrix Farrand was held by her colleagues was demonstrated in 1899, when she became one of the eleven founder-members – and the only woman – of the American Society of Landscape Architects. However, she always stressed that she considered herself a landscape gardener rather than a landscape architect;

The pebble garden at Dumbarton Oaks, Beatrix Farrand's
outstanding American garden where she fused an indigenous
style with her admiration for Gertrude Jekyll.

throughout her career she maintained that her work stemmed from the tradition of a garden as a personal, private domain in which horticulture took precedence over architecture and which lacked the social implications intrinsic in the Olmstedian view of the profession centring upon parks, gardens and other urban spaces for a more anonymous public. This was even true in the larger commissions that Beatrix Farrand carried out, including several university campuses, of which the most important were Princeton where she began work in 1913, and Yale where she began work in 1924.

Beatrix Farrand was nearly fifty when, in 1921, she was first consulted over the future garden of Dumbarton Oaks. The house and garden had been bought the previous year by Mildred Barnes Bliss and her husband. During many years in Europe, where her husband was at one time ambassador to Sweden, Mildred Bliss had been particularly influenced by formal French gardens. From the very outset the garden of over 20 ha/50 acres was conceived on an ambitious scale, as Lanning Roper has described: 'At the beginning it was agreed that as Dumbarton Oaks was to be the Bliss's permanent town residence, the garden must be beautiful during all seasons, relying heavily on the architectural framework. Emphasis was to be on design, the use of varied materials for paving, walling, pergolas and paths, and the incorporation of water features and decorative ornament. The design had to take advantage of the dramatic site with extensive terracing, flights of steps and vantage-points for seats to enjoy the garden vistas and the valley landscape. The planting, including copious groundcover, was to contain a high proportion of evergreens, both coniferous and broad-leaved, to be effective throughout the year.'[2]

While many of the ideas for the different areas came from Mildred Bliss and her enthusiastic desire to adapt what she had seen and enjoyed in Europe, as did most of the garden ornaments which she had collected, it was Beatrix Farrand who transposed the ideas into the landscape in a wonderfully flowing, heterogeneous style. Retaining the existing mature trees which, especially when the new areas were first created, gave the garden an enviable air of maturity, Farrand created an overall scheme whose simplicity of design served to heighten the effect of the garden's complex array of different features, plants and ornament.

Within the two main axes extending from the house at right-angles the central area of garden descends on the two angles through a series of enclosures. Below a small azalea garden lies the pool garden and beyond this the pebble garden, perhaps Dumbarton Oaks's most original enclosure where, within surrounding trellis hung with wisteria, a flowing scrollwork pattern in pebbles reproduces the Bliss family crest of a wheatsheaf, and at one end a fountain sprays its water into a pool and over the surrounding pebbles. Below the pebble garden, and linked with the urn terrace to the east of the house with a long narrow vista, a dramatic contrast is achieved by a rondel of pleached aerial hornbeams – reminiscent of the stilt garden at Hidcote in England – encircling a central pool fed by four mask fountains.

Dumbarton Oaks certainly evokes the French and Italian renaissance gardens that Mildred Bliss so admired, but Beatrice Farrand's great achievement was to mould the inspiration into something original and contemporary rather than derivative in the manner of James Deering's Vizcaya in Florida. She did this by an exemplary attention to small detail in the best traditions of the Arts and Crafts movement and of her mentor Gertrude Jekyll and by balancing the architectural ornamental influence from Europe with the existing setting and her horticultural input: the brick and grass steps linking the main north terraces which soften the overall vista; the patterns of brick, stone and pebble paths and of retaining or enclosing walls; the teakwood furniture which she designed herself and, most important, the planting, whether for single colour effect as in the emphasis on evergreens, or mixed highlights in spring borders, or autumn foliage of shrubs and native trees – all of which she recorded in meticulous detail in *The Plant Book for Dumbarton Oaks*. Towards the end of her life Beatrix Farrand considered that, of all her gardens, Dumbarton Oaks was, 'the best and most deeply felt of a fifty-year career'.[3]

Beatrix Farrand had already designed a garden for Dorothy Elmhirst and her first husband, Willard Straight, in Long Island but her commission to work at Dartington Hall in Devon arose also from the admiration Dorothy Elmhirst and her English second husband Leonard had for the developing garden at Dumbarton Oaks. The Elmhirsts had purchased Dartington Hall in 1925 with the express ambition of establishing a rural artistic community, and in 1932 were looking for someone to carry forward the first tentative redesigning of the gardens by H. Avray Tipping. The commission presented Beatrix Farrand with a quite different challenge from that of Dumbarton Oaks – not least the logistical one of designing a garden in England on the basis of annual visits: she paid her first visit to Dartington in 1933, returning annually until the outbreak of World War II, and her partnering with Dorothy Elmhirst is recorded in a copious correspondence. From her first visit when, as Dorothy Elmhirst recorded, 'she worked incessantly – scrutinizing every corner and angle – setting up her stakes, taking meticulous notes, planning, planning, planning every hour of the day and night – she finally departed for London, her mind clear as to what she wanted to do',[4] she was inspired by Dartington's history which stretched back to mediaeval England when Richard II's half-brother the Duke of Exeter had jousted on the sunken tiltyard to one side of the house, the focus of the whole garden. Her aspirations after her first visit were sent to the Elmhirsts: 'to allow Dartington to speak for itself, with its simple nobility of line and long human association.'[5]

Preliminary work had already been carried out by Tipping before Beatrix Farrand arrived. On one side of the hall, built around a courtyard, were a series of terraces, one a bowling green lined by the remains of 14th-century stone arches, and a lower one containing a line of clipped conical Irish yews called the Twelve Apostles. From here the ground dropped to the flat tiltyard, rising on the far side in grass terraces to a platform beyond which wood-land spread out, upward opposite the hall and around one end of the tiltyard to the perimeters of the garden and from the other end down to the sweeping line of a valley.

Farrand first concentrated on the courtyard which she resurrected from a semi-derelict state to provide a suitable foreground for the great hall and other enclosing buildings. The discrepancies in level which gave an unsatisfactory piecemeal appearance were removed to give an open expanse, and the central drive was replaced by a circular one around the courtyard's perimeter, its pattern of limestone flags and cobbles carefully planned. With the open area put down to one large lawn the courtyard once again related harmoniously to the surrounding buildings and Beatrix Farrand took care not to disturb the architectural balance by limiting her planting to selective wall plants and climbers. From the courtyard she moved out to areas closest to the hall, planting cedars on the south lawn and other trees in the area of terraces between the hall and tiltyard, siting new paths and flights of steps – notably the flights of steps leading out of the upper end of the tiltyard – widening the border between the arches and the Twelve Apostles known as the 'Sunny Border', and planting yew hedges around the tiltyard to complement and enclose the spatial formality.

In all her work at Dartington Beatrix Farrand aspired to fuse together the different areas of the garden without disturbing their natural individuality and this was most evident in her plans for the area of woodland beyond the tiltyard and grass terraces. Clearing undergrowth to reveal the trunks of mature trees, she laid out three parallel but meandering woodland walks, each with its own identity; one between rhododendrons and magnolias, another between banks of camellias, and the third planted with an array of woodland spring flowers.

As Reginald Snell has described, it was here that she allowed the direct influence of Gertrude Jekyll its most uninhibited play: 'it is in the Woodland that the English tradition is perhaps most clearly seen: her American disciple had begun the planting immediately after a visit to the elderly Gertrude Jekyll, and her use of colour, together with the grouping of the camellias and magnolias in particular, undercarpeted with wildflowers, is an open tribute to what she had recently admired in the garden of Munstead Wood.[6]

The correspondence between Beatrix Farrand and the Elmhirsts and between her and the agent James Luard – letters running to pages of politely worded instructions for specific planting or construction work, mixed with constant enthusiasm for his progress reports – are testimony to the work that she put into the garden at Dartington. The outbreak of World War II ended her direct connection, and from 1945 the Elmhirst's enlisted the help of Percy Cane (q.v. p. 194), but the continuing letters with advice and suggestions confirm how closely she was to remain involved, albeit from a distance.

The difference between Beatrix Farrand's approach to the garden and Percy Cane's was exemplified when he replaced the humble little zig-zag path running down the heath bank that she called her 'little goat track', with his magnificent flight of steps between banks of magnolias. For Percy Cane Dartington provided an opportunity for expansive gestures, while for Beatrix Farrand it was a place of historical romance that she was reticent about disturbing; but if she ever disapproved of his alterations she did so with the tact shown in one letter to the Elmhirsts written in 1957: 'Please – no more *Juniperus Pfitzeriana* (a favourite plant of Cane's), they always look as though their locks needed combing and they just don't go with the terraces. Is this dreadful to say?'[7] In the same letter she wrote: 'The unforgetten evening when Dartington was first opened to my eyes will live for as long as there is life and memory. The mild January misty dusk, the steep drops in the levels and equally steep rises, the splendid chestnuts and Monterey pines and the black mass of the holm oak. It is often before me.'[8] Her last letter was written in August 1958, some six months before her death. At Dartington, as at Dumbarton Oaks, it was the combination of personal involvement and her skills as a designer and plantswoman that gave her work such an impact; an impact that remains to this day.

NORAH LINDSAY (*1866-1948*)

BLICKLING HALL, *Norfolk;* GODMERSHAM PARK, *Kent;* PORT LYMPNE, *Kent;* SUTTON COURTENAY MANOR, *Oxfordshire*

NORAH LINDSAY was, like her contemporary Ellen Willmott, a *grande dame* of gardening, who carried the spirit of Edwardianism into the inter-war period at the same time as being an exceptionally accomplished plantswoman. In its obituary of her in 1948 *The Times* described how she would 'trace out a whole garden with the tip of her umbrella'. A granddaughter of the Earl of Mayo, born and brought up in County Galway, she married in 1895 Harry Lindsay, a grandson of the Earl of Crawford, later to become a colonel and early flying hero of the RFC during World War I. Her origins were reflected in the connections and friendships of her later life – at one time she advised the Prince of Wales (later Edward VIII) on his garden at Fort Belvedere – and as a gardener she became what Miles Hadfield describes as, 'one of the first of the amateur-professional garden designers who did so much to uphold the renown of English gardens during the years immediately preceding and succeeding World War I.'[1]

Norah Lindsay's own garden at the Manor House, Sutton Courtenay – which no longer survives – was unstintingly admired by her gardening contemporaries. Here she combined planting skill and imagination with the inspiration of classical Italy and she once wrote, 'I would have been a much lesser gardener had I not worshipped at the crumbling shrines of the ancient garden gods of Florence and Rome.'[2] Her forte, however, was the association of herbaceous plants in the borders so loved by Edwardian gardeners, and her most ambitious scheme was carried out for Sir Philip Sassoon at Port Lympne, probably the grandest garden created in England between the wars – laid out by Port Lympne's architect, Philip Tilden. Norah Lindsay was responsible for the huge double herbaceous borders that stretched down the hillside from one side of the house to the garden's edge, since replanted by Russell Page (*q.v.* p. 216) during the restoration of the garden in the early 1980s.

The garden where Norah Lindsay's work is most faithfully retained is at Blickling Hall in Norfolk, where she remodelled the great parterre by William Nesfield (*q.v.* p. 116) for the 11th Marquess of Lothian. Her treatment of the parterre combined practicality with sympathy for the original vista across the parterre through the rising ground of the woodland garden to the Doric temple in the distance, and her simplification of the foreground if anything increased the overall effect and harmony. In the main area of Nesfield's parterre only the four main square blocks were retained around the central fountain and these were replanted formally with herbaceous plants, the central areas forming a mound to match the domes of clipped yew on the outer corners. The rest of Nesfield's pattern was put to lawn, though the great blocks of yew shaped like grand pianos in the area further from the house and the four corner stone urns were retained. Below the retaining wall on one side of the parterre Norah Lindsay planned the long herbaceous border and today the whole parterre is carefully maintained by the National Trust.

THE HON VICTORIA MARY 'VITA' SACKVILLE-WEST
(*1892-1962*)

LONG BARN, *Kent*; SISSINGHURST CASTLE, *Kent*

THE GARDEN AT SISSINGHURST CASTLE in Kent, made by Vita Sackville-West and her husband Harold Nicolson, is universally considered to be the quintessential English garden of the 20th century. Clearly sustaining the influence of the Arts and Craft movement and closely moulded around the topography and history of its site it was an intensely personal creation that has become a model for the contemporary garden. The fact that the garden's reputation has inevitably increased in relation to the closely scrutinized lives of its creators is irrelevant in terms of its quality which shines out in a confidently independent manner. Encapsulating much that has come to be most admired in contemporary gardens, its unending appeal lies in its limited size and scale – the 'compartment' arrangement of gardens within gardens which creates an atmosphere of unintimidating ease; in its firm but understated architectural framework free of the decorative or ornamental features intrinsic to, for instance, a Lutyens and Jekyll garden; in its generally profuse style of planting and concentration of nostalgic, soft-shaded plants, in particular old-fashioned roses, climbers and wall plants, traditional herbaceous varieties and naturalized spring bulbs.

Vita Sackville-West was born the only child of the heir to the 2nd Lord Sackville, and brought up at Knole, the great historic family house that was to remain the passion and inspiration for her whole life. The death of her grandfather in 1908 brought the shattering revelation to the sixteen-year-old Vita that she would never inherit Knole; on her father's death it would pass with the Sackville title to his brother and thence to Vita's cousin Edward, ten years her junior.

It was from Knole and her solitary upbringing there that Vita derived her sense of history combined with a love of countryside in general and the Weald of Kent in particular. This sense of place, embedded to an unusual degree, proved her primary source of motivation, both as a writer – notably in her poem *The Land* – and as a gardener. (She would always have preferred to have been known as a writer rather than a gardener, and as a poet and biographer she achieved notably distinctions.)

Long Barn, which Vita and Harold Nicolson bought as their first home in 1915, provided the gardening apprenticeship to Sissinghurst. Originally a mediaeval timbered cottage, within walking distance of Knole, they virtually doubled its size by the addition of an old barn at right-angles. The garden was Vita's first concern and although groping her way as a beginner she soon showed the preferences which were to be repeated at Sissinghurst. In 1917 she visited Gertrude Jekyll at Munstead Wood with her mother (a visit arranged through Lady Sackville's friendship with Lutyens – whom they called 'McNed'), and the influence of the garden was soon evident at Long Barn. It was Lutyens who probably awakened Harold Nicolson's aspirations as a designer *manqué*; they designed the Dutch garden at Long Barn together, with its arrangement of L-shaped beds enclosed by low brick walls. Harold's interest in and understanding of the principles of garden design were later to be demonstrated in the layout at Sissinghurst as well as in his diaries, letters to Vita and other writing: 'The main axis of the garden should be indicated and indeed emphasised, by rectilinear perspectives, by lines of clipped hedges ending in terminals in the form of statues or stone benches. Opening from the main axis there should be small enclosed gardens, often constructed round a central pool, and containing some special species or variety of plant. From time to time this variation should be broken and an unexpected feature be introduced.'[1]

Vita's gardening combined her own inherent unconventionality with her veneration for certain traditions and the two apparent opposites produced a rich synthesis. Her gardening predecessors had long been advocating the unity of house and garden, but at Long Barn the garden flowed almost into the house, the walls covered in roses, clematis and buddleja, and herbs and scented flowers planted right up to the doors, while twenty sentinel columnar Irish yews planted on the first of two terraces with stone retaining walls combined with yew hedges further out to provide some formal framework; as did the brick edging of the Dutch garden. Following sympathetic restoration it all survives today.

Long Barn was idyllic in many ways, but various factors combined to make a move imperative by the end of 1929, and in May 1930 the Nicolson's bought Sissinghurst Castle, comprising the tower, the long entrance range – then divided into stables and cottages – two cottages and the neighbouring Castle Farm, which they let. The badly dilapidated buildings were in part survivors of the Elizabethan Sissinghurst Castle which had been built around two adjacent courtyards, of which a surviving wall was to be incorporated into the garden along the dry moat walk; a section of the moat itself also remained, full of water, marking the garden's boundary beyond the large central orchard. For Vita the tower alone was enough to captivate her; it was the twin of Bolebroke Tower in Sussex where the Tudor Sackvilles had lived.

Part of Sissinghurst's fascination for visitors has always been the knowledge that it was created from a completely derelict site – an accumulation of decades of farmers' rubbish and weeds – by Vita and Harold themselves, assisted by gardeners but with effectively no advice from professionals. While Vita began planting certain areas immediately, Harold worked out the plan that was to hold the garden together and make the most of its asymmetry. The tower was always to be the garden's architectural and spiritual centrepiece, with the courtyard on one side and a rectangle of lawn on the other. Beyond this lawn one of Harold's main vistas led from the white garden in front of the cottage called the Priest's House to the rondel of yew hedges in the rose garden, with the parallel long narrow axis of the yew walk. Other individual areas of the garden were arranged in interlinking progression from the rose garden: the cottage garden around the South cottage; the lime walk along the garden's boundary, leading to the nuttery which itself led to the neat little herb garden in the far corner; and the sunken moat walk roughly parallel to the nuttery which was eventually to be given the focus of a statue of Dionysius positioned on the far bank of the moat. The moat curved round two boundaries of the orchard which filled the largest area and whose pastoral simplicity was the perfect foil to the luxuriant planting elsewhere.

While the bones of the garden's structure were steadily being established they were given life by Vita's planting. By now assured in her knowledge and preferences, she was able to begin creating the series of different combinations which gave to each area of the garden its own identity while achieving an overall impression of unrestrained abundance and nostalgic beauty. She wanted the garden to be, 'a tumble of roses, honeysuckle, figs and vines. It was a romantic place and, within the austerity of Harold Nicolson's straight lines, must be romantically treated.'[2] In composition it was radically different from the traditional flower garden of Gertrude Jekyll's era and the plants that Vita used to best effect have become mainstays of contemporary gardens everywhere: there were none of the massed Michaelmas daisies that she disliked so much at Munstead Wood, nor the impressive purely herbaceous arrangements of the main summer border there; instead, old-fashioned roses everywhere – on the walls with clematis and in different beds and borders, underplanted with hardy geraniums and mixing with lilies, irises or selected flowering shrubs. The spring planting beneath the pleached lime walk was Harold Nicolson's particular domain, but the rose garden, white garden, the borders in the courtyard and the cottage garden were all clear evidence of Vita's desire for a medley of soft-shaded colour and scent.

The development of the garden was a continual process and by the 1950s its reputation was already spreading. In 1946 Vita had begun the column in *The Observer* that she was to write for nearly fifteen years. By the time of her death in 1962 Sissinghurst's fame was well established. Harold Nicolson died in 1968 and the previous year their son Nigel had bequeathed the garden to the National Trust. While the spontaneity, freshness and lack of restraint of a personal garden have inevitably diminished in the desire for preservation and in the accommodation of the hordes of visitors who fill the small garden every year, there is still plenty to show the genius behind its creation.

FLETCHER STEELE (1885-1971)

MISSION HOUSE, *Massachusetts, USA;* NAUMKERG, *Massachusetts, USA;* SMITH GARDEN, *Connecticut, USA;* STODDARD GARDEN, *Massachusetts, USA;* TURNER GARDEN, *Pittsford, USA*

FLETCHER STEELE was decisive before and after World War II in effecting the transition in American garden design from the Beaux Arts tradition of the late 19th century – which continued in demand with wealthy clients right up to the depression of 1929 – to a markedly less ornate and classical style that incorporated both abstract modernism and an appreciation of natural landscape. It was a breakthrough which the younger designers of the California style soon came to appreciate and admire; Steele became, as Garrett Eckbo described, 'the transitional figure between the old guard and the moderns'.[1] Steele became increasingly convinced that there was more to garden design than being impressively ornate – 'the chief vice in gardens is merely to be pretty'[2] – and this realization tempered his designs from the 1930s on. Steele's first garden design was carried out in 1915 and his last in 1970, although few of his five hundred or so gardens have survived.

The development of Steele's ideas can best be seen at Naumkerg in Massachusetts, where he began working for Mabel Choate in 1925 and continued to be involved through the 1950s. The name means in Indian 'haven of peace' and in characteristic American style the place takes its inspiration from the surrounding woods and countryside of the Berkshire Hills. Over the years Steele introduced an afternoon garden to the south lawn – America's first abstract landscape created by major earthworking; a Chinese garden and temple, to which he later added a curving surrounding wall with a moon gate (Naumkerg's last major addition); and his most innovative feature, the Blue Steps, laid out in 1939, a stairway of double flights, built in concrete and painted pale blue, which sweeps up between the ghostly trunks of paper birches and across a series of descending cascades into which a stream is channelled. The inspiration and bravado of the steps would appear to be straight from the Italian Renaissance and yet the style of construction and the naturalistic woodland setting is diametrically the opposite.

Steele's last garden design, for Nancy and Richard Turner, was close to his own home in Pittsford. He had officially retired in 1963 but this last project proved an intriguing finale to his career.

Around the austere Greek revival house he created a landscape with all the confidence of full maturity. In characteristic manner a majestic terraced vista stretched away from the north front between trees which curved round to form an apse some 200m/ 200yds distant, while Steele's narrowing of the planting as it extended away from the house, together with the drop in terrain, hugely increased the perspective.

Steele's ideas and were published in a series of influential books, *New Pioneering in Garden Design* (1930), *Landscape Design of the Future* (1932), and *Modern Garden Design* (1936).

By the latter stages of his long career he was widely revered among American garden designers as a figure who had pioneered radical progress and yet done so in sympathy with past traditions rather than in direct reaction against them, always maintaining the need for quality of overall design and small detail. He never lost sight of sound principles established in the past, or of the fact that the best landscape is usually produced by a simple, instinctive human response to the conditions of an individual site: 'The true gardener has abiding faith and must express it, if only by planting an acorn where the *genius loci* calls for an oak.'[3]

CHRISTOPHER TUNNARD (1910-79)

ST ANN'S HILL, *Surrey;* HALLAND, *Sussex*

CHRISTOPHER TUNNARD was the leading advocate in England between the wars of a move towards modernism in garden design, his work similar to that of Thomas Church (*q.v.* p. 173) and his colleagues in California. In England, however, Tunnard was up against deeply entrenched garden traditions and the preferred style of most of his contemporaries took the form of an evolution from the Edwardian garden and the styles of earlier periods, rather than something as radical as Tunnard was advocating. Tunnard achieved a considerable reputation within his profession and some of his principles were closely adhered to in early post-war and 1950s designs – in the landscapes of the New Towns, for example – but after five years of running his own practice in England, Tunnard felt himself to be swimming against the tide, and in 1939 he emigrated to the United States. There, modernism in both architecture and garden design was more sympathetically received, and after the war Tunnard taught landscape design at both Harvard and Yale Universities.

Tunnard trained at the Royal Horticultural Society's garden at Wisley before joining Percy Cane (*q.v.* p. 194) as an apprentice. He left Cane's office to set up his own practice as a landscape designer in 1934 and his flagged terraces flowing into grass and sparsely planted individual trees at St Ann's Hill and Halland survive as evidence from this time of his austerely modernist designs in which functionalism was combined with simplicity.

The reserve of Japanese gardens especially appealed to him, and the principles expressed in his book, *Gardens in the Modern Landscape* (1938), had an immense influence upon architects and landscape designers of the post-war decades. The book also stressed Tunnard's pessimism with the contemporary state of British garden design and his aspirations for the direction in which it should develop – aspirations that were to be largely unfulfilled in private gardens. 'Contemporary garden design has not even caught up with contemporary trends in architecture. It is to be hoped that in the near future garden-makers will become aware of this fact, and that instead of re-hashing old styles to fit new buildings they will create something more expressive of the contemporary spirit and something more worthy of the tradition to which they are the heirs.'[1]

Fletcher Steele's blue steps at Naumkerg, a design which exemplified his feel for both abstract modernism and natural landscape.

SIR (BERTRAM) CLOUGH WILLIAMS-ELLIS (1883-1978)

CORNWELL MANOR, *Oxfordshire;* DALTON HALL, *Cumbria;* NANTCLWYD HALL, *Clwyd;* OARE HOUSE, *Wiltshire;* PLAS BRON DANW, *Gwynedd;* PORTMEIRION, *Gwynedd*

CLOUGH WILLIAMS-ELLIS entitled his memoirs *Architect Errant*, and it was in this light, as a figure outside the mainstream and the establishment, that he considered himself; an image made manifest in his whimsical, picturesque creation at Portmeirion. Though in fact he was recognized by the establishment: he was appointed vice-president of the Institute of Landscape Architects and given a knighthood in 1971. Interrupted by service with the Welsh Guards during World War I, when he was awarded the MC, his formal architectural education was slender. He operated by a combination of panache and intuition added to a feel for building materials, and succeeded in establishing a fashionable architectural practice between the wars, almost exclusively building or altering private houses in a style that was described by John Martin Robinson as 'a cross between Cape Dutch and the sort of theatrical Italianate usually encountered only in the sets for opera'.[1]

His essays into garden work began at the family home, Plas Brondanw, which he inherited in 1908, and subsequently – and more ambitiously – at Portmeirion, on which he worked from 1925 to 1970. Decorated with architecture and ornament in an almost rococo manner, the gardens at Portmeirion are a vital part of the whole scheme, linking together the various buildings to give the overall coherence that was required by such a holiday community. In 1951 Plas Brondanw was gutted by fire and in the complete restoration which lasted two years the garden was considerably extended. In the unlikely setting of the Welsh hills, Clough Williams-Ellis's Italianate garden is strongly architectural in style, with columnar cypress trees adding height to the dense horizontal boundaries of yew hedges, and flights of steps of varying patterns linking the site's changing levels. In it, theatrically classical features such as almost over-sized swagged vases on stone piers are balanced by subtle refinements such as the classical group of a statue flanked by busts. The figures are set in arches in a wall at one end of yew allée, at the other end the arches are repeated in yew; while throughout the garden the quality of craftsmanship can be seen in the cobbled and flagstone paths. At one point there is a fountain in the form of a cherub wearing a fireman's helmet, squirting water from his hose into a formal pool. The garden's layout gives vistas in all directions to the spectacular surrounding hills – as from the belevedere roundel at one end of the long terrace stretching across the garden immediately below the house and from the fountain terrace which terminates one of the yew hedge-lined allées. Beyond the garden and approached by a path winding up the wooded hillside and past a picturesque old quarry wall and pool, Williams-Ellis produced his last flourish in the garden – 'Castel Brondanw', a castellated prospect tower built on an eminence which Christopher Hussey described in *Country Life*: 'There, in the authentic spirit of Squire Headlong and of all the view-mad Regency landowners, who turned their estates into landscape pictures, Mr Williams-Ellis has built perhaps the last of genuine follies, a prospect-tower surveying the panorama of estuary and mountains.'[2]

Clough Williams-Ellis's most successful and impressive garden work was carried out at Oare House in Wiltshire in a commission that must have been much to his liking. His work was essentially architectural, complementing the quality of the house and incorporated the details at which he excelled, such as gates and doorways, furniture, and the occasional flourish. On one side of the house he was commissioned to build a library; outside its bow windows he created a series of intimate garden enclosures approached from the main forecourt under a pergola and past a small formal lily pool with an urn set in a niche in a yew hedge on the far side. The path emerges into an enclosure on the side of the house surrounded by brick walls and yew hedges, with a vista from the house through the yew to pleached limes and a loggia-fronted summerhouse. Here he created a small secret terrace approached between closely planted yew hedges and a fine arched wrought-iron gateway.

Beside the house, a brick path leads across the bow front of his library extension to a gateway in a brick wall, from where the main area of garden is revealed. From the broad stone terrace in front of the house an enormous expanse of lawn sweeps down to a brick wall with borders in front, divided in the centre by a wide clairvoyée. Here, Williams-Ellis's work is given an instantly recognizable hallmark in either side of the clairvoyée's white-painted railings tall stone piers are surmounted by urns, and these are echoed by another pair on the piers of the gateway from the small enclosure, and by a quartet perched on the corners of the main block of the house. The gate in the centre of the clairvoyée leads through to the swimming-pool garden, plain and elegant, with matching wooden seats designed by Williams-Ellis at either end in front of curving yew hedges and protected on the lower side by a holly hedge. The view from the house terrace down the sweep of lawn to the clairvoyée and pool and parkland beyond is both impressive and theatrical in a manner that is typical of his style.

In an architect and designer of lesser skill, much of Williams-Ellis's work would have had an air of pastiche, but while there was certainly a light-hearted element, the quality of his design and craftsmanship was unmistake-able. In his love of classicism, his romantic view of an ornamented landscape and his semi-amateur status he harked back to the 18th century. During the latter years of his career, notably at his two major post-war country houses and gardens, Nantclwyd and Dalton Hall, his was a refreshing influence at a time when economic constraints were encouraging a more utilitarian attitude to architecture and when garden ornament was for most people either prohibitively expensive or very much a secondary consideration to plants.

THE CONTEMPORARY GARDEN
1950-

S INCE WORLD WAR II the Sissinghurst example has become something of a gardening ideal; its intimacy and romanticism, the balance of simplicity and ebullience – from single-colour planting schemes to the old-fashioned rose garden – have been aspired to by thousands; its nostalgic atmosphere has confirmed the requirement of post-war garden makers for the garden to be a retreat, a place of security and idyllic beauty. And yet its widespread influence has also been just one aspect of the increasingly hetero-geneous picture which gardens have presented since the war, not least because – as at Sissinghurst – they have been created by their owners who are perhaps happy to adapt an existing garden rather than start from scratch, whose personal taste is often the overriding influence on their garden's appearance and who may wish to incorporate features from many different places and cultures.

Vita Sackville-West (*q.v.* p. 179) also set an important example as a non-professional; through her success as an amateur gardener and garden writer she achieved a position of enormous influence over her contemporaries, an influence that continues to the present day. In her wake came other gifted amateurs such as Margery Fish (*q.v.* p. 204), Penelope

Margery Fish called her garden at East Lambrook,
'a cottage-type garden to complete a cottage-type house'.
It has inspired many imitators.

Hobhouse (*q.v.* p. 205), Christopher Lloyd (*q.v.* p. 212) and Rosemary Verey (*q.v.* p. 228) who, through their own gardens, their books, lectures and garden journalism have reached a wider audience of garden makers than any professional designers or landscape architects.

The slowing down of the evolutionary process of garden style evident through the first half of the 20th century has been more noticeable since World War II. Gardens have borrowed from the past in an increasingly unrestrained manner and mixed together different styles of planting with ever greater freedom. These factors, combined with the escalating costs of providing a garden with a firm architectural design and of maintaining anything remotely labour intensive, have often conspired to loosen the structure of contemporary gardens. Partly in response, the work of a number of professional garden designers, such as Russell Page and John Brookes has been characterized by a meticulous approach to both planting and garden architecture and constant stressing that the two are mutually dependent. Similarly the modernist movement has had greatest impact upon garden design through its ability to maximize simple spatial arrangements and the relationships of lines and abstract shapes. Thomas Church and his fellow designers of the Californian style introduced into garden design strongly geometric linear arrangements of paths, terraces and raised beds for planting, alternating them with more abstract curving shapes. Church's work often focused upon small, usually urban gardens, as does the work of the Danish-born Preben Jakobsen, who has worked in England since 1969. As Tom Turner describes, the secret of Jakobsen's skill is a fusion of elements: 'The geometry of abstract art has been blended with the various sensuous delights of Arts and Crafts gardens . . . Jakobsen's own work shows a love of geometry and a fine discrimination in the choice of hard materials. He also exploits the colours, patterns and textures of plant material with imagination.'[1]

Although his work has been confined to his native Brazil, the most internationally renowned figure of the second half of the 20th century among professional garden designers and landscape architects has been Roberto Burle Marx. According to Geoffrey Jellicoe Burle Marx, who was born in 1909, 'originated the transport of abstract art into landscape' and in doing so 'raised landscape design to a status that paralleled the modern art movements in Europe.'[2] The often lush native plants of Brazil have been ideal material for Burle Marx's painterly designs where plants are arranged and grouped to convey an abstract idea through their colour and texture, sculptural plants emerging out of brilliant single-colour carpets, and used in conjunction with water and sweeping lines. Much of his influence has arisen not only from his hugely innovative designs and techniques, but from the degree to which his work has provided successful large-scale surroundings for modern architecture.

In Britain and America small gardens have often provided the spark for innovative garden design, but at the other end of the scale innovation has come as a response to the challenges of landscape architecture. Two of the most distinguished post-war figures, Dame Sylvia Crowe (*q.v.* p. 202) and Brenda Colvin (*q.v.* p. 200), moved from garden design during their earlier careers before the war to practices dominated by large-scale landscape architecture projects. Both were involved with designs for new towns being built during the 1950s and 1960s and with the highly emotive work of siting potentially intrusive industrial features such as power stations. For both, the principles that had imbued their garden design continued to act as cornerstones of their landscape architecture and were passed on to pupils such as John Brookes and Anthony Du Gard Pasley.

As F. L. Olmsted during the 19th century had arguably introduced in the United States a more radical and adventurous approach to landscape architecture than existed in Europe, so a number of his American successors continued this trend in the 20th, some in careers which began before the war but which have blossomed and achieved full recognition since. Thomas Church's contemporaries from the California school, Dan Kiley and Garrett Eckbo have had a major influence, the latter in his writing – notably *Landscape for Living* (1950) and *The Landscape We See* (1969) – as well as in his landscape designs. Eckbo in particular has stressed the important of human involvement in landscape design and this priority has been equally strong in the work of Church's one-time pupil, Lawrence Halprin. Halprin's designs such as the now celebrated Lovejoy Plaza, in Portland, Oregon, laid out in 1961, with its vigorous water and abstract architectural form, demonstrates the strongly-felt belief that urban landscapes, imaginatively designed to a high standard, form a significant and enjoyable section of landscape for the community and are able to replace many of the past ills of urban planning.

Perhaps more important than anything else, however, the period has witnessed an increasing self-awareness in American landscape and garden design manifested in a desire to break free from the limitations imposed by European models and to capitalize on the United States' rich variation in regional natural landscapes and the styles of garden that this promotes. The most influential current example is the partnership of Wolfgang Oehme and James van Sweden (*q.v.* p. 213) whose 'New American Garden' style has been applied to widely varying landscape and garden designs and seeks to demonstrate the

Overleaf: *The swimming pool garden at Sutton Place, Geoffrey Jellicoe's most ambitious garden design in Britain.*

extent to which horticulture and plant composition can be incorporated into work on any scale, with a particular emphasis on seasonal change and low maintenance.

Unlike most of his contemporaries, who opted for one discipline or the other, Geoffrey Jellicoe (*q.v.* p. 206) continues to combine the dual roles of garden designer and landscape architect. Like both Crowe and Colvin he has been regularly involved in extensive landscape designs, but has maintained regular private garden design commissions throughout the post-war era. Jellicoe's work also shows how the fundamentals of good design can allow both modernism and classicism to be applied equally effectively at one and the same time either landscape or garden work. For his most ambitious private commission in England, at Sutton Place, he designed the garden as an allegory of human life. While the individual features incorporated in the design of the garden are clearly inspired by modern surrealist or abstract act – notably the Marble Wall sculpted by Ben Nicolson – the heroic concept of the garden can be compared to the succession of classical allegorical reference revealed in Henry Hoare's 18th century landscape of Stourhead. As if to demonstrate that landscape and garden design are in a constant state of evolution and cross-relation from one period and style to another, his most recent and largest project, the Moody Historical garden in Texas, is planned as a series of individual gardens from all over the world.

At Sutton Place Jellicoe was concerned to ensure that the garden did not take on the character of an historical restoration. Elsewhere, restoration has emerged as an important priority of the post-war era, as appreciation of historic gardens has been coupled with an awareness of the problems threatening their survival. In both England and the United States enormous efforts and often extensive campaigns have been mounted to effect the restoration of a derelict historic garden site or to safeguard its future – problems that never appeared to concern people in previous periods. The American Lanning Roper (*q.v.* p. 220), who established one of the most successful of all post-war garden design practices in Britain, was involved in planning the sensitive rejuvenation of a number of historic gardens owned by the National Trust; and as a body, the Trust has in recent years contributed enormously to gardening as a result of their conscientious curatorship. Many private owners, too, have played a similar role in their recreation of gardens in a manner faithful to their original periods.

The present Lady Salisbury has replanned the gardens of her family's two homes, Hatfield House and Cranborne, to evoke the work of John Tradescant the elder (*q.v.* p. 21) who planted both gardens during the 17th century; and the Painshill Park Trust have restored most of the major elements of Charles Hamilton's (*q.v.* p. 72) 18th-century garden at Painshill.

Conservation of historic gardens has been accompanied by an awareness of the need to foster and promote the use of old-established garden plants and often endangered species. The campaign to use indigenous plants begun in the 19th century by William Robinson and Gertrude Jekyll has been increasingly successful since World War II as manifested in the popularity of wild-flower meadow gardens and the romanticization of 'cottage garden' flowers. At the same time one side-effect of the flood of horticultural novelties in the form of hybrids and cultivators was a tendency to let the species themselves disappear, and it is these, whether indigenous or not, which have recently become increasingly championed by professional and private garden designers; by specialist nurseries and by the work of the National Council for the Conservation of Plants and Gardens. One of the first and most significant steps was taken by Graham Stuart Thomas in his ardent support for species of old-fashioned roses, a campaign which achieved the happiest possible outcome when Thomas designed a rose garden for the National Trust – for whom he was senior gardens adviser for some twenty years – at Mottisfont Abbey in Hampshire, to contain not only his own extensive collection of old-fashioned roses but also other varieties to make the collection fully representative of the history of the rose.

Increasing awareness of the importance of preserving historic gardens and conservationist concerns have certainly contributed to the fact that innovation in garden design has slowed down since World War II. Other factors have been economic constraints and the existence of a more transient population. Travelling more freely and influenced by garden writing and television, they have wished to adopt features and styles from many different places and cultures. The resulting tendency has been for professional designers to be more often called in to give ideas for the replanting of one area of a garden than to design the whole. While the base of gardening has broadened enormously in terms of those able to and interested in creating a garden, the apex of lasting, fashion-setting gardens has become increasingly hard to achieve. Therefore it is likely that future generations will see progressively smaller numbers of such gardens. But they will undoubtedly enjoy a rich kaleidoscope of historic gardens restored and preserved and a constant – if not increasing – flow of new gardens which show allegiance to any number of periods and styles; from the Renaissance to Islamic gardens, Japanese gardens or Abstract Modernism. They will probably continue the contemporary trend that the most interesting gardens usually focus upon plantsmanship.

JOHN BROOKES (1933-)

DENMANS, *Sussex*

JOHN BROOKES has been one of the most influential garden designers of the last two decades through his garden commissions, his writing and his teaching of garden design. His career has been of particular relevance during the post-war decades in that he has focused upon the treatment of small gardens, often in urban surroundings, emphasizing the principles first established in the United States that the garden should be treated in close unity with the house, often as an extension to the house in the form of an outdoor room. In this he has demonstrated skill in spatial arrangements and in the use of hard materials such as paving and gravel in conjunction with plants. He has also been influenced in his conception of the small garden as an intimate courtyard by an admiration for Islamic gardens, where architectural proportion serves to give an increased sense of space.

Brookes's professional training took place, first at the County College of Agriculture in his native Durham and subsequently with the Nottingham Parks Department. Most influential on his future work, however, were his periods as assistant to two of the most distinguished 20th-century landscape architects, first Brenda Colvin (*q.v.* p. 200) and then Dame Sylvia Crowe (*q.v.* p. 202) while studying landscape design at University College London. Both Brenda Colvin and Sylvia Crowe worked primarily on large-scale public projects rather than private garden design, and their influence instilled in Brookes his clearly discernible concern for the individual qualities of a site and for the importance of the surrounding landscape in the creation of a garden. The first of his books, *Room Outside*, was published in 1969 and has been followed by a steady output covering a wide range of aspects of garden design and planting, and contrasting garden situations.

In addition to lecturing extensively on garden design – in Britain at institutions such as the Royal Botanic Gardens, Kew and the English Garden School at the Chelsea Physic Garden, as well as in the United States and other countries overseas – Brookes has for some years run his own school of garden design at Denmans in Sussex. At Denmans he has also made substantial additions to the garden created by its owner, Mrs Robinson, which illustrate most effectively many of his ideas. Both he and Mrs Robinson firmly believe that plants should be grouped as much for their form and texture as for their colour – which may anyway be of little importance, as in the case of elegant ornamental grasses or luscious aquatic foliage – and that they should be planted in close association with hard textures, especially gravel, which is used extensively at Denmans instead of grass, and has plants growing through in a seemingly random fashion. This is best illustrated in a part of the garden where a dry gravel stream sweeps and curves through rough-mown grass: the 'river bed', dotted with foliage plants revelling in the free-draining conditions. The dry stream leads towards a water garden designed by Brookes, and where the flowing lines that he prefers to a more geometric style are continued. Immediately outside the house a paved terrace is partially shaded by a wooden pergola and fuses without break into gravel and areas of shrubs planting at its edges.

PERCY STEPHEN CANE (1881-1976)

DARTINGTON HALL, *Devon;* FALKLAND PALACE, *Fife;* HUNGERDOWN HOUSE, *Wiltshire;* MONTEVIOT, *Roxburghshire;* WEST-FIELDS, *Bedfordshire*

PERCY CANE'S CAREER in effect spans two periods of the book, for though he worked as a garden journalist between the wars, and also began his practice as a garden designer at this time, most of his major commissions came during the late-1940s and 1950s when he was already over sixty. Cane's latter years were impressively productive, but his whole career began late in his life; it was not until after

At Denmans John Brookes demonstrates his admiration for gravel as a medium for planting – an important innovation in the contemporary garden.

World War I that, in 1919 and aged nearly forty, he began studying at the School of Horticulture in his native county of Essex before establishing himself in London where he owned and edited two journals, first *My Garden Illustrated* and subsequently *Garden Design*.

One can see in Percy Cane's career the dilemma that confronted British garden designers in the middle of this century, a dilemma accentuated in Cane's case by the fact that his inspiration came from the more affluent periods before World War I and in the 1920s, while the majority of his work was carried out in the economically austere years of the 1950s. Michael Lancaster describes how 'the neo-classical and Arts and Crafts influences continued to dominate garden design'[1] in the post-war period – the influence of Harold Peto (whom Cane especially admired), and of Jekyll and Lutyens. Yet here there was a danger: in place of the architectural details, complexity of planting and occasional flourish that made the originals so alive, post-war conditions, demanded compromise; money was short, the labour market was in a state of revolution and the number of experienced gardeners that people could afford or even find had shrunk.

As a professional designer Percy Cane could rarely allow himself the luxury of dramatic gestures, and in his gardens we see for the first time the widespread use of design techniques and specific plants which became recognizable features of the 1950s and 1960s: modest-sized formal rose gardens planted with Floribunda or Hybrid Tea varieties – all neat, reliable and easier to look after than old-fashioned roses; smooth lawns edged with flowing plantings of mixed shrubs, to give a similar impression to an Edwardian herbaceous border but without the maintenance requirement; and – most especially – informal glades of ornamental or flowering trees such as cherries, birch and crab apples, planted with spring bulbs in the grass below.

Cane's career as a garden designer was short, but nevertheless enormously prolific, and the number of gardens that he designed – or for which he designed features – was well over a hundred. His commissions provided the material for his books on garden design, *The Earth is my Canvas* (1956) and *The Creative Art of Garden Design* (1967). All his complete gardens demonstrate that his primary talent was in the arrangement and grouping of plants, either close together and in impressive quantities in a formal border, or more selectively and informally in a glade. In a traditional manner he invariably favoured a formal arrangement around the house, with axes or vistas leading to larger informal surrounding areas.

The garden that Cane designed at Hungerdown House in Wiltshire is typical. A broad terrace runs along the main garden front of the house, from which steps descend to the long cross-axis of a narrow lawn between borders planted with a mixture of shrubs and herbaceous plants. At one end the walk terminates in the edge of the garden; at the other it leads via more steps to a circular formal pool surrounded by York paving in the right-angle with the garden's second formal axis which is shorter and leads up parallel to the side of the house to an impressive mature oak tree. Beyond the pool the garden merges into an informally planted area of glades, with Cane's favoured flowering trees and curving groups of massed shrubs.

At Dartington Hall in Devon, where he followed the American Beatrix Farrand (*q.v.* p. 174) who had developed the gardens before the war, Percy Cane was given the opportunity of working to a larger scale than in the great majority of his gardens and his response was unequivocably enthusiastic: 'Dartington Hall is not for the conventional type of garden, it demands landscape on the grand scale'.[1] His first visit to the garden was in 1945, and Dartington soon became the major project for the rest of his career; he continued visiting and advising well after his official retirement at the age of seventy and he paid over fifty visits in some twenty-three years. Like Beatrix Farrand, he also worked in close association with Dartington's owners, the Americans Leonard and Dorothy Elmhirst, and she in particular was deeply involved in the development of the garden and often the inspiration for its most successful features. In the immediate post-war years there was much restoration that needed to be carried out but thereafter Cane embarked upon the series of alterations to the informal and semi-woodland parts of the garden where his hand is most evident.

In both character and construction, Dartington was a daunting garden to take on. In spite of the fact that his approach to garden design was essentially practical and traditional, whereas Beatrix Farrand's had been more aesthetic and abstract (and her friendship with the Elmhirsts far more intimate and personal), Percy Cane succeeded in his intentions, although they were not always harmonious with Farrand's original work. As Reginald Snell wrote: 'Cane had come to allow the garden to breathe – he flung the windows wide to let in the air, and parted the curtains to let in the light. You could not have both mystery and clarity . . ..'[2] Cane paid his last visit to Dartington in his mid eighties and it was this garden that consumed more of his capacity for hard work than any other and which at times taxed his capabilities the most.

JOHN CODRINGTON (1899-1991)

ARTHINGWORTH MANOR, *Leicestershire;* EMMANUEL COLLEGE, *Cambridge;* MARSTON HALL, *Lincolnshire;* PENSHURST PLACE, *Kent;* ROSEMOOR, *Devon;* STONE COTTAGE, *Leicestershire*

JOHN CODRINGTON was by age the 'elder statesman' of British garden designers until his death in 1991, and yet his work in this field – a career to which he turned late in life – never demonstrated the sonorous tones associated with such figures, more often displaying an engaging originality. Initially Codrington was drawn to garden design by his interest in plants and plant collecting, and his commissioned planting often demonstrates an easy association of native species with rarities from foreign countries. Although the majority of his commissions were for private gardens in Britain Codrington also produced an unusual range of designs overseas; gardens in a number of African countries, including Madagascar and a courtyard garden for the Mali tourist board in Timbuktu;[1] the botanical gardens at the Papua New Guinea capital of Port Moresby; and gardens in Australia, the last of particular interest as a source of plants.

Codrington became a regular soldier as a young man towards the end of World War I, and remained in the army for twenty-six years, finishing as a lieutenant-colonel. He was for a time married to the painter Primrose Harley, who subsequently married Lanning Roper (*q.v.* p. 220). After working in films and for B.O.A.C., he began work in 1958 as a garden designer. Codrington's planting skill is matched by his painting skill and his clients have usually been able to retain the watercolour sketches of his plans. Much of his early work consisted of small London gardens but he also designed an interesting triangular herb garden in several compartments for Emmanuel College, Cambridge. In the 1960s one of his most successful garden commissions was Arthingworth Manor in Leicestershire, where the original house was abandoned due to advanced dereliction and the stable block converted into a home. The old house was retained as a semi-ruin in the centre of the garden, but the transfer of attention to the stables demanded major re-aligning of the garden's axes and focuses, as well as new planting in their immediate vicinity. Codrington suggested placing the forecourt to the side of the new house so that cars would not obscure the long view up the garden from the front door, and then enhanced the long stretch of lawn with a variety of winding borders on either side. In the borders bold groups of shrubs mix with herbaceous perennials, and elsewhere in the garden Codrington helped with the skilful design of the informal rose garden. Close to the house he designed a geometric herb garden clearly reminiscent of his work at Emmanuel College.

In the 1950s Codrington returned to his childhood home on the edge of Rutland Water, and at Stone Cottage, initially shared with his sister, he created the most original of all his gardens. Here he was free to indulge his own particular preferences and to allow the plants, rather than

At his own garden of Stone Cottage John Codrington was able to experiment in the planting ingenuity for which his work is particularly admired.

formal divisions of paths and hedges, to dictate the garden's shape and character. Protecting windbreaks of trees give the garden a secluded, enclosed atmosphere which Codrington cleverly enhanced by keeping the style of each area small-scale and intimate. This heightens the effect of the occasional views suddenly revealed through trees to the great expanse of Rutland Water. In most parts of the garden plants seed themselves freely, adding to the engaging cottage-garden atmosphere. Native perennials once common in the wild are one of the garden's specialities and are central to its informal character, while, growing alongside, are rare treasures collected by Codrington overseas, all carefully positioned in the most suitable conditions available. The overall naturalness of the garden disguises the expert skill involved in achieving the apparently random effect and, at a time when native perennials were enjoying a strong revival as garden plants, Codrington's work was totally in step with contemporary trends.

BRENDA COLVIN, CBE (1897-1981)

LITTLE PEACOCKS, *Gloucestershire*; OKEOVER HALL, *Derbyshire*; STEEPLE MANOR, *Dorset*; SUTTON COURTENAY MANOR, *Oxfordshire*

BRENDA COLVIN was a garden designer who became one of the pioneers of landscape architecture in Britain; she also personified the move forward for women from the old-fashioned amateur/professionalism of Gertrude Jekyll (*q.v.* p. 138) and Norah Lindsay (*q.v.* p. 178) to a position of fully accepted professionalism – she was a founder member of the Institute of Landscape Architects in 1929, the institute's first woman president from 1951 to 1953, and, in 1949, a founder member of the International Federation of Landscape Architects. Colvin's philosophy of landscape, which was integral to her whole career, was both rooted in her early work as a garden designer and

intensely humanist; it was argued with a foresight that heralded contemporary environmental concerns in her *Land and Landscape* (1948), a book of enormous influence, described by Hal Moggridge, for many years Brenda Colvin's partner: 'This classic work reviewed the state of the British landscape and foreshadowed today's movements towards applied ecology and countryside conservation as the backbone of a sophisticated design philosophy. Its opening lines sum up Brenda Colvin's views: "The control which modern man is able to exert over his environment is so great that we easily overlook the power of the environment over man. Perhaps we just assume that any environment, modified and conditioned by human activity, must inevitably be suited to human life. We know that this is not so, really, and that man can ruin his surroundings and make them unsuitable for future generations, just as he can make war; but we continue to act as if we did not know it, and we have not properly mastered the methods which the elementary knowledge should lead us to apply".[1]

Born and brought up in India, Brenda Colvin was first inspired when taught garden design by Madeleine Agar – also a founder member of the Institute of Landscape Architects – at Swanley Horticultural College. After a brief period in Agar's office Colvin set up her own practice and the inter-war years were devoted largely to private garden design, although very little of this work survives today. However, she often stressed in her later landscape work, how the lessons learnt designing gardens were simply re-applied on a larger scale – in particular in the use of space, the association of textures such as different foliages and the natural architectural qualities of trees. The importance that she attached to trees can be seen in her book, *Trees for Town and Country*, published a year before *Land and Landscape*, in 1947.

Colvin's garden design revolved around the use of plants rather than hard features, and writing about her own garden at Little Peacocks in the Gloucestershire village of Filkins, her description clearly outlines what she aspired to achieve in all her gardens: 'The planting is intended to give continuous calm enjoyment at all seasons, rather than dazzle the eye in the height of summer. The ground is well covered with low plants chosen for beauty of foliage: many are evergreen and there are masses of spring bulbs. In and over the ground-cover plants are many flowering shrubs, roses, viburnums, hydrangeas, tree peonies, etc, to provide flower through the year . . . . I have tried to get a feeling of quiet space in this small area, enclosed as it is by grey stone walls and farm buildings. I try, too, to engender a sense of anticipation and interest by the progression from one interesting plant group to the next in a rhythm, giving definite contrasts without loss of unity. But it is difficult to reconcile simplicity with one's enthusiasm for plants in so small a garden, and I probably let the plants jostle one another too much.'[2]

Purchased in 1954 when her practice was in London, Little Peacocks was initially a week-end house, but by the mid 1960s it had become Brenda Colvin's permanent home and office. Today it remains the office of the partnership Colvin and Moggridge and the style and planting of the garden remain true to her original aspirations. There is still the distinct anti-formality of sweeping lines that she advocated, the dense planting of perennials and spring bulbs that were particular favourites and which she planted to establish 'self-sufficient' plant communities. In many ways her garden was an early example of much that is fashionable and admired today, for instance in its use of small hardy perennials and bulbs, compromising many native and originally common wild flowers, and in its area of meadow grass containing anemones, narcissi, cowslips and white saxifrage and left uncut until mid July. She also insisted upon retaining the daisies on the main lawn for as long as possible and whenever a visitor to the garden was expected the lawn was mown three to four days earlier to give the daisies time to grow back.

Between the wars Brenda Colvin visited the United States where the landscape architect Thomas Adams introduced her to the design principles of Frederick Law Olmsted (q.v. p. 120) and his sons. In England after the war she was given the opportunity to apply the ideas in the many public landscapes that she was commissioned to carry out, predominantly in the landscaping of industrial sites, of power stations, reservoirs and the spoil from coal mines. These commissions often involved adapting potentially highly intrusive features, such as power stations, into the countryside, and her techniques demonstrated both unusual vision of the nature of large-scale landscape design and, as in her garden design, the idea that simplicity is often the key to success. At one power station she threw up a long grassed bank which effectively concealed the jumble of ancillary buildings at the foot of the cooling towers, so that when viewed from a distance the enormous towers appeared to rise straight from the ground. In her treatment of coal-mining waste in Yorkshire her design was historically inspired, as Hal Moggridge described: 'These silhouettes and forms derive from the patterns created by ancient lynchets on chalk downs. The hill's derivation from landforms created so long ago and the projection of an idea as a guide for such a long period of construction unite in a single work: Brenda Colvin's ideas about the connection between past and future, about time as a dimension in the creation of landscapes, about aftercare as an essential corollary to design.'[3]

In one of her few private garden designs to survive, Okeover Hall in Derbyshire, Brenda Colvin similarly demonstrated a sympathy with history. Okeover was an 18th-century house by Joseph Sanderson extensively remodelled during the 1950s by the distinguished architect, Marshall Sisson. The two major axes of the garden had both been created during the 18th century, stretching away from the house to classical temples, while the other most important feature, the walled garden, was of the same date. Brenda Colvin planned and supervised the replanting of all the major areas of the garden as part of the 1950s work, notably the pair of long herbaceous borders flanking one of the two main walks, from the house to the Temple of Pomona. The choice of plants, as much for shape and foliage as for flower colour, encapsulated her ideas on planting and moved away from the old border planting style of her predecessors such as Gertrude Jekyll.

Brenda Colvin's belief in the close interaction of garden and landscape design, her deeply felt philosophy of landscape, and the designs that she carried out, have all provided an important and enduring example for her successors, both professional landscape architects and more humble amateur gardeners. Her gardening legacy is lovingly perpetuated at Little Peacocks, where her elegant, tall figure and shy but quietly forceful character are remembered by many. At the end of a tribute to Brenda Colvin shortly after her death, Hal Moggridge wrote of her landscape architecture: 'These large and long-term projects have all been created on the basis of ideas developed through garden design. She believed that each garden went to the heart of the matter of landscape architecture, posing in miniature the problems to be solved in the largest project.'[4]

DAME SYLVIA CROWE (1901-)

SYLVIA CROWE once described private gardens as 'the gloriettas of the individual man'.[1], and although she moved away from garden design to the larger-scale work of landscape architecture, the garden, its history and planting, was an unceasing source of inspiration in her work. Her ideas and influence have been most widely propagated through her book, *Garden Design*, published in 1958 and one of the rare classics of post-war garden literature. Like Brenda Colvin (*q.v.* p. 200), Sylvia Crowe's many projects landscaping for industry and transport made her acutely aware of the need for a conservationist attitude to natural landscape at a time when unacceptable intrusion all too easily became a feature of the post-war reconstruction of Britain. As she herself discovered, most prominently in her work as the landscape architect for new towns and for the Central Electricity Generating Board, it was not always possible to accommodate happily the fierce demands upon the landscape made by post-war society, whether in urban or rural surroundings, and the mistakes of the 1950s and 1960s remain as lessons for today. She considered it to be a primary responsibility of the new profession of landscape architecture to safeguard the rural landscape from thoughtless exploitation and this protective attitude stemmed partly from her view of the garden as a haven of peaceful seclusion, the domestic manifestation of the natural landscape.

Her upbringing on a Sussex farm instilled in Sylvia Crowe her deep love of the countryside. Like Brenda Colvin she studied horticulture at Swanley before joining the office of a landscape architect. From 1927 to 1939 she designed private gardens but was becoming increasingly involved in the newly emerging profession of landscape architecture, both in its official bodies such as the Institute of Landscape Architects and the International Federation of Landscape Architects, both of which she served for many years, and in her own practice which demanded virtually all her attention after the war. By this time she was landscaping power stations and high voltage lines for the Central Electricity Generating Board – work that was highly unpopular – as well as reservoirs, oil refineries, motorways and new towns such as Harlow, Basildon, Warrington and Washington. In 1964 she was appointed landscape consultant to the Forestry Commission and advised upon the landscaping of nearly half-a-million acres of woodland, stressing the importance of wildlife preservation and public amenity; she was not, however, responsible for the extensive and controversial planting of non-indigenous conifers by the commission. The booklet she produced on the landscaping of areas of forest, in which she stressed the fundamental need to respect the natural contours of the land, has become a textbook not only in Britain but also in the United States and France.

As well as *Garden Design*, upon which her reputation and influence in the smaller-scale arena stand, Sylvia Crowe published a series of illuminating books on landscape, all of which voiced her concern for the safe preservation of natural beauty and the countryside. It was not

*Brenda Colvin's planting in her own garden at Little Peacocks
demonstrates how she was an early exponent of much that is
most admired in the contemporary garden.*

only the quantity and quality of her work but also this sympathetic attitude which ensured that, following a CBE in 1967, she became in 1973 garden design and landscape architecture's first and only Dame of the British Empire.

MARGERY FISH (1892-1969)

EAST LAMBROOK MANOR, *Somerset*

At a time of rapid popularization of gardening during the late-1950s and 1960s Margery Fish's books describing the creation of her garden at East Lambrook Manor in Somerset struck an immense chord with the burgeoning gardening public and catapulted her from being an enthusiastic amateur to being a figure of enormous and lasting influence. She did not begin gardening until 1938 and almost immediately her work was interrupted by the war years. But by the beginning of the 1950s the garden at East Lambrook was steadily emerging as the foremost initiator of the post-war craze for 'cottage' gardens and Margery Fish herself was ensuring that many of Gertrude Jekyll's most cherished principles were being perpetuated into the second half of the 20th century. Her enormous public appeal derived from the fact that she set out – like most of her followers – as an inexperienced beginner, because the garden at East Lambrook grew through a process of trial and error, and because of her ebullient ability to convey her enthusiasm through her writing. In 1956 she published her first book, *We Made A Garden* (which was to have been called *Gardening With Walter* in recognition of her husband's contribution, but he died before the book was finished). Other books followed, but none was to equal the popularity and reputation of this first one which struck just the right balance of personal experience, practical advice and adventurous ideas to become a classic of garden writing and to give its author admirers and devoted correspondents all over the world.

Margery Fish once said of East Lambrook, 'It is a cottage-type garden to complete a cottage-type house and lends itself to this type of informal planting'.[1] The garden was both considerably smaller and far less architectural than either Sissinghurst or Hidcote, relying on an unobtrusive framework of paths and hedges and the relationship of the Ham stone house to an old malthouse. It was, however, the plants and their associations and individual qualities which were always the primary interest. Not only did Margery Fish play a significant part in promoting many old-fashioned but often neglected plants, but she also illustrated in her work at East Lambrook what have become two important features of post-war gardens; extensive use of low, weed-smothering perennials and the desire to plant for year-round interest – as she herself explained, describing one area of the garden.

'As the house faces south *Iris unguicularis* in several varieties flower well all through the winter. The first, last and best to provide a succession of blossoms is "Walter Butt" with large, very pale flowers. In March the green and black flowers of *Hermodactylus tuberosus* show up well against the pale stone. The wild *Gladiolus byzantinus* has established itself here as in other parts of the garden but is more welcome as it grows in front of *Ceanothus veitchianus*. *Abutilon megapotamicum* is good too. *Oxalis floribunda* opens its pink flowers whenever the sun shines and it follows the gladiolus below the ceanothus and is still flowering when blue and white agapanthus are in bloom. Before that regale lilies follow spring bulbs in raised beds and in late autumn pale green *Eucomis punctata* has nerines as companions with the dark sword-like foliage of *Dianellas* as a background'.[2]

Today Margery Fish's considerable influence is perpetuated by the many plants which bear either her name or East Lambrook's, many of them seemingly modest but invaluably reliable perennials, or silver-foliaged or variegated plants whose use she constantly championed. During her lifetime she dispatched many of thousands of plants from East Lambrook to correspondents in many countries and this is continued by the current owners of the garden who have carried out an admirable restoration of her planting ideas and favourite plants. Above all else, perhaps, it was her maxim that plantsmanship need not be dry and rarified but was rather a question of combining personal taste with what best suited an individual site, and considering plants both individually and as part of a group and for their characteristics throughout the year, which was and remains at the heart of her widespread reputation.

PENELOPE HOBHOUSE (1929-)

BASS GARDEN, *Maine, USA;* BENCOMBE HOUSE, *Gloucestershire;* HADSPEN HOUSE, *Somerset;* HERRIARD PARK, *Hampshire;* NEW YORK BOTANIC GARDEN, *New York, USA;* TAUBMAN GARDEN, *Michigan, USA;* TINTINHULL HOUSE, *Somerset.*

LIKE MANY OF THE MOST INFLUENTIAL FIGURES of the 20th century Penelope Hobhouse's experience was built up as an amateur in her own garden. In 1967 she and her first husband moved into his family home, Hadspen House in Somerset, where the garden had been neglected for some thirty years after enjoying a hey-day before World War I and during the 1920s. She revitalized the garden around the surviving Edwardian framework at the same time as elevating its planting to a new level of quality and interest. In 1980 Penelope Hobhouse became the National Trust's tenant at Tintinhull, also in Somerset, where she took on responsibility for one of the classic English gardens of the inter-war period, created by Phyllis Reiss and comparable in both style and importance to Hidcote and Sissinghurst. Penelope Hobhouse's practical work in these two gardens was from the first and remains the cornerstone of her now wide-ranging career, as a writer, lecturer and designer. It is this firmly retained foundation of practical gardening and horticultural knowledge which, perhaps more than anything else, has accounted for the respect with which she is regarded, in particular in the United States.

Much of Tintinhull's quality derives from the work of Phyllis Reiss. She devised it as a small-scale compartmented garden – only extending to one acre – which compliments the architecture of the elegant stone Queen Anne house and instilled the superb balance between the orderly arrangement of enclosures, especially in the main vista from the west front of the house through the Eagle Court and Azalea Garden to the Fountain Garden, with stone walls, paved paths, clipped yew and box providing the framework, and finely detailed planting in the mixed borders. Penelope Hobhouse's achievement has been one of immense skill; to perpetuate the mood of the garden while adding to and enhancing the planting, thereby ensuring the place's healthy evolution. Her work has brought about the garden's enduring success and popularity and extended its reputation to an ever-widening audience. It also represents the continuity of a central theme of 20th-century gardening, the principle emphasized a hundred years ago by Gertrude Jekyll and repeated by Phyllis Reiss, that plant association should be as much of a priority as individual plant characteristics, in particular in terms of shape and foliage as well as colour.

While visitors to Tintinhull have been able to enjoy Penelope Hobhouse's work at first hand many more in Britain, the United States and on the continent have benefited from the ideas set out in her hugely popular and influential books. The first, *The Country Garden*, was published in 1976, *Colour in Your Garden* (1985) and *Garden Style* (1988), have become two of the most widely read books of the post-war period and many of the others, such as *The National Trust: A Book of Gardening* (1986), reveal a similar ability to combine expert knowledge with detailed description in a manner rewardingly instructive for the aspiring gardener. The definitive *Plants in Garden History*, published in 1992, represents a combination of Penelope Hobhouse's knowledge of both horticulture and garden history.

In addition to her books Penelope Hobhouse has extended her field of influence through lecturing, in Britain, Europe and Australia, but especially in the United

States. The regional plants and garden styles of the United States are a subject of which her knowledge is wide ranging and she has played an important role in the process of self-identification which American gardens have achieved with such success during recent decades. Her work as a professional garden designer, both in America and Europe reiterates the principles which have guided her whole gardening career; the importance of a formal, structural layout, the colour schemes of planting, affinity with the historical and landscape associations of a particular site, and inspiration from the great garden styles of the past, such as Islamic and the Italian Renaissance.

SIR GEOFFREY ALAN JELLICOE (1900-)

DITCHLEY PARK, *Oxfordshire*; EVERTON PARK, *Bedfordshire*; HARTWELL HOUSE, *Buckinghamshire*; MOODY HISTORICAL GARDEN, *Texas, USA*; MOTTISFONT ABBEY, *Hampshire*; ROYAL LODGE, *Berkshire*; SANDRINGHAM HOUSE, *Norfolk*; SHUTE HOUSE, *Wiltshire*; ST PAUL'S WALDEN BURY, *Hertfordshire*; SUTTON PLACE, *Surrey*

GEOFFREY JELLICOE'S FIRST LARGE-SCALE COMMISSION in England was Ditchley Park in Oxfordshire during the 1930s, the most recent was Sutton Place in Surrey during the 1980s, two gardens described respectively by Tom Turner as, 'The last major English garden to be designed in the Italian style', and 'the *magnum opus* of modern English garden design'.[1] Such diversity in the work of one man clearly illustrates the extraordinary span of Jellicoe's career which has led him to be generally acknowledged as the foremost British garden and landscape designer of the 20th century. The cornerstones of Jellicoe's work have been his philosophical belief that landscape and man's relationship with it is the basis of all art, and his ability to reconcile classical and modernist inspirations.

Throughout much of his life as a garden designer,

architect, town planner and landscape architect Jellicoe's immediate admiration has been for the work of modern artists and designers, many of whom – such as Henry Moore and Ben Nicolson – were his close friends. And yet this has always been reconciled with an awareness of the historical, evolutionary nature of gardens and landscape. Jellicoe's ability to fuse these elements is currently being demonstrated in the most ambitious project of his career, commissioned when he was eighty-four, the Moody Historical Gardens on a site of semi-tropical salt marshes at Galveston on the coast of Texas. Here Jellicoe is creating an epic portrayal of the global evolution of human landscape in a series of historically representative gardens. His attitude when questioned about the wisdom of taking on such a sizeable commitment at such a late age typifies the humour and energy that have always been prominent: 'Life begins at eighty.'

Geoffrey Jellicoe was born in London, educated at Cheltenham College, and did his training, in the 1920s, at the Architectural Association – at the time, the English focus for architectural modernism. Jellicoe has retained strong links with the AA throughout his life, teaching there and serving as principal. The balanced foundations of his work were established at this early stage when, following his time at the AA, Jellicoe travelled to Italy with a fellow student, J. C. Shepherd, for a detailed study of renaissance gardens – a visit resulted in their book, *Italian Gardens of the Renaissance*, published in 1925. As respectful and admiring as previous commentaries on Italian gardens, the book broke new ground in its closely analytical study of the gardens' spatial and intellectual inspiration, and has remained one of the most original and incisive studies of the well-covered subject.

During the 1930s Jellicoe's practice was essentially architectural, but always closely tied to his growing interest in landscape architecture and its formalization into a recognized profession, of which he was an early champion. In 1929 he was a founder member of the Institute of Landscape Architects and he served as the institute's president from 1939 to 1949. After the war he was the first

*The balance between architecture and planting which
Phyllis Reiss achieved at Tintinhull has been sensitively
perpetuated by Penelope Hobhouse.*

president of the International Federation of Landscape Architects, founded in 1948, and later became the federation's honorary president.

No doubt *Italian Gardens of the Renaissance* influenced Ronald and Nancy Tree's decision to commission Jellicoe to design a formal Italian garden for their impressive home, Ditchley Park in Oxfordshire, in 1935. The garden was to be in front of the east side façade of the house built by James Gibbs between 1720 and 1740. Responding to the inspiration of Gibbs's architecture, Jellicoe designed a geometric garden stretching away from the terrace below the house's east front. His original centrepiece, an elaborate rectangular parterre, has subsequently been removed and replaced by plain lawn, still flanked, as he planned, by yew hedges and pleached lime walks. At the far end a bathing-pool is screened from the house by a wall of fountain jets. The success of Ditchley played a part in Jellicoe's next garden commission, in 1936, to help King George VI and Queen Elizabeth, then Duke and Duchess of York, with the creation of a garden at the Royal Lodge, their home in Windsor Great Park.

After the war Jellicoe worked again for the King and Queen at Sandringham. Here George VI requested an enclosed garden stretching away from the north end of the house where the private apartments were, which would give privacy to the outlook from the house and provide a screen from the open view to the house from the Norfolk gates entrance. Jellicoe's response was one of classical simplicity which contained distinctive hallmarks of his garden style, in particular the pleached lime walks used at Ditchley – as well as at Mottisfont Abbey and later at Sutton Place – which flanked the central formal garden. This long narrow rectangle he designed as a succession of box-hedged enclosures where squares of lawn alternated with circular areas containing patterns of curving flower beds planted with roses and herbaceous perennials, including many of Queen Elizabeth's favourites.

The royal connection led to Jellicoe being approached by the Queen Mother's brother, Sir David Bowes-Lyon, to help with specific features in the restoration of the family's rare formal early 18th-century garden at St Paul's Walden Bury in Hertfordshire, work that has been carried on by Sir David's son Simon. As at Ditchley, Jellicoe greatly enjoyed working in such a distinguished historical setting. His new additions and resitings blend well with the old le Nôtre-inspired *patte d'oie* of three long hedged allées radiating from the house through woodland to distant focal points and include an impressive flight of curving stone steps leading up to an 18th-century copy of a famous Greek statue the Discus Thrower (known in the family as the Running Footman). Beyond the statue lies the marvellous original green theatre with its little domed temple on the far side.

Jellicoe has always happily admitted that he is not a plantsman, and in his early garden commissions he worked with other distinguished contemporaries. At Sandringham, Sylvia Crowe (*q.v.* p. 202) provided the planting scheme, and at other gardens he worked with Brenda Colvin (*q.v.* p. 200) and Russell Page (*q.v.* p. 216). Jellicoe and Russell Page were in partnership for a few years in the 1930s, and during this time designed an innovative public restaurant and garden for the Marquess of Bath at Cheddar Gorge. However, in 1936 Jellicoe married Susan Pares, a keen and knowledgeable plantswoman, and from the 1950s on they worked in close partnership on many schemes, she providing the planting for his designs. Their partnership also extended to writing and in 1975 they published one of the most ambitious and influential books on the history and ideals of landscape design, the splendidly illustrated *The Landscape of Man*.

During the 1950s and 1960s much of Jellicoe's work consisted of large-scale landscape architecture and town planning commissions: Oldbury-on-Severn Nuclear Power Station, the Blue Circle Hope Cement Works in Derbyshire, the Rutherford underground atomic research laboratory in Oxfordshire and Hemel Hempstead new town. At Rutherford Jellicoe moulded 350,000 cubic yards of chalk waste – excavated to build the underground laboratory – in the form of two gently rounded hills that blend in with the encircling downs. At Hemel Hempstead his most successful design was the water garden, created along the course of the small River Gade, in a long narrow space between car parks and shops. By capitalizing on the water, which he enlivened with bridges and a fountain jet and edged with paths and planting, Jellicoe managed to transform an unprepossessing and awkward site and fulfil the aspirations of public parks and gardens derived from Paxton's Birkenhead Park.

In the 1970s, and as a result of his work at Ditchley forty years earlier, Jellicoe was commissioned by the Trees' son and daughter-in-law, Michael and Anne Tree, to design one of his least-known gardens in England, but arguably his most successful, Shute House in the village of Donhead St Mary on the borders of Wiltshire and Dorset. The Trees bought Shute House in 1972, and moved there from Mereworth Castle in Kent, the Palladian villa designed by Colen Campbell. They wished to create a garden in harmony with the deeply rural surrounding landscape, to preserve the secretive woodland atmosphere of the main garden area, and draw inspiration from the major natural feature of the garden, an abundance of water provided by the source of the River Nadder, bubbling up in a series of natural springs into a pool in a grotto-like corner of the garden. The basic outline of the garden's ponds already existed, but the rest of the area was largely dense and inpenetrable wood.

Jellicoe has always maintained that the most successful gardens result from a close and sympathetic partnership between client and professional designer, and this partnership was to be as fruitful as he could have wished. Michael Tree is a painter and his wife – a daughter of the Duke of Devonshire and brought up at Chatsworth and other Devonshire homes – a talented plantswoman.

The main area of the garden lies through a gateway in a brick wall to one side of the lawn in front of the house. Jellicoe's most ingenious addition was a new water garden running at right-angles across the path into the garden, with the water channelled to flow downhill in a narrow rill, to fall over copper Vs in a series of musical cascades. A sheltered terrace looks down on the cascades edged with lush aquatic plants, old-fashioned roses and regale lilies. Flanking paths are spanned by arches draped with wisteria. Below this the mood changes dramatically and the water descends in sepulchral silence along a narrow rill through three descending pools, one square and the others octagonal. The simplicity of the grass banks on either side, contrasting with the rich planting above, is echoed by the bubble fountain in each pool, inspired by the Mogul gardens of Kashmir, the gravity-fed water constantly just breaking the surface. At the bottom stands a classical statue brought to the garden from Mereworth.

The path into the garden crosses the rill via a small stone bridge and beyond is the main flower garden, designed and planted in partnership with Anne Tree. Its layout of six box-edged squares, each filled with a mixture of summer perennials, ornamental vegetables and herbs beneath standard fruit trees, is reminiscent of an earlier and smaller design by Jellicoe at the garden of Bingham's Melcombe in Dorset. Along one side of the flower garden a beech hedge conceals one arm of an original pond which Jellicoe formalized into a canal. In a design reminiscent of William Kent (q.v. p. 41) at Chiswick House, another Devonshire home, he terminated one end of the canal with a pair of Palladian grotto arches and stone caryatids on the bank above. Two arches cut in the beech hedge allow wooden balconies to jut out over the water in a manner that he repeated at Sutton Place. At the other end of the canal the water flows round and out of sight to expand into one of the main ponds of the further areas of the garden, retained as semi-natural woodland with winding paths, the occasional suddenly revealed view of a classical statue, and an undisturbed atmosphere of mystery.

At the same time he was working at Shute, Jellicoe was also working on a very different scheme for Lord and Lady Pym at Everton Park in Bedfordshire. He was particularly intrigued by the fact that almost exactly a hundred years earlier Humphry Repton (q.v. p. 81) had prepared a *Red Book* for the park at Hasells Hall, the seat of Francis Pym Esq. Hasells Park had since been converted into flats by Kit Martin and the Pyms had built the neo-Georgian

Everton Park on the edge of the Hasells park in the late 1960s. Jellicoe commented: 'a comparison can be made, therefore, between the attitudes of two landscape designers nearly two centuries apart, towards the home of the same family.'[1]

Like Hasells, Everton Park stands on an escarpment from which there are wide views over the vale of Bedford to the west. Jellicoe's priorities were to retain the grandeur of the views, to give the garden a degree of intimacy and privacy, and to bind it historically to Hasells and the Repton park. The western edge of the garden was enclosed by a beech hedge, but with vistas from the house funnelled into spaces at either end: one out over the plain of Bedford, along which pass the Kings Cross to Edinburgh express trains – a modern landscape combining impressive natural and human features that greatly appealed to Jellicoe; the other across Repton's park, focusing upon an ancient cedar standing close to the old house. Screening on the garden's north and east sides has ensured privacy, while immediately to the south of the house Jellicoe positioned a seat in front of a protective yew hedge. From here long shrub beds (planned by Susan Jellicoe), stretch away on either side of a narrow lawn and the view from the seat extends across the Hasells park to the cedar beside the house.

Jellicoe's eightieth year witnessed an extraordinary acceleration in the pace of his career: 'In the 1970s I stopped full-time work and took a few holidays, but then at the age of eighty I experienced a sudden burst of ideas and became involved in several very large commissions.'[2] As well as being asked to produce extensive plans for civic landscapes and public gardens in the Italian cities of Modena and Brescia, unquestionably his major project was the new garden at Sutton Place in Surrey. Stanley Seegar, a reclusive American oil magnate, had purchased Sutton Place to display his collection of modern art, and in 1980 he commissioned Jellicoe with a view to creating an ambitious garden. It was an exciting project. Seegar's ideas were fully compatible with Jellicoe's own, and it was to be what Jellicoe described as 'a consummation of all the work I have ever done . . . I realized he would not be trying to restore the historical gardens (which I'm not interested in doing in the least), but would be trying to create a garden which expresses the modern mind, sympathetic to the ethos of the place, which comprehends the past the present and the future – considering a landscape design as a continuum and not as a restoration of the past.'[3]

Sutton Place provided a large enough canvas for Jellicoe to put into practice his growing conviction, partly inspired by Jungian philosophy, that gardens and landscape relate not only to the human senses but also to the subconscious: 'the landscape of Sutton Place is of the mind as well as the eye'.[4] His plan was for an allegory on human life, the stages portrayed by a series of gardens around the Elizabethan mansion. Creation was represented by 5ha/12-acre lake dug beyond the house's main front and shaped like a fish, while from the house the journey of life itself began: hazardous stepping-stones led across the moat to the paradise garden where paths wound between arched bowers covered in roses, and clematis and jasmine encircled fountains; from the secret garden the way continued through an octagonal gazebo built at the end of one of the new walls enclosing the paradise garden to the great terrace stretching across the house's garden front, where the symmetry was emphasized by pleached lime walks and a long traditional herbaceous border. On the far side of the house the terrace led into the surrealist garden inspired by a painting by Magritte, where five vast Roman urns along one side contrasted with a fragile magnolia tree just visible through a square window in the garden's boundary wall. From the surrealist garden an enclosed pathway leads to the garden's finale, a huge wall of white Carrara marble sculpted with a simple but monumental abstract design by Ben Nicolson, reflected in a lily pool and representing the transition from physical life to aspiration.

Stanley Seegar sold Sutton Place before the gardens were finished; the cascade and grotto that Jellicoe planned for the main garden front of the house between existing domes of yew never materialized; neither did the Henry Moore sculpture planned to overlook the lake; nor the redesigning of the old walled garden on the opposite side

The water garden at Shute House, Geoffrey Jellicoe's most delightful garden design.

of the house from the paradise garden, where only Jelli-coe's swimming-pool garden was carried out. Jellicoe him-self remains philosophical about the non-completion of his work, appreciating that commissioned garden designs are always dependant upon the patron and that unfinished projects can be cited on numerous occasions in the past. His work has been meticulously maintained by the new owner of Sutton Place. His approach to the commission of equal scale that followed immediately after Sutton Place, the Moody Historical Gardens in Texas, is equally realistic but has not detracted from his commitment to the project: 'I don't suppose I'll be around to see it completed, but that hardly matters. I know in my mind exactly what it will look like. I have walked through every inch of it already.'[5]

Jellicoe's long career has been productive and influen-tial and will remain of lasting importance. He will be remembered for his ability to reconcile traditions from the past with contemporary aspirations, so that classicism and modernism, often presented by others in dichotomy, have had an easy co-existence in his work. His humanist approach to gardens and landscapes has reflected his own warm personality and his belief that all landscape has an inherent human element, a message of increasing relevance in today's threatened world.

CHRISTOPHER LLOYD (1921-)

GREAT DIXTER, Sussex

CHRISTOPHER LLOYD is one of the select number of amateur gardeners whose influence on contemporary gardening has come as a result of both their own garden-ing prowess and their garden writing. Christopher Lloyd's column in *Country Life* – heading towards its thirtieth year – is one of the most enjoyed perennials of gardening journalism while his books include acknowledged classics of current garden literature. The originality and unam-biguous views that he expresses in his writing are put into

practice at Great Dixter, the garden that his parents had already made a gem of the Arts and Crafts movement.

Christopher Lloyd's father, Nathaniel Lloyd, sub-scribed to the ideas of Philip Webb and William Robinson. After purchasing Great Dixter in 1910 he commissioned his friend Edwin Lutyens (*q.v.* p. 146) to assist in the restoration and transformation of the 15th-century tim-bered manor house and its surroundings. The house was to become the centrepiece of the garden around it, and old farm buildings were drawn into the design – a cowshed was adapted into a loggia and an oast house provides the backdrop to one side. Lutyens was responsible for archi-tectural features of this kind, and for marvellously detailed brick walls and gateways, but Nathaniel Lloyd was always firmly in charge of the overall plans and responsible for the yew topiary that has become such a feature of the garden, while his wife introduced the naturalistic meadow style of gardening that has been retained in areas ever since.

Christopher Lloyd returned to Great Dixter during the late 1950s, where he soon developed the garden and estab-lished a nursery specializing in clematis and unusual hardy perennials. Before long he had also begun to pro-duce the elegantly written books which have achieved such a reputation: *Clematis* (1965) and *The Well-Tempered Garden* (1970). Whether writing on a specific subject, such as *Hardy Perennials* (1967), or more broadly using Great Dixter for subject matter as in *The Well-Chosen Gar-den* (1984) authority and sharply attuned humour is always evident.

At Great Dixter he has maintained the most important features of his parents' garden while adding his own sub-stantial contribution. This has been provided by a catholic yet discerning choice of plants and is especially effective in the immensely long mixed Long Border stretching away from the house. Here, over the years, many of Lloyd's firm-ly held principles of planting, plant association and cham-pioning of unusual plants have been put into practice. Small trees, shrubs and hardy perennials are grown togeth-er and he has demonstrated how best to achieve a vigorous mixture that gives year-round interest and enjoyment.

WOLFGANG OEHME (*1930-*) and
JAMES VAN SWEDEN (*1935-*)

DRAPER GARDEN, *Washington DC, USA*; FRANCIS SCOTT KEY PARK, *Washington DC, USA*; GELMAN GARDEN, *Maryland, USA*; GERMAN-AMERICAN FRIENDSHIP GARDEN, *Washington DC, USA*; GRATZ GARDEN, *Maryland, USA*; HESTER HEADQUARTERS, *Virginia, USA*; NEW AMERICA GARDEN (**US National Arboretum**), *Washington DC, USA*; NORTH PARK, *New York, USA*; OFFUTT GARDEN, *Maryland, USA*; PENNSYLVANIA AVENUE LANDSCAPES, *Washington DC, USA*; ROSENBURG GARDEN, *New York, USA*; SCHNEIDERMAN GARDEN, *Washington DC, USA*; SHOCKEY GARDEN, *Virginia, USA*; SLIFKA GARDEN, *New York, USA*; UNIVERSITY OF MINNESOTA (**Telecommunications Plaza**), *Minneapolis, USA*; VIRGINIA AVENUE, *Washington DC, USA*; VOLLMER GARDEN, *Maryland, USA*.

BOTH WOLFGANG OEHME AND JAMES VAN SWEDEN enjoyed distinguished careers as horticulturists and landscape architects before establishing their partnership in 1977. It is since then, however, that they have become increasingly acknowledged as a leading force in the development of contemporary American landscape and garden design.

Their partnership has been credited with the creation of the 'New American Garden' style which, according to one commentator, 'seems to be moving away from the aristocratic European model toward a reflection of the egalitarian United States and its great plains heritage'.

At a time when American gardeners have sought to break away from traditional European influences and assert their varying regional individualities, it is this indigenous American element which has been central to the work and reputation of Oehme and van Sweden. To some extent they have built upon the example of the evolving tradition of American landscape design evident in the work of, for example, Fletcher Steele (*q.v.* p. 181), Thomas Church (*q.v.* p. 173) and Jens Jensen, but with increasing attention to the use of plant materials and their harmonious balance with the hard architectural features of any single design. They see the 'New American Garden'

style as being a metaphor for the American meadow, reflecting the quality of natural landscape and seasonal change and using, in particular, perennial plants and ornamental grasses.

It is a style which they have employed equally successfully in large-scale public schemes such as Pennsylvania Avenue and Virginia Avenue Gardens, both in Washington DC, and in private gardens. In the latter they have demonstrated an honest recognition that most people's gardens are not purely horticultural havens and as a result incorporated potentially intrusive features such as swimming pools and children's play areas to enhance the overal scheme of a garden, rather than detracting from it and needing to be hidden away.

Wolfgang Oehme was born in Germany and James van Sweden in the United States, but both men worked extensively in Europe before embarking upon their mainstream careers in the United States, Wolfgang Oehme in 1957 and James van Sweden in 1964. Thereafter they both specialized in urban landscape, designing parks and schemes of urban regeneration, as well as fulfilling private garden design commissions.

Since 1977 their partnership has combined horticulture and landscape architecture in a pioneering and adventurous manner, which has aimed to bring together human requirements – whether of a single, private client or a far larger public audience – with recognition for individual plants which have a link with the natural landscape and the balance of clearly defined, but not classically ornamental, hard or architectural features.

Another important priority which reveals the degree to which their work is contemporary is emphasis on the year-round appearance of plants and on varieties which require low maintenance and little or no artificial pesticides or fertilizers.

Perennials and ornamental grasses are planted in bold groups within a framework of hard features to give immediate impact on both horizontal and vertical planes. Spring bulbs, in particular tulips, are also a vital ingredient in many of their gardens, whether planted in great massed

Overleaf: The innovative work of Wolfgang Oehme and James van Sweden is notable for the planting of perennials and ornamental grasses in bold individual groups.

swathes as in the gardens of Pennsylvania Avenue, or in a smaller-scale but equally effective manner as in the Schneiderman Garden in Washington DC. Favourite perennials and grasses such as the ground-covering *Ceratostigma plumbaginoides*, tall pink-flowered *Lythrum salicaria* 'Morden's Pink', the aptly-named black-eyed Susan, *Rudbeckia fulgida* 'Goldstrum', and among the grasses, varieties of *calamagrostis* and *miscanthus*, reappear throughout Oehme and van Sweden's work and do perhaps more than anything give it an individual and immediately recognizable style.

In both public and private commissions their treatment of plants arranged in sweeping groups of single varieties marks an immediate step forward from a traditional arrangement of lawn, formal vistas and plants arranged in mixed beds or borders. This is heightened by the relationship with hard features, in particular paths or open terraces, the colour and texture of whose material is carefully chosen for maximum effect, by the introduction of water into their gardens either in formal pools or natural streams and cascades over boulders, and the choice of ornamental trees – most often outstanding native American species such as magnolias, cornus, swamp cypress or different oaks and ilex.

In 1990 Oehme and van Sweden published *Bold Romantic Gardens*, a book which draws together and illustrates their ideas on garden and landscape design and their major commissions during the last two decades.

At a time when American gardens are truly enjoying freedom from European influences and looking instead to their more immediate surroundings for inspiration, the Oehme and van Sweden partnership demonstrates how successful this can be and what a rich vein this will be in the future.

They continue the now long-established tradition that private and public commissions of the highest quality have evolved side by side in America and confirm the extent to which the two areas are intrinsically linked, often with the only major factors of separation being a difference in scale and the contrasting demands of privacy and public access.

RUSSELL PAGE (1906-85)

COPPINGS FARM, *Kent;* THE COTTAGE, *Badminton, Avon;* FLETE, *Devon;* FRICK MUSEUM, *New York, USA;* LEEDS CASTLE, *Kent;* LITTLE MYNTHURST FARM, *Berkshire;* LONGLEAT HOUSE, *Wiltshire;* OWLEY, *Kent;* PEPSICO PARK, *New York, USA;* PORT LYMPNE, *Kent*

EARLY IN HIS CAREER, in the 1930s, Russell Page worked in partnership with Geoffrey Jellicoe (*q.v.* p. 206) but after World War II moved to France where he established one of the most successful international practices of any contemporary garden designer. Gaining experience in other European countries, especially France, before expanding his work to countries all over the world, Page absorbed and transmuted many different national styles and conditions. The hallmarks of his work were an elegant formality and a belief that simplicity is the key to garden design; as he described in his immensely influential semi-autobiographical *The Education of a Gardener* (1962), whose language is as impeccable as his garden designs: 'All the good gardens I have ever seen, all the garden scenes that have left me satisfied were the result of just such reticence; a simple idea developed as far as it could be . . . a lovely or impressive site is apt to tempt a garden designer, make him elaborate his plans and work out sumptuous schemes to match his setting. In such cases he would usually do better to discipline any tendency towards exuberance and let the site tell its own story.'[1]

Russell Page was at school at Charterhouse in Surrey, whose grounds he was to redesign in one of his earliest commissions before the war, before going on to the Slade School of Art in London and subsequently to study painting in Paris. Although he had already decided that his inclination was towards gardening, his painter's eye for form and colour was to be a dominant feature of his garden designs. The need to know the individual qualities of plants in order to assess their suitability for an overall scheme was an early priority which led to Page's formidable horticultural knowledge; while his familiarity with the Mediterranean was to make him deeply aware both of the importance of light and its potential for creating contrast, and of the qualities of water, used either as a formal architectural feature or in conjunction with planting.

As he makes clear throughout *The Education of a Gardener*, the inspiration of garden styles from past periods and of different countries is of little interest if reproduced in a purely derivative, repetitious manner, and he highlights the problems of an accumulation of historical examples which can weaken a garden's basic form, a problem exacerbated by the embarrassment of plant riches available to modern gardeners: 'Another reason for the frequent lack of consideration given to the underlying structure of contemporary gardens is that modern gardeners have a far greater choice of plants. The élite among them know and care for rare and unusual plants which they collect and cultivate with care and skill. However, they tend to be less interested in the visual relationships of form and colour.'[2]

One of Russell Page's earliest and most influential gardening introductions was to Mark Fenwick and his garden at Abbotswood in Gloucestershire. Before World War I Fenwick had commissioned Edwin Lutyens (*q.v.* p. 146) to extend the house and create the garden immediately surrounding the house, which Lutyens did in characteristic and highly successful style with a series of terraces decorated with planting, gazebos, a formal lily pool and a canal garden. By the 1920s Fenwick was an old man and confined to a wheelchair, but was still developing new areas of the garden beyond Lutyens's terraces. Page assisted him in the creation of a spring garden along the banks of a narrow stream that tumbled through a series of miniature waterfalls to the main water at Abbotswood, a tributary of the River Windrush, and in the process he himself learnt much from Fenwick's skill and enthusiasm for the positioning and blending of different plants – spring narcissus, anenomes, scillas and fritillaries in great quantities.

While in partnership with Geoffrey Jellicoe Page was commissioned to work at Longleat in Wiltshire, a connection that continued until the 1960s. Initially he advised on removing intrusive 19th-century planting of exotic conifers and rhododendrons from 'Capability' Brown's 18th-century park and perimeter woodlands, and replanting with more suitable species. One of the earliest areas successfully replanted was Longcombe Drive, along which visitors now approach the house. Later, during the decades after the war, the formal areas around the house were replanned and Russell Page's major achievement was in radically simplifying the mid 19th-century planting schemes (which had accommodated some 40,000 summer annuals), while retaining the necessary formality and air of dignity befitting the house's immediate surroundings.

With large numbers of public visitors in mind, Page's approach was to enlarge the scale of features, broadening paths and having fewer, larger and less intricate flowerbeds. This was particularly successful in the area between the house and the classical orangery. Here Page flanked a simplified scheme of flowerbeds and lawn with a broad allée running between clipped yew hedges, rows of columnar cypress trees and pleached limes to an urn at the far end. There was enjoyable historical continuity in this scheme, for in George London's (*q.v.* p. 46) correspondence (1685-1711) with Viscount Weymouth (who spent £30,000 on the Longleat garden – one of London and Wise's most ambitious commissions) there is detailed discussion of 'planting limes' for the great parterre that London was laying out. In front of the orangery a terrace was decorated with a central fountain surrounded by tubs and urns in a style typical of Page who always attached great importance to well planted containers.

The Longleat work introduced Page to the Marquess of Bath's daughter, Lady Caroline Somerset (now the Duchess of Beaufort) and with her he designed the garden of The Cottage, at Badminton in the 1960s. This became one of the most admired of post-war gardens, embodying many of the principles and characteristics held in highest esteem in recent years. John Sales describes it: 'The strong formal outline bounded by neat hedges and climber-covered walls; the clever variety of intimate enclosures; the wide range of plants used at the same time; it is all here, a worthy development of the Hidcote style and a rare achievement in every way.[3] The planting, notably the ebullient mixture of old-fashioned roses, climbers and white and silver foliage plants was largely devised by Lady Caroline, while Page's contribution was the garden's structure of axes linking the various enclosures and the architectural features: smart white-painted open-panelled wooden doorways and the similar trellised rose arbour in the centre of the French-style *potager* – soon to become hugely fashionable in country-house gardens; the extensive use of clipped box hedging both to enclose beds and to provide parterre-like patterns; the sheltered simplicity of the swimming-pool enclosure concealed inside yew hedges; and the formal use of evergreen in a variety of ways such as the balls of clipped box in Versailles tubs, pleached limes and yew clipped into pyramids.

When Lady Caroline's husband inherited the Beaufort dukedom in 1984 they moved to Badminton House where she immediately began planning new gardens, in particular to the south and east of the great house. Russell Page was consulted from the earliest days, but died a year later after providing a series of enclosures, long borders and walks in the foreground of the endless view away into the Badminton park. Very late in his life Page was also involved in the most ambitious scheme of his career, the landscaped park around the Pepsi-cola offices in New York known as the Pepsico Park. The scheme could not have been in sharper contract to the warm English country house style of Badminton and the Cottage; the priority at the Pepsico Park was the display of contemporary sculpture, both figurative and abstract. Page designed much of the garden's planting and its major axes; one of the most impressive runs from a formal square pool with willows growing on square islands to David Wynne's Boy with a Dolphin pool and on to a broad walk between pleached limes.

The exhilarating modernism of the Pepsico Park was a challenge to which Russell Page was well suited with his style of fastidious formality with its clean-cut architectural lines, soft single-colour planting, clipped evergreens and restrained water features – a style partly inspired by and certainly with a close affinity to the French gardens where he worked for much of his career. Page's work in England was limited but closely related to the mainstream development of landscape and garden design in Britain: he was awarded the OBE for his design for the Festival Gardens in Battersea Park for the 1951 Festival of Britain.

ANTHONY DU GARD PASLEY (1929-)

OLD PLACE FARM, *Kent;* THE POSTERN, *Kent;* WADHURST PARK, *Sussex*

ANTHONY PASLEY'S EARLY YEARS as a garden designer combined training as assistant under the two leading landscape architects, Brenda Colvin (*q.v.* pp. 00) and Sylvia Crowe (*q.v.* pp. 00), with work for R. W. Wallace of Tunbridge Wells, a firm of nurserymen whose practice was incorporated garden design as well as the supply of plants. Since the war traditional nurseries have been increasingly pressurized by economic conditions and competition, and their involvement in garden design has declined accordingly. Pasley's work, which has consisted predominantly of private commissions for gardens in England, combines a formal structure of terraces, lawns, hedges and paths, with carefully planned borders and varied planting of trees and shrubs for different seasons of the year. In recent years he has been a resident lecturer at the English Gardening School at the Chelsea Physic Garden in London.

While working with Wallaces during the 1950s Pasley took on the design of his most successful garden, The Postern, where he planned the garden in conjunction with the owner, John Phillimore, Pasley's design improved the relationship between the 18th-century house and garden by the addition of paved terraces along the east and south fronts with wide steps down at the corner. In the main area of garden he created series of formal enclosures on

At Woolbeding House, Lanning Roper demonstrated his skill at creating a border with bold mixtures of perennials and shrubs.

either side of central herbaceous borders backed by yew hedges, the enclosures surrounded by other trim hedges of hornbeam and green and copper beech which are strongly reminiscent of Hidcote. At the far end of the herbaceous borders a classical pavilion with trellis pillars, designed by Phillimore, opens to the cross-axis of a pleached lime walk, leading in turn to a rose walk where rambling roses swathe tall tripods along a gravel path. The formal structure of the garden is nicely balanced by the collection of ornamental trees underplanted with spring bulbs which replaced an old orchard.

The Postern is in many ways a traditional country house garden with its different enclosures, rose garden, hedged walks and spring garden. Quite different is the garden that Pasley designed for Wadhurst Park, a strikingly modern house built by John Outram. Around the house the treatment is far more linear and restrained, with paving and grass balancing sculpture and stone ornaments. The new house replaced a Victorian one and an innovative feature is the recreated Victorian winter garden at one end of the house, transformed into a temperate conservatory and blending with the architecture of the rest of the house.

Anthony Pasley's teaching of garden design for the English Gardening School and his actual garden designs have helped to continue the tradition of the most characteristic English 20th-century gardens.

LANNING ROPER (*1912-83*)

ANANOURI, *New York, USA*; CHARTWELL, *Kent*; CONISTON COLD, *Yorkshire*; FARNSWORTH HOUSE, *Illinois, USA*; HALL PLACE, *Hampshire*; HILLBARN HOUSE, *Wiltshire*; THE LAINES, *Sussex*; LOWER HALL, *Shropshire*; MULGRAVE CASTLE, *Yorkshire*; THE OLD RECTORY, *Suffolk*; THE OLD VICARAGE, *Sussex*; PENNS IN THE ROCKS, *Sussex*; SCOTNEY CASTLE, *Kent*; WOOLBEDING HOUSE, *Sussex*

FEW RECENT GARDEN DESIGNERS have been given the accolade of a biographical study. The fact that such a book, *Lanning Roper and His Gardens*, by the distinguished garden historian Jane Brown, appeared within five years of his death is an indication of the respect and affection that scores of garden owners and eminent horticulturists felt for Lanning Roper.

He was something of an enigma: an American with an extraordinary feel for English gardens, who established in England a one-man-band that was probably the most wide-ranging garden practice of the post-war decades. His career was completely in tune with contemporary demand, and his reputation was secured not by a small number of ambitious long-lasting projects but by his involvement in nearly two hundred gardens during the relatively short period of some twenty-five years.

Roper's design work revolved around his enjoyment and knowledge of plants; he appreciated that few contemporary garden owners either wanted or could afford 'complete' design schemes for their gardens. Most wanted help with details, usually of planting, and this was his forte and the work he enjoyed. In the list of commissions at the end of Jane Brown's book a majority of the entries are for 'brief garden advice' or 'planting advice',[1] and it was in this way that his influence was spread. Jane Brown pin-pointed the demand which Lanning Roper responded to: 'The English love of gardens was reviving after the war and there were many gardens to be restored and made anew. Who would help the hard-pressed owners? The horticultural students that became Lanning's friends at Kew and Edinburgh Botanic Gardens would cultivate wonderful plants and work in grand gardens; the small English landscape architecture profession would reorganize itself, but its sights were set upon recognition for work in public landscapes, in parks, schools, hospitals and factories. Somewhere between these two there was a gap: whether Lanning ever precisely identified that gap and aimed to fill it, I do not know; but he did come to fill it, both usefully and successfully.'[2]

Lanning Roper was born in New Jersey and it was via

a long and at times circuitous route that he arrived at the point in 1957 when he began practising in England as a 'garden consultant' – a description he always preferred to designer. He nevertheless maintained contact with the United States throughout his life and designed a number of gardens there; his own family provided a connection with the American landscape design tradition, for his brother's wife was Laura Wood Roper who in 1973 published her authoritative biography of Frederick Law Olmsted (q.v.p. 120).

After studying fine arts at Harvard and architecture at Princeton – which he gave up after a year – teaching English in New York took Roper up to World War II when he served in the US Navy and established his first real contact with England. Although he did not appear to make a conscious decision that there might be greater opportunity for him to pursue his gardening interests in England, after returning briefly to America he established himself in London. He felt that landscape architecture was not the path he wished to follow as it seemed to preclude the practical plant-orientated gardening that would become his primary interest, and by the late 1940s had enrolled as a student at Kew. In 1950 he moved to the Edinburgh Botanic Garden where he remained for a year before joining the Royal Horticultural Society as assistant editor of their monthly journal, *The Garden*.

It was as a writer that Lanning Roper first made his mark in the gardening world. In addition to his work for the RHS he began writing the articles for *Country Life* that continued right up until his death. More significantly, in 1962 he became gardening correspondent of *The Sunday Times*. As Jane Brown points out, it was the year that Vita Sackville-West died. Her column in *The Observer* had dominated the Sunday reading of garden enthusiasts, and Lanning Roper was soon to take over this position. In 1957 he published *Successful Town Gardening* which struck an immediate chord with the 1950s readership. The book was written around the garden of the London home he shared with his artist wife Primrose Harley (who had previously been married to John Codrington (q.v. p. 197),

though before he became a garden designer), until their separation in 1964. However, his most successful and influential book was *The Sunday Times Gardening Book*, published in 1968, one of the first – and to many people the best – of a new type of mass-market garden book publishing that has proliferated ever since.

Describing Roper's success as a *Country Life* writer, Jane Brown commented: 'It was typical of everything that Lanning did that quietly, so quietly that it seemed effortless, he joined the ranks of the *Country Life* stylists, and became a habitué of the country house and garden world.'[3] This description says a great deal about Roper. First, it was the unfussing, confident ease with which he worked that appealed to his gardening clients. Second – and more decisive – it was through the network of the country house world and its seemingly endless connections that the commissions appeared, one after the other, in ever-increasing numbers as his reputation grew. This is not to say that his work was limited to the narrow confines of the traditional country house garden; far from it.

Lanning Roper did much to free such gardens from their uninteresting confines of lawns, rose gardens and shrubberies. He also worked right across the board: from small town gardens in London to historic National Trust properties whose preservation was to become an increasingly important part of his career, to gardens for modern architecture such as the Sainsbury Centre at East Anglia University, designed by Norman Foster, and Farnsworth House in Illinois, designed by Mies van der Rohe and owned by Peter Palumbo, a friend and client of Roper's for many years.

Being an American proved a constant advantage; it gave his attitude and ideas an important element of detachment which fostered great clarity. When, as was often the case, he was presented with an existing or part-existing garden, or an old garden in need of rejuvenation, he was able to pare away unwanted or detrimental features and judge what additions would be most suitable. The style of his work was also significantly different from that of many other designers, and followed closely that of his compatriot Beatrix Farrand (q.v. p. 174), whose work he admired enormously; he wrote articles about both Dumbarton Oaks and Dartington Hall for *Country Life*. Like Beatrix Farrand, Roper believed strongly in a professional designer's responsibility to retain a long-term involvement in his commissions. Like Farrand, he too preferred to make plans and designs on site, and instead of painstaking and decorative drawings his plans were essentially practical, emphasising the details of planting schemes and accompanied, after regular visits, by written reports and advice.

As many of his gardens still demonstrate, Lanning Roper excelled as an original and highly accomplished border plantsman, his best schemes containing a mixture of plants – usually both shrubs and herbaceous perennials – with lively colour combinations and an emphasis on shape and contrasting foliage. In the right setting, stretching along an expanse of lawn or in front of a warm wall with an attractive house façade in the background, the effect was imbued with an intangible quality of 'Englishness' that Roper instinctively seemed able to conjure up. By contrast, his American origins also made him appreciative of the qualities of autumn foliage in the garden, and more informal areas were often planted with carefully selected trees to give this effect. Herb gardens were another favourite feature, to which he devoted much care; he was able to put this into practice most rewardingly at Scotney Castle in Kent where he planned a new herb garden in the court of the ruined castle.

At Hillbarn House in Wiltshire Lanning Roper was able to design and plant a 'complete' garden. He worked there for three successive owners who each added new areas. The house faces onto the village street and the garden, initially was L-shaped on two sides of the house. The later expansion formed a large rectangle on different levels. Each part has its own distinct flavour: the small area to the east of the house is enclosed by pleached limes on two sides, cleverly heightening the screen of the roadside wall; to one side of the main lawn behind the house a miniature box-edged parterre in front of a summerhouse has gravel paths dividing the beds and running between

great domes of yew; but the most successful area was the last to be added to the garden. Here, steps down from the main lawn lead into a hornbeam tunnel with windows looking down onto the swimming-pool in a secluded walled court on one side. On the other side a rectangle of paths enclosed a large *potager*, part of which has now been made into a chessboard pattern herb garden. One path along a mixed border leads under a series of metal arches over which pear trees are trained, while at the far end Roper devised an ingenious split-level hornbeam hedge to screen a tennis court. The lower hedge is on one side of a path and the taller on the other, behind a deep border planted in characteristic Roper style with bold groups of shrub roses, daylilies, agapanthus and peonies surrounded by grey-leafed foliage plants, while behind, the hornbeams have bare trunks up to the height of the border planting, above which the neatly clipped foliage extends. The longest border was planted along the fourth side of the *potager* beneath the retaining wall of the upper main lawn, its planting scheme another colour variation of mixed shrubs and herbaceous perennials.

Lanning Roper's work in English country gardens was so extensive and so well received that he might be assumed to have become completely anglicized. He never lost sight of his American identity, however, and his close affinity with America was best demonstrated in the select number of gardens that he designed there. They were quite different from his English gardens, harmonizing instinctively with their surroundings and with American garden ideals, not least in their naturalistic flow from house to garden to untamed landscape, and in their close attunement with each seasonal mood. For one of his most successful gardens, Ananouri, he returned to a spiritual cradle of American gardens, the Hudson River valley, where a century earlier A. J. Downing (q.v. p. 108) had worked. The modern house at Ananouri had been built in the 1960s by Alexander Perry Morgan, a pupil from Roper's schoolmastering days in New York. Working in close partnership with the house's owners and inspired by the house and its relationship with the spectacular surroundings of

At Vanbrugh's brooding masterpiece, Seaton Deleval,
James Russell laid out a box-edged parterre on a scale suitable
to the house's architecture.

apparently endless wooded hills along the broad river, Roper guided them towards achieving the garden they envisaged. It was a simple garden, with stylistic planting kept to a minimum around the house and for the rest dependent upon the native trees and grass framing views out to the river valley. In one of his earliest reports to its owners he analyzed the priorities of the site, embodying some of the most dearly held ideals of American gardeners: 'Seasonal aspects of landscape are all important. Near the house there should be evergreen planting for year-round effect, and obviously it is essential for the screening of the intrusion of buildings on boundaries and other undesirable features. However, the native trees are essentially deciduous. Autumn colour, the pattern of bare branches against the winter sky, and the haze of tender green in spring are essential to the river valley. Native shrubs, wild flowers and ferns are to be encouraged where they seem natural, and bulbs naturalized in key places.'

In the last years of his life Lanning Roper's work was interrupted by the cancer which eventually proved terminal but by this time he had shown in scores of gardens that his talent lay in an ability to adapt to changing circumstances and clients' wishes – whether planning a garden around two magnificent Henry Moore statues, as he did during the 1960s at the Old Vicarage, Bucklebury in Berkshire, or incorporating a neo-Georgian house built during the 1970s into the old setting of the previous Victorian house, as he did at Coniston Cold in Yorkshire. At Coniston Cold he first cleared an overgrown bank between the house and its lake and surrounding park to restore the severed link between house and landscape remaining, and then skilfully mapped out planting to follow the traces of the old house, retaining walls, terraces and the theatrical doric columns of the old portico which became a magnificent folly. His last – and most prestigious – commission was to assist the Prince of Wales in the creation of a garden at Highgrove House. His failing health prevented him from fulfilling the task, but he did give the initial all-important advice which provided the ground rules for the garden's development.

JAMES PHILIP CUMING RUSSELL (1920-)

ASCOTT, *Buckinghamshire*; CASTLE HOWARD, *Yorkshire*; CHOLMONDELEY CASTLE, *Cheshire*; SEATON DELAVAL, *Northumberland*; WEST WOODHAY HOUSE, *Berkshire*

JAMES RUSSELL has been one of the few post-war figures to come to garden design from a background of nursery work rather than landscape design or architecture. A primarily horticultural approach has been evident in all his gardens and his most important commissions, where old-fashioned gardens were in need of extensive restoration and new features, show a judicious choice of plants. After studying botany at Cambridge his ambition to make a career in horticulture was interrupted by World War II, but after the war he focused his attention upon the restoration of the once-famous Sunningdale Nurseries in Surrey where, in 1956, he was joined by Graham Stuart Thomas (*q.v.* p. 224). From then until 1968, when Russell sold the nursery, the partnership enjoyed a leading reputation both for supplying quality plants and also for garden design. In the early years some of the work came as a result of wartime neglect, as Russell explained: 'After the war there were huge opportunities, total neglect had ruined many large estates and there was the question of replanting on a considerable scale'.[1] In addition, requests for garden designs often followed from an initial requirement of plants.

A typical garden from the Sunningdale Nurseries period was West Woodhay House in Berkshire, where Russell was commissioned to help in the extensive rejuvenation of a depressed garden around the superb 17th-century house. One of the place's great assets was the view southwards across a great expanse of lawn to a ha-ha boundary, beyond which parkland stretched up to the Berkshire down. Percy Cane had carried out some work in the garden before the war and Russell advised on the restoration of certain features such as the rose garden. More importantly he advised on the replanting of groups of trees in the park to enhance the view, and the creation of an informal spring and early summer woodland garden along one side of the main lawn where, beneath mature oak and beech trees, he planted rhododendrons – one of the Sunningdale Nursery's strengths – camellias, magnolias and pieris.

Russell has also worked on the gardens of two of Vanbrugh's major houses, first at Seaton Delaval Hall and subsequently and more extensively, at Castle Howard. At Seaton Delaval he created an enormous box-edged parterre below the broad terrace along the west side of the house, harking back to the original early 18th-century gardens and on a scale suitable to the house's monumental architecture. Within enclosing yew hedges and obelisks great circles of box enclose grey-leaved santolinas around sombre classical urns and at the far end, centred on the house, a statue of David and Goliath by Baccio Bandinelli was positioned behind a seat. The overriding air of grand formality was continued in a box-edged rose garden on another side of the house.

It was to the old dairies at Castle Howard that Russell moved with his stock of plants when he sold Sunningdale Nurseries in 1968, and in partnership with Lord Howard he carried out extensive replanting of various parts of the gardens and surrounding landscape, including planting rare ornamental trees and shrubs in Ray Wood and designing bog and water gardens along the lakes that lead to the Roman Bridge. Most impressive, however, was the old-fashioned rose garden in one of Vanbrugh's original walled gardens, only rivalled by the garden created at Mottisfont Abbey by Russell's former partner, Graham Stuart Thomas, as the most comprehensive collected of old shrub roses in England. Although the total of over five hundred different varieties inevitably makes it a collection, Russell's great skill was to make it equally a garden: capitalizing upon the ornamental features of the surroundings, such as Vanbrugh's Satyr Gate in one wall and the statue of Venus that is the centrepiece of one of the four symmetrical areas; adding architectural features to enhance the plant effect, such as tall trellis-work pillars supporting ramblers and climbers, and the magnificent pergola around two sides of the Venus garden; and adding variety to the planting with a mixture of climbers and long border edges of lavender, and emphasizing the framework with hedges, columnar cypresses and weeping pear trees. In its magnificent setting the Castle Howard rose garden is one of the best examples of the garden restoration and preservation that has assumed such increasing importance in recent decades, and is also a tribute to James Russell's flair as both plantsman and designer.

GRAHAM STUART THOMAS (1909-)

MOTTISFONT ABBEY, *Hampshire*; SEZINCOTE, *Gloucestershire*

EVEN BY CONTEMPORARY STANDARDS when most of the influential figures in the garden world have combined careers as writers, designers and plantsmen, Graham Stuart Thomas has been an exceptional all-rounder: a plantsman, designer, painter, conservationist, historian and journalist. He first studied horticulture at the Cambridge University Botanic Garden, before going on to nursery work, notably as the partner of James Russell (*q.v.* p. 224) at the Sunningdale Nurseries, and during his long career has steadily built up a reputation of enormous authority. As gardens adviser to the National Trust from 1955 to 1974 he held one of the most important positions with regard to historic gardens and their preservation, and during that time masterminded for the National Trust a number of outstanding garden restorations: at Claremont, Cliveden, Westbury Court and Shugborough, for instance. At the same time he helped the Trust cope with rapidly increasing maintenance costs and numbers of visitors.

As a plantsman Thomas's most significant and enduring contribution has been his championing of old-fashioned shrub roses, and he did much towards returning them to popularity in the face of competition from new varieties.

Overleaf: *The Indian-inspired bridge and Snake pool at Sezincote, where Graham Stuart Thomas skilfully introduced planting that would enhance the existing architectural and water features.*

After the war he began to build up a collection of these old-fashioned roses and, in 1972, achieved a long-held ambition when he was able to design a rose garden for the National Trust at Mottisfont Abbey in Hampshire, for which his own collection provided the initial nucleus of plants. The rose garden was laid out in Mottisfont's walled garden, where a formal pattern of generous-sized box-edged beds and borders contained a comprehensive representation of pre-1900 roses; and today the rose garden contains the national collection of old-fashioned roses. Thomas's love and knowledge of roses inspired a series of books on the subject of which *The Old Shrub Roses* (1955) remains among the most popular and definitive of post-war garden books. But his scope is far wider than that, and *Plants for Ground-Cover* (1970) and other books have been followed by such essential reference books as *Perennial Garden Plants* (1976) and *Ornamental Shrubs, Climbers and Bamboos* (1992).

After World War II Thomas assisted in the restoration of the garden at Sezincote in Gloucestershire, the unique Mogul-style house built by Samuel Pepys Cockerell in 1805 and surrounded by a park laid out by Humphry Repton (*q.v.* p. 81).

Thomas's work here demonstrated his skill as both designer and plantsman, especially in the formal 'paradise' garden laid out on one side of the house, with its right-angled Mogul canals meeting at a central octagonal fountain, and in the planting along the descending edges of the stream garden. On either side of the succession of ponds bold groups of shrubs were arranged for shape and foliage effect, along with Japanese maples and other ornamental trees.

Thomas's wide-ranging career illustrates the extent to which contemporary gardens involve a combination of sensitive preservation, restoration and rejuvenation by adventurous planting. Whether in his books – the text usually illustrated by his own delicate drawings and water-colours of plants – in his garden designs or in his knowledge of plants, Thomas's emphasis on quality and authenticity has been largely responsible for his far-reaching influence.

ROSEMARY ISABEL VEREY (*1918-*)

BARNSLEY HOUSE, *Gloucestershire*; HIGHGROVE HOUSE, *Gloucestershire*; LITTLE HOUSE, *Gloucestershire*; OLD WINDSOR, *Berkshire*

ROSEMARY VEREY exemplifies the manner in which amateur gardeners and garden writers have profoundly influenced the development of the contemporary garden. 'Rosemary Verey', wrote John Sales, 'is indeed a worthy successor in the honourable British tradition of artist-gardeners.'[1]

Rosemary Verey's gardening career began in earnest some thirty years ago in her own garden at Barnsley. During the ensuing three decades the garden has developed to universal admiration, her books and lectures have proved hugely popular both in Britain and the United States, and she has carried out commissions as a garden designer in both countries. A fascination with garden history and increasing love of plants have provided the two foundations of her garden work and she has always been acutely conscious of the need to achieve a balanced harmony between design and planting. Her studies of garden history have encouraged her enjoyment of period features from Tudor and formal 17th-century gardens, and one of her great successes has been to demonstrate how well these can be incorporated into the modern garden in an original fashion.

Until his death in 1984, the development of the garden at Barnsley relied very much on the partnership of Rosemary Verey and her husband David, a distinguished architectural historian. The house had been a village rectory for centuries and the Vereys made sure that this historical continuity was retained in the atmosphere of the garden, in a manner that immediately strikes a chord with visitors. Admirably the garden illustrates much that is best in the evolution of contemporary gardens in the Hidcote, Sissinghurst and Tintinhull tradition: great variety, both in design and planting, but subtly well organized within a surprisingly small area. The garden at Barnsley, including a largish area in front of the house which is not really part of the main garden, only extends to 1.2 ha/3 acres.

Rosemary Verey is always happy to acknowledge the debt she owes to previous garden writers, in particular to Russell Page, Gertrude Jekyll and the selection of treasured 17th-century authors whose volumes are the jewels in her library. The garden perpetuates historical traditions but in no derivative way. Rosemary Verey's knowledge and individual flair have produced at Barnsley a rich diversity; and yet the garden does not divide into areas, rather flows together around three sides of the house, from mature trees on the entrance front, to the lawn sweeping away from one side, to a collection of ornamental trees planted as a 'wilderness', and on to the main flower garden at the back of the house, which is walled on two sides. A castellated verandah on the side of the house facing the wilderness is now complemented by the intricate pattern of a miniature knot garden, with hedges of box and wall germander forming tight diamond patterns in gravel, and surrounded by hedges of rosemary with clipped spirals of holly on the corners. Another historically inspired feature at Barnsley is the ornamental vegetable garden or *potager*, the idea for which came partly from seeing the famous garden at Villandry in France, but also from a book published in 1617, *The Country House-Wife's Garden*, by William Lawson, which contained plans and ideas for just such a garden – and on a suitable reduced scale for the space available at Barnsley.

From the main garden front of the house a paved path leads away between columnar Irish yews, parallel with a herb garden from the kitchen door to one side. On either side of the yews deep borders filled with a mixture of small flowering trees, shrubs and flowers curve around the lawns' edges. The yews lead to a splendid major axis at right-angles, that opens up a new and unexpected dimension. At one end is a Doric temple that originally stood at Fairford Park but was given to David Verey and re-erected by him stone by stone. From here a vista extends across a lily pond and away along a grass walk to double mixed borders leading to a pool and a fountain sculpture of frogs spouting water against a tablet carved with two rams, made by Simon Verity. Verity's work, which also includes a superb statue of a lady in a hunting habit standing partly concealed by trees, is an important feature at Barnsley, and provides a contemporary decorative element.

In 1980 Rosemary Verey was co-editor with Alvilde Lees-Milne of *The Englishwoman's Garden* (1980); since then her other widely read books have included *The Scented Garden* (1981), *Classic Garden Design* (1984), *The Garden in Winter* (1988) and *Good Planting* (1990). As well as complete garden designs, she has designed borders, knot gardens or formal *potager*-style kitchen gardens for places such as Ascot Place, Fort Belvedere, Longleat, Luton Hoo, Mount Stewart and Sudeley Castle. In each case her new additions have fitted harmoniously into the surroundings of an existing garden and in them she demonstrates her skill at plant association and in recreating period features.

Rosemary Verey has used her garden at Barnsley to provide much of the material for her writing, and her influence rests on the combination of garden and writing. The garden at Barnsley will surely be regarded in the future as one of the finest successors to Hidcote and Sissinghurst – gardens whose principles and scale make them adaptable to almost any conditions, be it in Britain or the United States.

Equally important, it also illustrates how garden designs and features from past periods can become an inspiration today; at Barnsley this is encapsulated by the formal vista parallel to the main double borders, where pleached limes lead into a laburnum tunnel underplanted with alliums. At the far end is a sundial given to her husband David on his sixtieth birthday and inscribed by Simon Verity with a quotation that goes back three centuries to John Evelyn: 'As no man be very miserable that is master of a garden here; so will no man ever be happy who is not sure of a garden hereafter . . . where the first Adam fell the second rose.'

Overleaf: The laburnum walk designed by Rosemary Verey in her own garden at Barnsley House.

NOTES

THE FIRST PROFESSIONALS

THE REV JOHN BANISTER
1 Miles Hadfield and others, *British Gardeners*, 1980.

ISAAC DE CAUS
1 *Country Life*, vols 133-4, 1963.
2 *Country Life*, ibid.

JOHN EVELYN
1 & 2 Miles Hadfield, *Gardening in Britain*, 1960.
3 *Journal of Garden History*, vol 4 no. 1, 1976.
4 *Country Life*, vol 121, 1957.
5 Stephen Switzer, *The Nobleman, Gentleman and Gardener's Recreation*, 1715.

CHRISTOPHER HATTON
1-3 Miles Hadfield, *Gardening in Britain*, 1960.

JOHN TRADESCANT, THE ELDER
1 *ex info.* Marchioness of Salisbury.

EDMUND WALLER
1-5 *Country Life*, vol 91, 1942.

THE EMERGENCE OF AN ENGLISH STYLE

1 Joseph Addison in *The Spectator*, 1712.
2 Tom Turner, *English Garden Design*, 1986.
3 Miles Hadfield, *Gardening in Britain*, 1960.

JOHN AISLABIE
1-3 *Country Life*, vol 70, 1931.

GUILLAUME BEAUMONT
1 William Sawrey Gilpin, *Practical Hints for Landscape Gardening* (1832).

THOMAS BROWNE DUNCOMBE and THOMAS DUNCOMBE
1 *Country Life*, vol 122, 1957.

JOHN JAMES
1 *Country Life*, vol 85, 1939.
2 Howard Colvin, *Biographical Dictionary of British Architects*, 1954.

WILLIAM KENT
1 Alexander Pope, *The Correspondence of Alexander Pope*, 5 vols ed. G. W. Sherburn, 1956.
2 English Heritage, *Register of Parks and Gardens of Special Historic Interest in England* (Greater London vol.), 1988.
3 Sir Thomas Robinson to Lord Carlisle, 1734.
4 Horace Walpole, *On Modern Gardening*, 1785.
5 Michael I. Wilson, *William Kent*, 1984.
6 Horace Walpole, *ibid*.

GEORGE LONDON AND HENRY WISE
1 David Green, *Gardener to Queen Anne*, 1956.
2 F. L. Colvile *The Worthies of Warwickshire* (1869), quoted in Green.

PHILIP MILLER
1 Miles Hadfield, *Gardening in Britain*, 1960.
2 Miles Hadfield, *ibid*.

STEPHEN SWITZER
1 Whistler, Laurence, *The Imagination of Vanbrugh and his Fellow Artists*, 1954.
2 Switzer, Stephen, *Ichnographica Rustica*, 1742.
3 Switzer, Stephen, *Ibid*.

SIR JOHN VANBRUGH
1 Christopher Hussey, *The Picturesque*, 1927.
2 Horace Walpole, *Correspondence*, ed. W. S. Lewis, 1937.

THE FLOWERING OF THE LANDSCAPE MOVEMENT

1 Thomas Jefferson, *Garden Book* (annotated by Edwin Morris Betts), 1985.

2 Tom Turner, *English Garden Design*, 1986.

LANCELOT 'CAPABILITY' BROWN

1 David Watkin, *The English Vision* (1982).

2 Dorothy Stroud, *Capability Brown*, 1950.

3 Humphry Repton, *The Theory and Practise of Gardening*, 1803.

4 Richard Payne Knight, *The Landscape*, 1794.

5 Dorothy Stroud, *ibid.*

SIR WILLIAM CHAMBERS

1 Howard Colvin, *British Architects 1660-1840*, 1954

2 Howard Colvin, *ibid.*

3 Christopher Hussey, *The Picturesque*, 1927

4 Sir William Chambers, *Plans, Elevations, Sections and Perspective Views of the Gardens and Buildings at Kew, Surrey*, 1763

5 Howard Colvin, *ibid.*

6 Miles Hadfield, *British Gardeners*, 1980

THE HON CHARLES HAMILTON

1 Sir Uvedale Price, *Essay on the Picturesque*, 1794

2 J. C. Loudon, *Arboretum et Fruticum Brittanicum*, 1838

HENRY HOARE

1 English Heritage, *Register of Parks and Gardens of Special Historic Interest in England*, Wiltshire vol, 1987

2 David Watkin, *The English Vision*, 1982

3 Henry Hoare Correspondence, 1762. Quoted in Kenneth Woodbridge, *Landscape and Antiquity*, 1971

THOMAS JEFFERSON

1 Geoffrey and Susan Jellicoe, *The Landscape of Man*, 1975

2 Ann Leighton, *American Gardens of the Nineteenth Century*, 1987

3 Thomas Jefferson, *Garden Book* (Annotated by Edwin Morris Betts), 1985.

4 *ibid.*

5 *ibid.*

SANDERSON MILLER

1 Lord Dacre correspondence 1749, in Newdigate papers, Warwickshire Record Office. David Watkin, *The English Vision*, 1982.

2 Horace Walpole, *Correspondence*, 1937.

HUMPHRY REPTON

1 Edward Hyams, *'Capability' Brown and Humphry Repton*, 1971.

2 Humphry Repton, *An Inquiry into the Changes of Taste in Landscape Gardening*, 1906.

3 Edward Hyams, *ibid.*

4 Edward Hyams, *ibid.*

5 Edward Hyams, *ibid.*

6 Mark Girouard, *Life in the English Country House*, 1978.

RICHARD WOODS

1 Humphry Repton *Theory and Practice of Landscape Gardening*, 1803.

2 Hugh Prince in *The Oxford Companion to Gardens*, 1986.

THOMAS WRIGHT

1 O. A. Sherrard, *Lord Chatham and America* (1958), quoted in Mavis Batsy and David Lambert *The English Garden Tour* (1990).

THE HIGH VICTORIAN ERA

SIR CHARLES BARRY

1 Miles Hadfield, *British Gardeners*, 1980.

2 Miles Hadfield, *Gardening in Britain*, 1960.

JAMES BATEMAN

1 Geoffrey and Susan Jellicoe, *The Landscape of Man* (1975).

2 Peter Hayden, *Biddulph Grange* (1989).

3 Brent Elliott, *Victorian Gardens* (1986).

DAVID DOUGLAS

1 Sandra Raphael in *The Oxford Companion to Gardening* (1986).

2 Miles Hadfield, *Gardening in Britain* (1960).

3 Miles Hadfield, *British Gardeners* (1980).

ANDREW JACKSON DOWNING

1 Andrew Jackson Downing, *A Treatise on the Theory and Practice of Landscape Gardening*, 1841.

2 Jane Loudon, *Gardening for Ladies and Ladies' Companion to the Flower Garden*, edited by A. J. Downing, 1843.

3 Ann Leighton, *American Gardens of the Nineteenth Century*, 1987.

4 *Ann Leighton, ibid.*

JOHN CLAUDIUS LOUDON

1 John Claudius Loudon, *Encyclopaedia of Gardening*, 1822.

2 Miles Hadfield, *British Gardeners*, 1980.

3 Brent Elliott, *Victorian Gardens*, 1986.

WILLIAM ANDREWS NESFIELD

1 Olive Cook. *The English Country House*, 1974.
2 Christopher Hussey, *English Gardens and Landscapes 1700-1750*, 1967.

FREDERICK LAW OLMSTED

1 Laura Roper, *FLO: A Biography of Frederick Law Olmsted*, 1973.
2 F. L. Olmsted, *Walks and Talks of an American Farmer in England*, 1852.
3 Laura Roper, *ibid.*
4 Laura Roper, *ibid.*

SIR JOSEPH PAXTON

1 John Cornforth, *Country Life*, vol 144, 1969.
2 Miles Hadfield, *Gardening in Britain*, 1960.
3 Miles Hadfield, *British Gardeners*, 1980.
4 John Cornforth, *ibid.*
5 F. L. Olmsted, *Walks and Talks of an American Farmer in England*, 1852.
6 Brent Elliott, *Victorian Gardens*, 1986.

INTERNATIONAL INFLUENCES

1 David Ottewill, *Edwardian Gardens*, 1989.

SIR REGINALD BLOMFIELD

1 Sir Reginald Blomfield, *The Formal Garden in England*, 1892.
2 Sir Reginald Blomfield, *Memoirs of an Architect*, 1932.
3 Clive Aslet, *The Last Country Houses*, 1982.
4 Sir Reginald Blomfield, *ibid.*
5 Sir Reginald Blomfield, *ibid.*

ACHILLE DUCHÊNE

1 Monique Mosset, in *The History of Garden Design*, 1991.
2 Hugh Montgomery-Massingberd, *Blenheim Revisited*, 1985.
3 Hugh Montgomery-Massingberd, *ibid.*
4 Hugh Montgomery-Massingberd, *ibid.*
5 Hugh Montgomery-Massingberd, *ibid.*

GERTRUDE JEKYLL

1 Jane Brown, *Gardens of a Golden Afternoon*, 1982.
2 Edwin Lutyens in Foreword to *Gertrude Jekyll: A Memoir*, by Francis Jekyll, 1934.
3 David Ottewill, *The Edwardian Garden*, 1989.
4 Gertrude Jekyll, *Home and Garden*, 1900.

MAJOR LAWRENCE WATERBURY JOHNSTON

1 Edward Hyams, *The English Garden*, 1964.
2 Alvilde Lees-Milne, *Lawrence Johnston, Creator of Hidcote Garden*, in *Hortus*, vol 1. no 2, 1987.
3 John Sales, *West Country Gardens*, 1980.

SIR EDWIN LUTYENS

1 Jane Brown, *Gardens of a Golden Afternoon*, 1982.
2 David Ottewill, *The Edwardian Garden*, 1989.
3 David Ottewill, *ibid.*
4 Edwin Lutyens to Emily Lutyens 1908. Quoted in Jane Brown, *ibid.*

THOMAS HAYTON MAWSON

1 David Ottewill, *The Edwardian Garden*, 1989.
2 Thomas Mawson, *The Life and Work of an English Landscape Architect*, 1927.
3 2nd Viscount Leverhulme, *Viscount Leverhulme*, 1927.
4 Thomas Mawson, *ibid.*
5 Thomas Mawson, *ibid.*
6 David Ottewill, *ibid.*

HAROLD AINSWORTH PETO

1 *Country Life*, vol 52, 1922.

WILLIAM ROBINSON

1 David Ottewill, *The Edwardian Garden*, 1989.
2 David Ottewill, *ibid.*
3 William Robinson, *The English Flower Garden*, 1911 ed.

SIR GEORGE RERESBY SITWELL

1 Sacheverell Sitwell in *Hortus Sitwellianus*, 1984.
2 Sir Osbert Sitwell, *Left Hand! Right Hand!*, 1945.
3 Sir Osbert Sitwell, *ibid.*
4 Sir George Sitwell, *On the Making of Gardens*, 1909.

FRANCIS INIGO THOMAS

1 David Ottewill, *The Edwardian Garden*, 1989.

BRITISH AND AMERICAN STYLE

THOMAS CHURCH

1 Michael Lancaster in *The Oxford Companion to Gardens*, 1986.

BEATRIX (JONES) FARRAND

1 Dorothy Elmhirst in Dartington Hall Trust Records Office, 1959.

2 Lanning Roper, *Country Life*, vol 155i, 1974.

3 Georgina Masson, *Dumbarton Oaks: a Guide to the Gardens*, 1968.

4 Dorothy Elmhirst in Dartington Hall Trust Record Office, 1933.

5 Beatrix Farrand in Dartington Hall Trust Record Office, 1933.

6 Reginald Snell, *From the Bare Stem*, 1989.

7 Beatrix Farrand in Dartington Hall Trust Record Office, 1957.

8 *ibid.*

Norah Lindsay

1 Miles Hadfield, *British Gardeners*, 1980.

2 Norah Lindsay, *Country Life*, vol 69, 1931.

The Hon Victoria Mary 'Vita' Sackville-West

1 Harold Nicolson in Introduction to *Great Gardens of Britain* by Peter Coats, 1967.

2 Anne Scott-James, *Sissinghurst: The Making of a Garden*, 1975.

Fletcher Steele

1 Robin Karson, *Fletcher Steele, Landscape Architect,* 1989.

2 Robin Karson, *ibid.*

3 Robin Karson, *ibid.*

Christopher Tunnard

1 Christopher Tunnard, *Gardens in the Modern Landscape*, 1938.

Sir (Bertram) Clough Williams-Ellis

1 John Martin Robinson, *The Latest Country Houses,* 1983.

2 *Country Life*, vol 122i, 1957.

The Contemporary Garden

1 Tom Turner, *English Garden Design*, 1986.

2 Geoffrey and Susan Jellicoe, *The Landscape of Man*, 1975.

Percy Stephen Cane

1 Michael Lancaster in *The Oxford Companion to Gardens*, 1984.

2 Reginald Snell, *From the Bare Stem*, 1989.

Brenda Colvin

1 Hal Moggridge in *The Garden*, vol 106, November 1981.

2 Brenda Colvin in *Modern Private Gardens.* edited by Geoffrey Jellicoe, 1968.

3 Hal Moggridge, *ibid.*

4 Hal Moggridge, *ibid.*

Dame Sylvia Crowe

1 Crowe, Sylvia, *Garden Design,* 1958.

Margery Fish

1 Margery Fish in *Journal of the Royal Horticultural Society*, vol 90 (1965).

2 *ibid.*

Sir Geoffrey Alan Jellicoe

1 Sir Geoffrey Jellicoe, *The Guelph Lectures on Landscape Design,* 1983.

2 Sir Geoffrey Jellicoe, interview in *The Independent*, 1990.

3 *Sutton Place* (Guidebook for Sutton Place Heritage Trust, 1983).

4 *ibid.*

5 Sir Geoffrey Jellicoe, article in *The Independent*, 1990.

Russell Page

1 Russell Page, *The Education of a Gardener*, 1962.

2 Russell Page, *ibid.*

3 John Sales, *West Country Gardens*, 1980.

Lanning Roper

1 Jane Brown, *Lanning Roper and His Gardens*, 1987.

2 Jane Brown, *ibid.*

3 Jane Brown, *ibid.*

4 Jane Brown, *ibid.*

James Philip Cuming Russell

1 *ex info* James Russell.

Rosemary Isabel Verey

1 John Sales, *West Country Gardens*, 1980.

Amherst, Hon Alicia. *A History of Gardening in England.* Bernard Quaritch, London. (1896).

Anthony, John. *The Gardens of Britain vol 6: Derbyshire, Leicestershire, Lincolnshire, Northamptonshire, Nottinghamshire.* Batsford. (1979).

Aslet, Clive. *The Last Country Houses.* Yale University Press, New Haven and London. (1982).

Batey, Mavis and Lambert, David. *The English Garden Tour.* John Murray, London. (1990).

Bisgrove, Richard. *The Gardens of Britain vol 3: Berkshire, Oxfordshire, Buckinghamshire, Bedfordshire, Hertfordshire.* Batsford. (1978).

Blomfield, Reginald and F. Inigo Thomas. *The Formal Garden in England.* Macmillan and Co., London. (1892).

Blomfield, Reginald. *Memoirs of an Architect.* Macmillan and Co., London. (1932).

Brown, Jane. *The English Garden in Our Time.* Antiques Collectors Club, Woodbridge. (1987).

Brown, Jane. *Gardens of a Golden Afternoon.* Allen Lane, London. (1982).

Brown, Jane. *Lanning Roper and his Gardens.* Weidenfeld and Nicolson, London. (1987).

Brown, Jane. *Vita's Other World.* Viking, London. (1985).

Browell, M. *Alexander Pope and the Arts of Georgian England.* Oxford University Press, London. (1978).

Cane, Percy S. *The Earth is my Canvas.* Methuen, London. (1956).

Cane. Percy S. *The Creative Art of Garden Design.* Country Life Books, London (1967).

Colvin, Brenda. *Land and Landscape.* John Murray, London. (1948).

Coats, Alice M. *The Quest for Plants. A History of the Horticultural Explorers.* Studio Vista, London. (1969).

Colvin, Howard. *Biographical Dictionary of British Architects.* John Murray, London. (1954).

Cook, Olive. *The English Country House.* Book Club Associates. (1974).

Crowe, Dame Sylvia. *Garden Design.* Country Life Books. (1958).

de Figueiredo P. and Treuherz J. *Cheshire Country Houses.* Phillimore and Co., Chester. (1988).

Desmond, Ray. *Bibliography of British Gardens.* St. Paul's Bibliographies, Winchester. (1984).

Downes, Kerry. *Vanbrugh.* Zwemmer, London. (1977).

Downing, Andrew Jackson. *A Treatise on the Theory and Practice of Landscape Gardening.* Fourth edition, revised, G. P. Putnam, New York. (1859).

Elliott, Brent. *Victorian Gardens.* Batsford, London. (1986).

English Heritage. *Register of Parks and Gardens of Special Historic Interest in England.* English Heritage, London (county volumes 1983–88).

Girouard, Mark. *Life in the English Country House.* Yale University Press, New Haven and London. (1978).

Girouard, Mark. *The Victorian Country House.* Oxford University Press, Oxford. (1971).

Gothein, Marie Luise. *A History of Garden Art 2 vols.* English Edition, J. M. Dent, London. (1928).

Green. D. *Gardener to Queen Anne.* Oxford University Press. (1956).

Hadfield, Miles (and others). *British Gardeners. A Biographical Dictionary.* Zwemmer, London. (1980).

Hadfield, Miles. *Gardening in Britain.* Hutchinson, London. (1960).

Harris, John. *The Artist and the English Country House.* Sotheby Parke Burnet, London. (1979).

Harvey, John. *Early Nurserymen.* Phillimore and Co., London. (1974).

Hobhouse, Penelope. *Private Gardens of England.* Weidenfeld and Nicolson, London. (1986).

Hollis, Sarah. *The Shell Guide to the Gardens of England and Wales.* Andre Deutsch, London. (1989).

Hunt, J. D. *William Kent, Landscape Garden Designer.* Zwemmer. (1987).

Hunt, J. D. and Willis, P. *The Genius of the Place. The English Landscape Garden 1620–1820.* Paul Elek, London. (1975).

Hussey, Christopher. *English Gardens and Landscapes 1700–50.* Country Life Books, London. (1967).

Hussey, Christopher. *The Picturesque.* Revised edition, Frank Cass, London. (1967)

Hyams, Edward. *Capability Brown and Humphry Repton.* J. M. Dent, London. (1971).

Hyams, Edward. *The English Garden.* Thames and Hudson. (1964).

James, John. *The Theory and Practice of Gardening.* London. (1712).

Jefferson, Thomas. *Garden Book.* Annotated by Edwin Morris Betts. American Philosophical Society, Philadelphia. (1985)

Jekyll, Gertrude. *Home and Garden.* Longmans, Green and Co., London. (1900).

Jekyll, Gertrude. *Wood and Garden.* Longmans, Green and Co. (1899).

Jekyll, F. *Gertrude Jekyll: A Memoir.* Jonathan Cape, London, (1934).

Jellicoe, Geoffrey. *The Guelph Lectures on Landscape Design.* University of Guelph, Ontario. (1983).

Jellicoe, Geoffrey and Susan. *The Landscape of Man.* Thames and Hudson, London. (1975).

Jellicoe, Geoffrey and Susan, and others. *The Oxford Companion to Gardens.* Oxford University Press, Oxford. (1986).

Jellicoe, Susan and Geoffrey. *Modern Private Gardens.* Abelard Schuman. London and New York. (1968).

Jones, Barbara. *Follies and Grottoes.* Revised edition, Constable, London. (1974).

Jourdain, Margaret. *The Works of William Kent.* Country Life Books, London. (1948).

Karson, Robin. *Fletcher Steele, Landscape Architect.* Harry N. Abrams/Sagapress, New York. (1989).

Langley, Batty. *New Principles of Gardening.* London. (1728).

la Rochefoucauld, Francois. *Mélanges sur l'Angleterre: A Frenchman in England.* New edition, translated by S. C. Roberts. Cambridge University Press, Cambridge. (1933).

Leighton, Ann. *American Gardens of the Nineteenth Century.* University of Massachussetts Press, Boston. (1987).

Leith-Ross, Prudence. *The John Tradescants, Gardeners to the Rose and Lily Queen.* Peter Owen, London. (1984).

Lemmon, Kenneth. *The Gardens of Britain vol 5: Yorkshire and Humberside.* Batsford, London. (1978).

Loudon, J. C. *Arboretum et Fruticum Brittanicum.* 8 vols. Longman, Orme, Brown, Green and Longmans, London. (1838).

Loudon, J. C. *Encyclopaedia of Gardening.* Longman, Hurst, Rees, Orme and Brown, London. (1822).

Loudon, J. C. *The Suburban Gardener and Villa Companion.* Astor Arboretum, London. (1838).

Mawson, Thomas. H. *The Art and Craft of Garden Making.* Batsford, London. (1900).

Mawson, Thomas. H. *The Life and Work of an English Landscape Architect. An Autobiography.* The Richards Press, London. (1927).

McGuire, Diane Kostial. *Gardens of America.* Thomasson Grant, Charlottesville. (1989).

Mosset, Monique and Teyssot, Georges (eds). *The History of Garden Design.* English edition, Thames and Hudson, London. (1991).

Olmsted, F. L. *Walks and Talks of an American Farmer in England.* David Bogue, London. (1852).

Ottewill, David. *The Edwardian Garden.* Yale University Press, New

Haven and London. (1989).

Page, Russell. *The Education of a Gardener.* New edition, Collins, London. (1983).

Paterson, Allen. *The Gardens of Britain vol 2. Dorset, Hampshire and the Isle of Wight.* Batsford, London. (1978).

Payne Knight, Richard. *The Landscape.* London. (1794).

Plumptre, George. *Collins Book of British Gardens.* Collins. (1985).

Plumptre, George. *The Latest Country Gardens.* Bodley Head. (1988).

Pope, Alexander. *Correspondence.* (ed G. W. Sherburn). Oxford University Press, Oxford. (1956).

Price, Sir Uvedale, *Essay on the Picturesque.* London. (1796).

Repton, Humphry. *A Inquiry into the Changes of Taste in Landscape Gardening.* London. (1806).

Repton, Humphry. *The Theory and Practice of Landscape Gardening.* London. (1803).

Robinson, John Martin. *The Latest Country Houses.* Bodley Head, London. (1983).

Robinson, William. *The English Flower Garden.* New edition, John Murray, London. (1911).

Sales, John. *West Country Gardens.* Alan Sutton, Gloucester. (1980).

Schinz, Marina and von Zuylen, Gabrielle. *The Gardens of Russell Page.* Stewart, Tabori and Chang, New York. (1991).

Scott-James, Anne. *Sissinghurst, The Making of a Garden.* Michael Joseph, London. (1975).

Sedding, J. D. *Garden Craft Old and New.* Kegan Paul, Trench, Trabner and Co., London. (1891).

Sidwell, Ron. *West Midland Gardens.* Alan Sutton. (1981).

Simpson P. and Bell. C. F. *Designs by Inigo Jones.* (Walpole Soc. xii) Oxford. (1923-24).

Sitwell family. *Hortus Sitwellianus.* Michael Russell, Salisbury. *(1984).*

Sitwell, Sir George. *On the Making of Gardens.* John Murray. (1909).

Snell, R. *From the Bare Stem.* Devon Books, Exeter. (1989).

Strong, Roy. *The Renaissance Garden in England.* Thames and Hudson, London. (1979).

Stroud, Dorothy. *Capability Brown.* Country Life Books. (1950).

Stroud, Dorothy. *Humphry Repton.* Country Life Books. (1962).

Summerson, Sir John. *Architecture in Britain 1530–1830.* Penguin, London. (1953).

Switzer, Stephen. *Ichnographica Rustica.* London. (1742).

Synge, Patrick. *The Gardens of Britain vol 1: Devon and Cornwall.* Batsford, London. (1977).

Thacker, Christopher. *The History of Gardens.* Crom Helm, London. (1979).

Thomas, Graham Stuart. *The Gardens of the National Trust.* Weidenfeld and Nicolson, London. (1979).

Tunnard, Christopher. *Gardens in the Modern Landscape.* The Architectural Press, London. (1938).

Turner, Tom. *English Garden Design. (History and Styles since 1650).* Antique Collectors Club, Woodbridge. (1986).

Walpole, Horace. *Correspondence.* (ed W. S. Lewis). Oxford University Press, London. (1937).

Walpole, Horace. *Essay on Modern Gardening.* Strawberry Hill Press, London. (1785).

Watkin, David. *The English Vision.* John Murray, London. (1982).

Wharton, Edith. *Italian Villas and their Gardens.* English edition, Bodley Head, London. (1904).

Whistler, L. *The Imagination of Vanbrugh and his Fellow Artists.* Batsford, London. (1954).

Williams-Ellis, Sir Clough. *Architect Errant.* Constable. (1971).

Willis, Peter. *Charles Bridgeman and the English Landscape Garden.* Zwemmer, London. (1977).

Wilson, Michael. I. *William Kent.* Routledge and Kegan Paul, London. (1984).

Woodbridge, Kenneth. *Landscape and Antiquity, Aspects of English Culture at Stourhead 1718–1838.* Oxford University Press, Oxford. (1971).

Wright, Tom. *The Gardens of Britain vol 4: Kent, East & West Sussex, Surrey.* Batsford, London. (1978).

ACKNOWLEDGEMENTS

The publisher thanks the following photographers for permission to reproduce photographs in this book.

2 *Dartington Hall* Kate Mount 6 *Castle Howard* Anthea Beszant 10 *Hampton Court* Heather Angel 19 *Euston Hall* Andrew Nicholls 23 *Cranborne Manor* Harry Smith Horticultural Photographic Collection 26 *Bramham Park* Boys Syndication 31 *Studley Royal* Anthea Beszant 35 *Levens Hall* Hugh Palmer 39 *Rievaulx Terrace* Andy Williams 43 *Rousham House* Hugh Palmer 47 *Melbourne Hall* Hugh Palmer 54 *Stowe* National Trust Photographic Library/Jerry Harpur 59 *Chatsworth* Clive Boursnell 63 *Bowood* Photos Horticultural/Michael and Lois Warren 67 *Chillington* Hugh Palmer 71 *West Wycombe Park* National Trust Photographic Library/Vera Collingwood 74/75 *Stourhead* National Trust Photographic Library 79 *Monticello* Elizabeth P. McLean 82/83 *Farnborough Hall* Anthea Beszant 87 *Sheringham Hall* Rod J. Edwards 91 *Mount Vernon* Hugh Palmer 94 Chatsworth A-Z Botanical Collection 98/99 *Westonbirt* Jim Merryweather 103 *Shrubland Park* Hugh Palmer 106/107 *Biddulph Grange* Hugh Palmer 111 *Scotney Castle* Harry Smith Horticultural Photographic Collection 115 *Broughton Hall* Clive Boursnell 118/119 *Castle Howard* Rolf Richardson 123 *Birkenhead Park* Will Curwen 126 *Vizcaya* Hugh Palmer 131 *Renishaw Hall* Hugh Palmer 134/135 *Mellerstain* Elizabeth Whiting Associates 139 *Blenheim* Heather Angel 142/143 *Hestercombe* Jerry Harpur 147 *Abbotswood* Hugh Palmer 151 *Thornton Manor* Country Life Picture Library 155 *Buscot Park* Hugh Palmer 159 *Gravetye Manor* Hugh Palmer 163 *Athelhampton* Hugh Palmer 166 *Hidcote* National Trust Photographic Library/Andrew Lawson 171 *Sissinghurst* A-Z Botanical Collection 175 *Dumbarton Oaks* Hugh Palmer 183 *Naumkerg* Positive Images/Margaret Hensel 186 *East Lambrook Manor* Hugh Palmer 190/191 *Sutton Place* Hugh Palmer 195 *Denmans* Photos Horticultural/Michael and Lois Warren 198/199 *Stone Cottage* Hugh Palmer 203 *Little Peacocks* Hugh Palmer 207 *Tintinhull* National Trust Photographic Library/Neil Campbell-Sharp 211 *Shute House* Hugh Palmer 214/215 James A. van Sweden 219 *Woolbeding House* Harry Smith Photographic Collection 223 *Seaton Deleval* Horticultural Photo Library/Michael Warren 226/227 *Sezincote* Hugh Palmer 230 *Barnsley House* Eric Crichton

Picture research by Cathy Stastny.

INDEX

Bold entries denote biographical entry; italic entries denote illustrations.